Featuring: **LED ZEPPELIN ★ GUNS N' ROSES ★ BON JOVI BLACK SABBATH ★ DEEP PURPLE ★ DEF LEPPARD MÖTLEY CRÜE ★ METALLICA ★ IRON MAIDEN & MORE!**

M&G Publishing Ltd.

Copyright © Mick Wall 2006

The right of Mick Wall to be identified as the author of this work has been asserted by him in accordance with the Copyright, Designs and Patents Act 1988

First published in Great Britain in 2006 by M&G Publishing Ltd
MickWall.com PO Box 47241, London W7 3YE

First impression 2006

ISBN: 0-9552780-0-7
978-0-9552780-0-6

All rights reserved. Apart from any use permitted under UK copyright law, this publication may only be reproduced, stored or transmitted, in any form, or by any means, with prior permission in writing from the publisher or, in the case of reprographic production, in accordance with the terms of licenses issued by the Copyright Licensing Agency.

This book is sold subject to the condition that it shall not, by way of trade or otherwise, be lent, re-sold, hired out, or otherwise circulated without the publisher's prior consent in any form of binding or cover other than that in which it is published and without a similar condition including this condition being imposed on the subsequent purchaser.

A CIP catalogue for this book is available from the British Library

Design by Julie Bennett www.juliebennett.co.uk
Printed and bound in Great Britain by Printhouse Corporation, London

Every effort has been made to fulfil requirements with regard to reproducing copyright material. The author and publisher will be glad to rectify any omissions at the earliest available opportunity.

Additional copies of this book can be purchased from
www.mickwall.com

Contents

Foreword

In April 1987, I rang *Kerrang!* magazine to ask if I could go for some work experience. I was at the London College of Printing at the time, studying journalism. One of *Kerrang!*'s straplines was 'the Bible of heavy metal'. For me, it was. I owned every issue. Just the thought of calling the number, which I had memorised, provoked days of fear. But when I got through, all they said was, "How long do you want to come for?"

"Er, a week?"

"Okay then."

A month later I was in Hollywood, interviewing a hair band about living their dream. We were at the Sunset Marquis hotel, known locally as "the loser's Hilton", outside one of the little cabanas drinking free beer on a record company tab. Bruce Springsteen was in the swimming pool. The band looked at Bruce and they felt immortal. I took a look at Bruce and felt a bit immortal too.

Kerrang! had a sensibility that the other music magazines didn't, probably because its first issue had been produced on someone's kitchen table and its name was an onomatopoeia taken from the sound a loud guitar made. It was edited by the guy who'd invented it, Geoff Barton, a man who grew up obsessing over Stan Lee comics and Kiss. Geoff had made it big writing about heavy metal for *Sounds*, so he got the chance to start his own magazine. Within four years, *Kerrang!* was bigger than *Sounds*, which in turn was bigger than the *Melody Maker*. *Kerrang!* didn't take any notice of reader research or marketing departments or any of that stuff. If Geoff liked a band, or if they made him laugh, he'd put them on the cover. He'd listen to any pitch from any writer or PR. *Kerrang!* got bigger and bigger, but it was still a fans magazine. If its writers hadn't been writing for it, they'd have been reading it.

It was Geoff that I'd phoned to ask for work experience. I had an idea in my mind of what he'd be like. (I already knew how he looked. I knew how all the writers looked, because *Kerrang!* quite often published their pictures). I visualised the office, with all of the writers I read sitting there writing: Mick Wall, Dave Dickson, Derek Oliver, Dante Bonutto, Xavier Russell, Steve Gett, Pete Makowski, Steffan Chirazi and the rest. But when I arrived, there were no rows of writers. They didn't write in the office. They were all out on record company trips to America and Europe. When the writers did show up to pick up the great piles of free records they were sent every week, they were nothing like I'd imagined either. Dave Dickson was about five feet tall. He dressed entirely in black. He always wore black eyeliner and he always carried an umbrella whatever the weather. He was acknowledged as the magazine's expert on Satanism. When he wasn't writing, the others intimated, he was making his studies of the dark side. Derek Oliver was an obsessive record collector. He had so many, he'd had to reinforce the floor of his house. Xavier Russell – son of legendary film director Ken – was a film editor. Steffan Chirazi was a kid from Surbiton who'd moved to San Francisco to cover the scene close-up. Pete Makowski was addled from his years on tour buses and in airports. And Mick Wall I saw barely at all. He was the magazine's star writer. His interviews were almost always cover stories, and Geoff would run them at great length over two or three issues. They were terrific. He seemed to be permanently on the road on one record company expense account or another, accompanied by a ferocious photographer called Ross Halfin. They came as a pair, Mick and Ross, and what a pair they made.

I learned how it worked on the hoof. Geoff didn't really mind what you wrote as long as it was funny. The record companies didn't care what you said, just as long as you said it at length. The bands rarely read it properly either; they just liked to see their faces over several pages. There was a trick to it. Mick told me that the trick was simple: give the people what they want. They wanted rock stars who acted like rock stars, who spoke like rock stars, who did the stuff that rock stars did. And they wanted to feel like they were there when they did it. The bigger the band, the easier it was. Mick was unbeatably good. Things happened to him that other writers dreamed of: he'd be in LA, staying with Ross at the Sunset Marquis, and rock stars would turn up to see *them*. He'd be invited not to record company offices but to band members' houses, or on their jets. He'd ask them questions and they'd actually answer properly, not with an answer that they gave to every other chancer with a tape recorder.

The question I was asked most by people who read the magazine – and by bands who'd not yet made it – was always, "So this Mick Wall then. What's he really like?" The answer was always the same too: "He's exactly like you imagine..."

So what did they imagine? Well, he was small. Any picture of Mick with a band usually placed him at about a foot shorter than anyone else. He didn't look like a wannabe or a pseudo band member. He had this look of his own, with not-quite long hair and not-quite rock star clobber. He was first-generation

Anglo-Irish from a rough part of Ealing and he never really looked as though he was going to be surprised by anything that happened to him, either.

From his writing you could learn a little (but not much) more. As you'll see from the pieces collected here, he quickly coined a style that came to encapsulate the times. He was a hard, fast wise-guy observer whose empathy with his subject came with a sub-text: that all were somehow implicit in a game in which Mick understood the rules better than they did. Unlike some writers, he revealed little of himself directly. Instead he developed a persona that made the bands feel safe but that offered the latitude to poke a little fun without breaking the bond between magazine and reader (the famous Poison piece here became known for pushing the limits of that bond).

Inevitably it was all more complex than that. Beyond the pages of the magazine, there was all of the usual politicking and egoism. As he acknowledged in his cult memoir of the times, *Paranoid*, Mick was as guilty as anyone of that. And yet when Ozzy Osbourne tried to kill his wife Sharon, in 1989, and got sectioned for his trouble, it was Mick that he summoned to the hospital to tell his story. When Mötley Crüe cancelled a UK tour with an excuse dripping in bullshit it was Mick that they phoned, first to offer it and later to sheepishly withdraw it. When W. Axl Rose, puffed up with hubris, needed to have his mighty thoughts recorded, it was Mick he asked over to his LA apartment in the dead of night to do so.

Mick turned me onto lots of writers, Charles Bukowski amongst them. Bukowski was a hero of Mick's long before his was a name worth dropping. One day in the *Kerrang!* office, Mick told me that Anthony Kiedis, the Red Hot Chili Peppers singer and another Bukowski fan, had said that he knew "where Bukowski hung out" in LA, and had offered to take Mick down there to see him. Mick declined. At first I couldn't understand why, but I overcame my thickness eventually: when you'd seen lots of heroes at close-hand, when they'd just tried to strangle their wives, or fuck over their band-mates, or take their fans for a bunch of wankers, it didn't do to go off and meet your own.

So the answer to that question asked all those years ago is, thankfully, that Mick Wall is nothing like you'd imagine. Most of the bands included here, I'm afraid, are a different story. So enjoy the monstrous little fuckers in all their glory once again... they're well worth the price of admission, and so is Mick Wall.

Jon Hotten, Classic Rock

These days, whenever it comes up that I was actually backstage at the American version of the 1985 Live Aid concert, even I have to admit it sounds quite impressive. At the time, though, I saw things rather differently. The whole thing seemed so obviously driven by rock star vanity that I found it impossible to get behind it wholeheartedly. I grudgingly accepted that there did indeed seem to be money being sent to Africa, and that the dreadful 'Do They Know It's Christmas' single might, after all, be a 'good thing', in that respect. But I hadn't quite got my head round the fact yet that almost everything in the music business is driven by rock star vanity. I still thought it was a bad thing and I cringed every time Geldof came on telly, doing his righteous give-me-your-fuckin'-money thing, or your butter-mountain or whatever it was. I was convinced that if his group the Boomtown Rats hadn't been a busted flush he would never have come up with Band Aid. Like that mattered.

For some reason, it did matter to me, though, and nothing would have pleased me more than to discover the whole thing was a sham. Hence the rather large chip I appear to be wearing throughout the story.

All that said, I still found myself squirming as I sat at home watching the Live 8 show in Hyde Park in 2005. Was it just me or did the whole thing make the original 1985 version look like a genuinely innocent, heart-warming occasion, really and truly designed to give a hand to the poor and the dying? Without being asked to send money, what the 2005 version was about, I don't know. Ending poverty? What does that mean? Does anyone know? Apart from Bob Geldof and Bono I mean?

Maybe I'll need another 20 years to get that one…

Live Aid, Philadelphia, August, 1985

'Not since those star-spangled, guilt-edged nights in 1970-71 when Leonard Bernstein threw his Black Panther party and George Harrison organised the Concert For Bangladesh have so many of the rich and famous stepped out for the poor and famished...' The Observer

'By mid-morning the American Telegraph Company reported that the toll-free telephone line it had set up to receive pledges, 1-800-LIVE AID, was overloaded. The 1,126 circuits allocated were simply getting more traffic than they could handle...' – New York Times

"Who the fuck are the Hooters?" – Ozzy Osbourne

Ah yes... who indeed? But that's a question you may never get answered. Not here certainly, not this time. No, we are, after all, professionals with a money-down obligation to address ourselves to only the most important issues, at whatever the cost. So when the boss dished this dirty assignment my way I sat there fingering the soft flesh tyre hanging from my belt, dreaming of pizza and wondering flatly just what a moonage daydream like me could possibly say about this whole meals-on-mega-wheels deal Mr Geldof had christened Live Aid? Gimme a menu and I'll think about it, you know?

Forty or so different singers, bands, actors, comedians and over 90,000 people paying between 35 and 50 dollars a ticket just to see it, to finally believe in it, and to go home that night and tell the folks that, yes, they actually witnessed it – Live Aid! History in the making, my little mascara snakes! And why not? Indeed. I remember watching the evening news one night on TV way back in the foul arsehole of last winter, and screwing up my nose when Bob Geldof bounded before the camera with the news that he had assembled his "friends in the pop business" to record this one song good old Bob had written called 'Do They Know It's Christmas?', proceeds of which would most certainly go, and that means every penny, to the starving Africans in Ethiopia, where the sun always shines and the rain has not fallen in three years. There followed the most atrocious video-clip of several puff-pastry pop bimbos looking dead sincere and as fascinating as a turkey's bollocks, singing this awful, trite little ditty, and blow this for a game of marbles, says I. Waves of cynicism came hurtling from my heart; this is too much, this is just too fucking perfect, they've gone too far this time if they think they can have me choking and weeping on the perfect sincerity of a plan as plainly obnoxious and damned decent as this baby. What's that you see in my eye, Bob? Grass? You bastard…

We all know what happened to the record and, it's only fair to point out, we all know what's happened to the money. What Thatcher and her storm-troopers didn't steal in VAT, Geldof and his newly appointed Trust Committee (higher-ups included people like Michael Grade, head of BBC1; Maurice Oberstein, then president of CBS Records; and Lord Gowrie, officially a sponsor) set up to protect the public's money, took care of. The Trust's formation came from a special lesson learnt after the bitter experience of George Harrison's Bangladesh Appeal. The project disintegrated when it got tangled up in the tortuous relationship between Allen Klein, the erstwhile Beatles' manager, and the US Inland Revenue. Twice a week, the famine-relief co-ordinator in Ethiopia, Brother Gus O'Keefe, telephones through a shopping list of vital supplies needed to the London offices of Band Aid, in Burton Street WC1, and according to Geldof, "It's out there in ten hours!"

That information cancelled my argument somewhat, but I am a grossly cynical bastard at the best of times and I would not give in. Not yet, not so easily this time, friend. But when Big Mama America took up the idea, the £8.5 million already raised by Geldof and 'pop friends' started to look like cold spaghetti. 'We Are The World', featuring some genuinely heavy talent indeed – Quincy Jones, Michael Jackson, Stevie Wonder, Diana Ross. That kind of money doesn't haul ass out of leopard-skin couch in Malibu for some dog-shit small-time hustler idea. No, they move when their fine and sophisticated instinct for a deal they cannot refuse wafts by their security-guarded front porch. As a result, to date – and right now I'm talking about the night before the Wembley and Philadelphia concerts kick off, in approximately five hours – Geldof's little Christmas present to the starving children of Africa has already raised many millions of dollars, a lot of it now stretching into the empty stomachs of Chad, Mozambique, Angola and the Sudan.

So the action is already heavy, and only a certifiable bed-wetter or a cheap stinker out to seriously party-poop this whole nervous deal should raise a hand against it. Only I just can't quite get off on the notion of looking at Live Aid like the good little punter a lot of this material is aimed at. Everybody loves a circus, every man, woman and child wants to join the carnival, and a lot of people like ABC Television network in America know it, and what they know they grow good healthy crops of bucks from. For example, ABC paid an alleged figure of $4 million for the legal rights to broadcast the last three hours of the Philadelphia Live Aid concert. As a result from 8 pm to 11 pm Eastern Time, ABC would be the only channel the people of America would watch, and a solid piece of history right there on the video-tape too, while the company dished out their 30-second commercial spots to potential sponsors across the world for figures reportedly starting at around $250,000 a throw. Of course, they would also be obliged to run a Telethon, but what the hell, this is good television, so let's roll!

And strange expressions passed across the faces seated in the bar of the Four Seasons Hotel in Philadelphia where all the acts and organisation people are holed-up, when the press report went out that Huey Lewis And The News had decided to withdraw from the concert after what the official document described as 'disturbing news reports about the handling of the food by the Ethiopian government'. A week before the event, local TV news bulletins featured an item that claimed Russian nuclear arms were getting unloading preference over Band Aid food supplies at crucial Ethiopian air-landing sites. It went on to suggest that crates of food were left to rot on abandoned gang-planks, completely and wilfully wasted, man...

All I know is, Huey Lewis is a man of conscience, and his band the News are so popular in America and around the world that, unlike one or two names I want to throw around later in this piece, they certainly don't crave the added precedent of massive point-to-point around-the-world-in-a-day publicity. So they thought about it seriously and then they said no. Bear in mind, Huey Lewis had already personally contributed to the 'USA For Africa' single and accompanying video; with the band, together they had contributed a track gratis to the million-selling album that followed, so there was obviously complete agreement with the sentiment expressed, but now they say they will not be convinced sufficiently to perform again until they get hard evidence that the project is being seen through to its ultimate and Godly end.

There's something happening here. I mean, where's Michael Jackson today, at home playing with his pet snakes? Where are you, Stevie Wonder, and what have you seen that we can't see? I mean, I don't believe Stevie Wonder isn't here. Like, why not? It can't be the weather, not today with the sun promising us 80 degrees of slow burn and so many silly motherfuckers like me wandering around with their best smiles on. Whatever the reasons, I hope we never find out. Because if those people I saw at the Live Aid concert in Philadelphia ever get to hear of any scams going down about misappropriated funds by any government, or any one-eyed jacks they can put a dirty name to, then I don't wanna be sitting around on my ass somewhere bashing the keys and telling this foul stinking world, well, you know, I fucking told you. No, that would mean nothing. I hope we would lynch the bastards and slit their throats right down to their rotten putrid gizzards!

Ah... but hang on here. How much bile does a person need to suck on before it all just starts to sound like one long bitch of crummy complaints? Let's put the sunglasses on and take a walk round the gig, the weather's nice after all…

'By mid-afternoon, Phil Collins had finished his duet with Sting in London and was headed across the Atlantic on a Concorde jet to perform in Philadelphia and, more important... more than 20 million dollars had already been pledged'
– New York Times

'David Bowie, Sting, Tina Turner, Mick Jagger… there they all were, in glorious, full-colour satellite Dollarvision, being, of all things, nice!'
– The Observer

I feel like a goddamn fool, but I'm humping around in the queue for the hot dog stand – hoping to lay my molars on some of that fine South Philly cheese-steak... Mmm-hmmm, with some of those hot cheese fries to go – and I figure, what the hell and why hot, so I lean over and with a sudden flash of my bad-teeth smile I am talking to a local Philly Southsider, who says, "Shit, I know it's for a good cause and all, and I'm glad that's where my money's going, you know, to help people, but like, why I'm here is to see Led fuckin' Zeppelin! You know what I mean?"

You got it. The JFK Stadium – a huge sports arena that in its prime was the home of the big local Philadelphia football team, the Flyers, before the team took their crowd two blocks down the street to the more modern sports complex recently erected – is rarely used these days, except for the biggest events. It is in fact the only stadium capable of holding almost 100,000 people out here on the East Coast, and today the old girl look likes she's bought herself a brand new pair of pantyhose, hitched up her drawers and dragged a comb through her hair. The place is alive with colour, rich in good vibes, and swinging on the once-in-a-lifetime security of knowing that what you're doing is right. Straight as a bleeding arrow, mate.

Backstage, the atmosphere is equal to anything going on outside. When Ozzy has finished his three number set with Sabbath he tells TV interviewer after TV interviewer that no, he wasn't really sure about his feelings before he arrived in Philadelphia, but now, oh now, well that was different... and Ozzy was right. The picture changes when you see the action going on, and fully righteous with it, right there in front of your eyes. Jack Nicholson chats to Ozzy and the two old rogues end up laughing at each other. Rick Springfield you wouldn't know until the TV cameras start to cluster up close, while Bryan Adams walks around in shorts with his girlfriend by his side. Even the loathsome Thompson Twins drop the pop-fart facade for this one special occasion and don't bother the locals too much.

"Good morning, children of the '80s," announced Joan Baez, at the very start of the concert. "This is your Woodstock, and it's long overdue." We stuck our fingers down our throats for that one, but when the old biddy cranked out a nice and sensible rendition of 'Amazing Grace' I could forgive her those wrinkles around the throat, and anyway, it was only one number, and as a professional I could cope with that.

The Hooters followed and... yes, but who are the goddamn Hooters? Local boyos snuck through the back door of course, should anybody care to enquire. But so what? The Four Tops are a real belly-wobble; quite superb sound, raunchy vocals and saxes hotter than July; no question about it now Sergeant, we're on our bloody way this time. Why, there are thousands of people over there shaking their booty like Mama ain't never coming home... And then Billy Ocean, followed by Black Sabbath! Yeah, why not? Let's fuckin' go...

It's almost 11 o'clock on this sweltering morning and Crosby, Stills and Big Nose are crying into their guitars. David Crosby is going to jail in Texas before the year is out say the police and court reports, a five-stretch say the wise, for getting caught with a room full of guns, cocaine, and... dirty socks, who knows? Stephen Stills looks like Benny Hill on Mandrax for the first time, but they do their bit and what the hell. Judas Priest follow and kill me stone dead. I like this group of Band Aid banditos so much, and when they open their set with 'Living After Midnight', well, here's my fiver, take it to the deserts of Africa with my blessing. When the revolving stage wheels Bryan Adams into view, and the news goes out that we are now – ta-ra! – live and linked, via satellite, to London, the place experiences its first really dangerous explosion of the day. By noon, young Bryan is dipping into the honey with 'The Kids Wanna Rock' and, all right, I give in. Gimme two of those 14 dollar T-shirts, I'm all yours...

As the day turns into dusk the stars all come and go. Simple Minds, the Pretenders, Tom Petty, the Beach Boys, Eric Clapton, all introduced so warmly by, uh, Sonny from Miami Vice, Chevy Chase, Bette Midler, Jack Nicholson, Jeff 'Whoa! Rock'n'roll!' Bridges... still no-one is burned out, no-one is anywhere near ready to quit the good and wholesome action, the tone is growing ever-more mellow, not ready to make the jump yet to deep and respectful, but not far to go.

For that final piece of our hearts that says, "Yup Bob, I gotta hand it to you, I think you did us all a favour there!" we have to wait for Led Zeppelin. Oh yes, you remember, the daddies of them all... Led Zeppelin! That name is worth pure gold in America. The small talk about the Beatles may come and go, but when it was announced that Zeppelin was to reform, albeit minus their deceased former drummer John 'Bonzo' Bonham, replaced for this event by Phil Collins and Tony Thompson (Power Station/ Bowie/Chic drummer), you could feel the anticipation an ocean away. Was it true? Led Zeppelin, the biggest, the best, and the baddest, just this one last time?

The crunch came as I was standing chatting to Ozzy and Geezer, along the backstage alleyway concourse that led to the stage. All day long the star attractions had wandered amiably around unaffected and wholly uninterested in unveiling their own petty vanities before people who were, after all, suitably regarded as their peers, the least temporary contemporaries, and who would be ass enough to stomp around and play up the whole star-star-superstar boogie, for who would it impress? And then suddenly large black voices behind our knotty little gathering began yelling: "Qutta the way there! Outta the way! People comin' through here!"

And we shift ass very quickly, being smart, and on turning round to see just who the people are causing this rash disturbance, we spy three no-shit uniformed spades providing a human shield to the angular distorted crab-like vision of 'Little' Jimmy Page, glassy eyes slitted and raw, his jerky spasmodic gestures a testament to the powers of modern science. Heading up the back with his own court of bully-boy jesters and sprightly laymen, comes Robert Plant, looking every month his true age (15 and-a-half) and bursting with a rouged good health it is hard to ignore.

"Hey, Rob! You big girl's blouse!" cries Ozzy as Plant swishes past, swanning his own unique song for every red cent it's worth (which is at least double any number you or I could come up with, kid). "Ozzy!" cries Robert. "Bloody hell! And Geezer too!" And Robert breaks rank, much to the obvious bafflement of his armed guards, and ambles over to greet the two (temporarily) reunited Black Sabbath kingpins. Nice guy, Rob Plant, if he played his cards right I'd really like to interview him…

Minutes later, up on stage, the red, white and blue curtains wind back as Jimmy Page hits the opening chords to 'Rock And Roll' and there isn't a dry brain cell left in the house. Madness! Great huge waves of it erupt into the sky and Band Aid be damned, they really did it this time, and good. 'Whole Lotta Love' follows and the whole thing starts to take on the aspect of some crazy dream. Page looks out of it, Plant looks superb, pencil thin, knows what he's doing, knows why, too.

At the finale of 'Stairway To Heaven', when Plant closes his eyes and sings, "And she's buy-uy-ing… a stairway… to… heaven', the crowd all come in on the buy-uy-ing part and cold tingles go up and down the neck of the world. Afterwards, the applause is huge, not just from the crowd of terminal hysterics out front, but from the hard-nosed pay-check dependent herds of worker ants backstage, me included.

Much later, I am rolling down the highway from Philly, sitting hunched up in the front seat of Ozzy's limo, and on the miniature TV in the back Bob Dylan is sealing the fate of history with his finest old waltz, 'Blowin' In The Wind'. And then Ozzy says: "Turn that bloody TV off, Sharon. I'm tired."

Off it goes, the screen dies, and so do my thoughts…

'The international accounting firm of Howarth And Howarth, in co-operation with its United States affiliate, Laventhal And Howarth, is to prepare a complete public disclosure of the Live Aid finances' – New York Times

First published in Kerrang! No.100, August 8, 1985

Never having interviewed 'Diamond' Dave before, I was hoping for something special – or at least something a little outside the normal bullshit. Well, he certainly gave me that.

Ushered into a room backstage after the show, I was treated to Jack Daniels, cocaine, a huge sack of grass, even a naked dancing girl. All this before we'd even sat down to start the interview. Not that I was complaining. The Average White Band blared from a ghetto-blaster and every now and then Dave would turn to me with that mile-wide smile familiar from all those Van Halen videos, and howl like a wolf. Beyond words, I just howled right back.

From there the night just got longer and stranger. The naked dancing girl eventually put her clothes back on and left, as did everyone else in the room bar me, Dave, and photographer Ross Halfin. For the next eight hours we were treated to what amounted to a long stream-of-consciousness rap from the Diamond. Laugh? My face and neck muscles ached for days afterwards. I wished I'd taped it but he wouldn't allow me to. I wish Ross could have got a shot of it but Dave wasn't having any of that either. It was probably just as well. When the demon's eye is upon you, the last thing you need is reminding of it the next day, let alone 20 years later.

The sun was already high in the sky by the time we eventually left the gig – definitely a first for me. Ross, who was off drugs and booze at the time, later complained that it had been one of the most boring nights of his life. Not being off anything myself in those days, I thought it was one of the most exciting. Maybe even a bit too exciting. For when we got back to the hotel and Dave tried to talk me into joining him in his suite for "a nightcap" I practically ran to the elevators to get away. By then even I had had enough. Only Ozzy Osbourne at his worst had ever made me feel the same way.

If there was ever a real-life Rock School, David Lee Roth would be the headmaster.

David Lee Roth, Massachusetts, August 1988

Maybe two-thirds of the way through the show, the stage-lights dim, drummer Gregg Bissonette strikes up a lookin'-for-trouble cha-cha-chasshhh on the cymbals, and Diamond Dave saunters out from the wings under cover of a lone spotlight. He sashays like Humphrey Bogart up to the mike, lights one, rolls his shoulders and pulls his trilby an inch further down over his face, then looks the audience straight in the eye and holds it. He's about to go into a rap. You can tell. Somewhere far off a sleazy saxophone begins to wail like a police siren.

"My name is Roth. I'm licensed to carry a microphone," he begins, the crowd already laughing. "I was in my office over on Main Street in Worcester, Massachusetts (cue huge roars of approval, Worcester being where the show is taking place) working kind of late one night when I got the call..."

He pauses, takes a drag, continues... "She sounded like she needed help, so I told her to come on over. She said OK... Sometime later there's a knock on my door. I said, come in. She said OK ..." More pauses, more knowing looks.

"She walked in and blew me a kiss so hot I could feel the breeze go right through the buttons on my 501 jeans... She was wearing a dress so tight it looked like she'd been poured into it and somebody had forgotten to say when... She looked me over and said: 'Nice gun'. I said, 'Nice holster...' We got to talking and she told me she was having trouble with the law and wanted to know if I could get her off..."

Saxophone sighs deeply as the crowd titter. He continues. "I said, 'I don't know nothin' about the law, sweetheart, but I know I can get... you... off!' She looked at me and said, 'Oh, Diamond Dave! You're just a GIGOLO!'..."

BANG! The band womp into the song. The lights are up, the crowd are dancing and wiping the tears from their eyes at the same time. We've got a real show on our hands here! Songs, jokes, props and lights; the raps and the razzle-dazzle and the blessed rock'n'roll... What hasn't this show got?

Seeing David Lee Roth perform live for the first time since he last stepped onto the stage with the rest of the Van Halen boys at Donington four years ago, really brought home to me how mundane and street-average most rock bands are by comparison.

There's nothing humourless and tense about a David Lee Roth show; it's just straight up, high times excitement from start to finish! Nothing ever stops moving – the music, the band, the lights, him least of all... Kid, you gotta be ready when this stuff comes at ya, otherwise you'll miss something and get left behind!

It begins with a simple announcement, mostly obscured by the surge of noise from the 10,000-strong Worcester crowd, and by the time the words DAVID... LEE... ROTH!! are boomed from the speakers the band are suddenly already there and into 'The Bottom Line', Roth in full Diamond Dave mode, the familiar look of complete and utter astonishment on his face as he throws one leg and then another high into the air, which makes him look as though he is flying across the stage...

With the crowd already eating it up, the band go almost without pause into 'Ain't Talkin' 'Bout Love', the old but bold Van Halen hit, pumping out the riff like they were shaking hands with an iron bar: Steve Vai, sleek and immaculately underdressed, patrolling the boundaries of the stage, trying to keep up with his guitar which seems to go where it pleases. His opposite number, bassist Matt Bissonette, hawking it around like Billy The Kid in shades. And on risers deeper into the stage, keyboard wizard Brett Tuggle, knee pumping, grin in place, and drummer Gregg Bissonette, arms flailing like a drowning man, half out of his seat, wild like the wind.

Standing atop half a dozen lighted steps leading to the drum riser, Roth suddenly cuts the number dead with a single wave of his arm, leans heavy into the mike, and breathes: "We ain't just talking 'bout lurrvwe here tonight... We're talking about going right up to the edge and gazing DOOWWWNNNN!" The crowd whoop and cheer; girls scream and throw their panties at the stage; one throws a red rose which Roth picks up, sniffs, laughs, then tosses it back into the stalls. He launches into a rap about his early days living right here in Worcester, which he did for a couple of years as a child. "That's right, no shit! I fucking know this town, baby!" The crowd, for most of whom this is news indeed, go completely over the top, trying to climb the air with clawing fingers, eyes white, voices howling like hungry wolves...

The band break into 'Just Like Paradise', Roth starts flying into mad, acrobatic shapes again, the rhythm section kick-in and Vai strolls out into the spotlight cradling that baffling but impressive-looking triple-necked guitar thing – just like in the video, ma – and takes it for a spin around the jaw of the stage. Against a backdrop of some vague cityscape outlined in silhouettes, the lighting rig – a row of gigantic diamonds, hovering like a crown above the stage – begins throwing out yellow beams of light into the balconies that trim the stage, and Roth runs the band hard through 'Knucklebones', twirling the mike-stand so fast it starts to flash like a hot strobe ("an old Kung Fu trick," he tells me later).

A trés butch little strut through the kitsch and beguiling old chestnut 'Easy Street' followed, played for laughs. It got them all singing along, before Gregg Bissonette began pummelling out the raw Red Indian beat that signals the introduction to 'Hot For Teacher'; Vai's spidery guitar lines perfectly matching the original Eddie Van Halen interpretation, but adding something around the edges that is all his own; Roth in his element as he wrestles with the footlights and springs like a cat from side to side of the stage.

'Stand Up', the new single, goes down like cold vanilla on a hot day, the Worcester kids and me cranked high enough to hang ourselves, Vai taking off into some Prince-style humping of his guitar, which he lays on its back – still screaming, still itching – across the top of one of the amps in a way only the little girls would understand. Before the guitar solo has grown cold though, its echo returns to grow into 'Skyscraper', a veritable tour-de-force, Roth descending on a rope from high up in the lighting rigging down the sheer face of the stage in time to reach the mike for the first verse...

After that, it's straight into the hilarious 'Just A Gigolo' routine. 'Crazy From The Heat' is next up and proves to be an unexpected highlight when, halfway through the guitar break, the band suddenly cut out and the lights zero in on the lip of the stage where Diamond Dave is poised behind seven steel drums, whistle in mouth, sticks in hand, ready to blow up a storm of marimba-maramba-let's-go-yamma-yamma! Eventually, the entire band are at it on the steels, rattling it out like veterans; synchronised, cool; coaxing the house to the tips of its toes...

"Stevie, can you spell Massa-fuckin'-chusetts for me?" asks Dave when the band are back in position behind their instruments. Stevie spells MASSAFUCKIN'CHUSETTS for him with his guitar and the crowd goes right with him. The bass starts thumping and the drums start to swagger, and 'Yankee Rose' comes rolling like a wagon-train from the valley of stage. The number dovetails into an extended guitar break while Roth vanishes from the stage, only to reappear five minutes later at the mixing desk, which is positioned on a five-foot riser in the centre of the arena.

Back on stage, Vai cuts into a camp and over the top arrangement of 'The

Star Spangled Banner', while Roth begins to climb a rope ladder like Weird Jack right up the giant's beanstalk, pausing every 20 feet or so to swing by one hand and wave, like an outer space ham, to the audience below, which can barely control itself. About 100 feet up he disappears from view once again onto a platform seemingly the size of a matchbox. The band strike like queer lightning into 'Panama' and the platform begins to descend from the sky. As it floats down into view you can see it's actually a boxing ring Roth is riding: ropes, corners, the US flag hanging from one end. The crowd are beyond wild by this time and Dave gives it the full Muhammad Ah-Lee Roth treatment, pausing the number at one point just to receive the adulation of the adoring crowd, arms outstretched just like the real prize fighters do…

And so began the finale. In time for 'California Girls', Roth climbs out of the ring onto a giant surfboard, smoke billowing from its tail, also suspended by wires from above the mixing desk, gliding down to the stage above the heads of the crowd. He's the futuristic lounge-lizard with the Blade Runner smile, still singing, still kicking his legs, the Crazy Man who knows something…

The first encore is 'You Really Got Me', which Vai practically reinvents in places, knocking new life into the old standard in a way that would have Ray Davies reaching for the Valium. And then to finish, what else of course but 'Jump'. Preceded by a synthesised excerpt from the theme tune to the movie, *2001: A Space Odyssey*, the parping synthesiser intro to 'Jump' is still the one that exerts the most feeling in the crowd here tonight. But Dave knows that, which is why he sensibly saves it for last. Anything after that would be impossible, even now. In that knowledge, Roth and the band squeeze it for every drop it's worth, the way only real pros know how. Breathtaking! She was right, you know. Diamond Dave, you are a gigolo!

We had come face to face for the first time the previous evening; when he spun into the room in which I was propping up a beer table, next door to the dressing room, shortly before he went on stage. It was like a hurricane suddenly hit the room. Stomping around in big desert boots, as he talked his body shuddered and jolted, head thrown back in a mile-wide grin, the famous permanently astonished visage mostly concealed beneath a black, floppy beret, dark, impenetrable shades, and the long yellow mane that falls down his back. He was all angular comic gestures and spitting speed-freak satire, hurling the jazzy one liners out of the side of his mouth and laughing like a drain before I had time to get a fix on all the punch-lines; turning it on for me in his guise as the Guru of Good Times and the reigning King of Ramalama...

"Great, man!" he cried. "That's fuckin' great! So this shit is gonna be on the cover of the 200th edition of *Kerrang!*? Oh, that's COOL! I fuckin' love *Kerrang!*, man. You guys gotta really BAD attitude! HAHAHA! Take no fuckin' prisoners, baby!"

He spun round on his heels and threw out his arms. "Jesus, I feel high! I'm fuckin' flying here! It musta bin that orange I ate before coming down to the gig. It's that fuckin' sugar, man. It goes to my system like that – zap! Pow! HAHAHA! Somebody fuckin' hold me down, quick, before I explode..."

At first I couldn't decide whether this guy was a suitable case for treatment or if he was just putting down a rap – for all I know it was probably both – but I took to him immediately. You'd have to be nine-parts dead not to. When something tickles, you laugh. And when Diamond Dave sings you his song, you listen.

Later, after the show, we got shit-faced together taking turns on his bottle of Jack Daniel's. With the shades off and his gig over, he talks a lot slower, but his conversation is no less animated; standing up and striking poses to explain the point of a certain story, or crouched on the edge of his seat barking with laughter at another, the conversation rambling all over the place like a drunk looking for the way home.

At one point, we got started in on some travelling stories. When he's not working, Roth likes to take off on his own sometimes. "Just to see which way the wind blows," he said. "Travelling around, you can learn a lot about people and places, and through that you can learn a lot about yourself too, just by the way you react on the spot to new and different situations. And you can land yourself in some funny shit, too. And that's good for you! You shouldn't be afraid to try and put yourself some place you've never been before..."

He tells me a story. "I remember driving through the Midwest with a friend one time, we were right out in the middle of nowhere, late at night and looking for a place to stop and have some drinks, maybe. Suddenly we see a truck-stop with a light on, so we decide to pull over and take a look. We walk inside and the place is completely empty except for this one old woman mopping up behind the counter. We ask her for a couple of beers and some sandwiches and she says sure, no problem.

"She brings the stuff out and we get to talking and she's pretty cool, this old gal, so we invite her to sit down and join us for a drink. Well, we put a couple away and I take out a handful of nickels and dimes and tell the old gal to put some sounds on the juke while I went and got us a couple more drinks. I get the drinks, she gets up and puts the money into the juke, then comes back and sits down. Now she doesn't know me from Adam, but the first record that comes on is 'Just A Gigolo'! I think, wow, the old gal digs my music!

"I turned to her and said, 'You like this song?' She said, 'Oh, you mean number I5A? I just love I5A! It's one of my favourite songs on that old jukebox!' I couldn't believe it. 15A, she called it: the button you had to push on the juke to get the record. Didn't know what it was called, didn't know who it was by, just liked it a lot. So I told her. I said, 'That's my song and that's me singing', and she freaked and said, 'You mean you're I5A? You!? You're I5A?Oh, my!' I said, 'That's me all right, baby – MISTER FIFTEEN A!' HAHAHA!"

He takes another pull on the bottle. "At first she got real excited about actually meeting I5A, you know what I mean, but then she turned quiet. I asked her what was the matter and she said: 'Oh, I just wish Old Sal was here to meet you. He just loves 15A, too. Old Sal loves that song more than anybody I know'. I'm thinking, who the hell's Old Sal? I mean, this lady has got to be pushing 70, so this Old Sal dude has got to be hitting at least 90!

"Meantime, she carries on with her story... 'Old Sal comes in here most nights of the week and just sits there at that bar, nursing a beer and just playing that old 15A over and over, with a kind of knowing look in his eye'. I said, 'Oh, yeah? How do ya mean?' She paused, looked straight at me and said, 'I think it's because Old Sal's a bit of a gigolo himself'. HAHAHA! I tell ya, man, that old girl was worth her weight in gold..."

Somehow we stumbled onto the subject of videos – I think we were talking TV. I was probably trying to sell him on idea of hosting his own chat-show. Anyway, it transpires that the reason why the colours are so eye-stingingly vivid on the Van Halen 'Hot For Teacher' video is that, "I was wearing shades the whole time we were editing it and I couldn't see a goddamned thing!" he laughed. "We'd be shooting segments in which I was wearing these things, then in-between times I would be racing over to the playback console to take a look at what we'd got. Only I never once thought to take off my shades. And I'd be standing up there going, 'Hey, man, this looks a little dull. Turn the goddamned colour up!' And it wasn't until much later when I saw the thing on a TV screen that I though, my god, what is this? How come the colours are so fuckin' high? And then I remembered… Oh shit! Oh yeah…"

He grins and continues. "I'll tell you something else I bet you didn't know about that video," he said, tapping me on the knee with the bottle of JD. "You know that bit right at the end, when I'm standing there pretending to be a game-show host? Next time you see that video take a good look at my trouser leg – I'm not telling you which one, you'll have to see for yourself. But if you look real close, you'll see a stain down my leg. That's a piss stain, man! HAHAHA! We were working so hard I didn't even have time to take a piss – literally! So a little got on my leg, so I'm a slob… HAHAHA! Take a look next time you see it, though. I guarantee you'll never be able to watch that video again without that piss stain sticking out a mile!"

At another point, I asked Roth if he ever got nervous clambering around on those ropes he uses in his show.

"No, never. Shit, I'm used to floating around at the end of a rope on the side of a mountain, so crawling around in the stage-rigging 50 feet above a stage is not about to faze me. Plus, I've got a guy up there to be on hand if ever I did get in any serious trouble. In fact, he's more nervous than I am. One night I was just about to climb onto the rope and get ready for the part where I lower myself down onto the stage, and I suddenly grabbed him and said, 'Oh my God, something's wrong, man…' You shoulda seen his face. Immediately he was like, 'What is it? What is it? What's up, Dave?' And I was like, 'Oh my God, give me your arm!' By this time he's going crazy. 'WHAT IS IT, DAVE? WHAT IS IT, MAN? WHAT, WHAT, WHAT?' And I grabbed him by the wrist and said, 'It's your watch, man. It's running a little slow, I think…' HAHAHA! Now he doesn't listen to a word I say, so we're both totally safe!"

I asked him how he was looking forward to his coming appearance on the bill with Iron Maiden at the Donington Monsters of Rock festival?

"It's gotta be better than the last time I played there with Van Halen," he said, shaking his head. "Man, we were not going through happy times. Everything was going wrong between us, we were barely talking. The most fun I had all day was actually being onstage, and even that was a little strained. I remember one particular point, I was starting to get into a number and really fly. I glanced over to the side of the stage and I saw this female photographer with her back to me bending over, searching around in her bag for something. Man, I was already working on my high, trying to get into the set, and then I saw this cute little ass wiggling at me and I just went for it! I ran right over to one the side of the stage and got down on my knees and planted a kiss on that sweet little butt.

"And do you know what she did? She spun around like someone had just kicked her in the ass and hit me – whammo! – straight in the jaw! HAHAHA! And that chick packed a wallop, man. It almost knocked me off my feet! I thought, Jesus, this day is doomed..."

The night died a lot quicker than the bottle of Jack Daniel's, and it was past dawn before we had crawled out of the dressing room and into Roth's waiting limo, coarse yellow sunlight like needles in our eyes. And now here I stand 24 hours on, beer-handed and perspiring a little too heavily in the hospitality room backstage, waiting for Roth to emerge from his post-show dinner of lobster, barbecued ribs, salad, rice and fries, and give me that wave of the hand that tells me it's time to unravel the cellophane from another bottle of old granddad's favourite and turn on the machine.

Suddenly the door flies open arid there he is, wise-ass grin in place, eyes a little tired maybe, but still bouncing around on his feet and loose. "Let me get us a couple of beers and some of this," he says, indicating the JD on the drinks table. It is, in fact, the only spirit stocked backstage at a David Lee Roth show.

"OK, follow me…" We take off down the corridor and Roth leads us into an empty room closes the door behind him. "Awright, I'm open for business," he smiles. "Go for it."

I want to start by asking you a little bit about your current tour. You've always been very athletic, almost acrobatic, onstage, but how did you come up with the idea of a rope-ladder and being hoisted back down into the arena in a boxing ring?

"Well, that, and when I lower myself down a rope onto the stage, or when I ride the surfboard over the audience's heads, they're what I call my tricks. They're not special effects. A special effect is something you buy in a box, that when you take out you need a technician to put together for you. The stuff I do is more pure than just using another set of lasers that anybody with the money can buy. These are tricks that could have been done 20 years ago for roughly the same cost and the same effect.

"I remember when I was a kid going to see a production of 'Peter Pan' with my sister, and here was this woman dressed as a man flying from one side of the stage to the other on the end of a wire, and I just thought this was the greatest thing I'd ever seen! There's a certain kind of character displayed in theatrics like that that appeals to me greatly. I don't mean like a cartoon character, I mean in the sense that there's some soul there, there's some heart in stuff like that. And I don't mind having a little bit of that same soul in my show..."

There comes a moment in the show when the boxing ring hovers above the mixing desk in the middle of the arena, and the music cuts out and you stand there soaking up the applause and adulation for minutes at a time. The audience seems to be at its craziest at that moment. What is going through your mind as you stand there with your arms in the air taking it all in?

"I'm not really thinking too hard at that point. HAHAHA! I'm more just reacting. But I think the people are cheering more from all the combined years of conditioning that seep into your system when you see a boxing ring. And what we have is the real thing. It's a regulation-ring we've got flying around up there. So when you see it, all those years, decades, of watching boxing rings on TV, or seeing pictures in magazines and newspapers or having them described on the radio, when you actually see one it hits you straight away. Question: what happens in the boxing ring? Answer: life, man! You know what I mean? We all deal with the boxing ring on a daily level. Meaning, there is always great hope and potential and there is always potential disaster every time you step into the boxing ring. But like it or not we all have to take that step every day to survive. Just reading those words trigger off something in people they didn't have when they started reading this interview! HAHAHA!

"It's man against man, that's what that symbolises. But both guys can get crushed by time, by the great invisible opponent..." He pauses, self-conscious suddenly. "Hey man, can you imagine certain people reading this shit? 'What's that the dude said about an invisible opponent? Fuck that! I wanna buy a T-shirt!' HAHAHA! But it's in there all the same, buried deep, and that's what makes people go hysterical every time they see me in that thing."

You're often accused by your critics of camping things up too much as a rock'n'roll performer, and there's obviously a lot more going on in your head than just wham-bam-thank-you—ma'am mindless metal. Do you ever feel that you have to tie yourself down occasionally, so that you don't go too far above your audience's heads?

"Communication is an art, and music is nothing but communication: how ya feel on a given day and why. That's all music is, and you don't even need words to get the story..."

People seem to either love you or hate you, though. They're either fanatical or they can't stand you. What is it about you that provokes them?

"If they hate me it's because they don't understand me. Either we haven't had a chance to sit and get to know one another, or I'm screwing up on the transmission end. Or maybe they just don't like the changes I've been through with my music over the last 10 years. But I never wanted to be a performer that stood for just one thing, one style, one set of moves and that's it. How boring! Nobody reading this right now wants to spend the rest of their lives doing the same thing over and over, so why should I?"

I know from our conversation last night that you're quite a literary person. Do you get many of your ideas for lyrics from the books you read? "No. Wait a minute... I'm such a contrary prick, sometimes. There I go saying no without even paying attention to the question. HAHAHA! I shoulda bin a lawyer... Anyway, yeah, I get inspired by books and magazines. They inspire me to pay attention to things that I wasn't paying attention to before. But I get ideas cooking in my head about all sorts of things – I meet a type of person I never met before, I see something in society I never noticed before...

"Anything, man, anything that moves me. I'm always finding new things to get interested in. Sometimes it's a book, sometimes it's other things. You gotta remember, I'm not a natural anything. I got it all out of books, I got it all off a screen, I got it all off the radio, I got it all off other people and put it all together. I hate that term 'self-improvement' but that's kinda how it is with me. I'm always looking for something new that's good to add to the stew, you know?"

I'd like to get your opinion, as a renowned live performer, on some of your contemporaries, OK? "OK, but I'm going to have to say something upfront first. I'm only going to talk about other bands as a music fan, not as someone comparing what anybody else does to me. So if I end up cutting up another band in the press, I want the readers to know that I'm only doing it to complain as a music fan, just the same as they do when they don't like something OK?"

First off then, Prince. Do you find what he does exciting? "I think he has a lot of great ideas but most of them are unfinished. I think that... ah...

working with some outside people might flesh out some of his ideas. A lot of his music sounds like jams in the studio that an engineer refined later on in the day, or a remix artist pasted together. And the chief thing about it is it's primarily dance music, very simple chord structures and so on, which to me is a little too much like wallpaper. You use it to change the feel of the room, and not much more. As a live performer I think Prince has got a lot of energy and he's got a lot of heart. But he's hyper derivative and that I don't find intriguing. I see right dead straight who it is he's copying, and I find that boring, and boredom is the cardinal sin."

What about Michael Jackson, what do you make of him? "With Michael there's a more definitive style. Whether you like it or not, it sounds like him. It's definitely his kind of music, it's all his trip. You can't see through the weld marks like you can with someone like Prince. Now that's intriguing to me. Good songwriting, man, and good performance, you know. It's something you've either got or you haven't got. On the other hand, I get the feeling that nobody ever stole this kid's lunch money at school, nobody ever threw a baseball bat at him too hard during recess, and that's an important part of growing up, too. All of that going in the front is what comes out of the back end in your music later on in life. And I'm kinda missing that with Michael's approach. HAHAHA! Some of that man stuff has gotta go into the stew too! Jesus, stop asking me about other people, the readers will think I don't have a god word to say about anybody. HAHAHA!"

All right. What about your own career as a performer – where do you take it from here? You surely don't plan to spend the rest of your life on the road? "Well, if I want to I could carry this act around for another 20 years, give or take an act of God or Ferrari. I'm certainly in shape for something like that if I want to take things that way. But the next logical step is movies. You know, as one half of the fabulous Picasso Brothers [the other being Roth's manager, Pete Angelus] we made more than three Jack Nicholsons combined, apiece, for the movie we never made! [Crazy From The Heat.] I mean, hey, we were ready to shoot but CBS went out of the movie business, so suddenly I had to get Darth Vader & Sons as my attorneys and wage doom war on the company.

"But that movie will be made, eventually. I know I talk about a million things at once, but talk don't mean a thing. Come pay day, there's my new record, there's the new tour – that's where my heart is. And up until now there hasn't been enough time to mobilise 150 people on a movie set for months and months at a time. What can I tell you? You bet we're gonna get the movie situation together, though. But, typically, I'm already looking forward to recording the soundtrack!"

Is there ever going to be a David Lee Roth that could be a quiet, family man with a wife and kids etc? They say it can happen to the best of us, Dave. "I surprise people a lot in that I actually spend most of my time by myself. I lived with a girlfriend for a couple of years, but we broke up about a year and a half ago. Before that I lived by myself for 12 years. And I do again now. And this is... how I'm happiest."

Hence, he said his passion for climbing mountains and going on jungle expeditions. "This is all introspective stuff, and I brood. A lot of times people are very surprised if they run into me on the streets. It can be very different from what they expect me to be like in public, or on a stage. I can be the most outgoing, public person in the world or I can be the most private dude you've ever come across. And I like both extremes."

Do you find, though, that you can adopt the Diamond Dave persona at the drop of a hat when you want to? "It depends. I mean, I know how to misbehave right on cue! HAHAHA! That's the trooper part of it. But luckily, I've managed to work most of my reality directly into the music, directly into the show, and for the people out there that are familiar with what I've been doing over the years, they know it's never been just one face I've worn, one approach.

"Spirit is the thread that winds all the way through all the chaos, but the faces are different. The face of the person singing 'Damn Good' is very different from the person who's singing 'Bottom Line', although the spirit is the same."

The first time I read the lyrics to 'Damn Good' I thought they might have been written about your time in Van Halen. Were they? "No, definitely not. I guess they could be interpreted that way, and sitting here looking in rear-view mirror with you, Mick, I see that in the middle of the road, too. HAHAHA! I felt the bump, but I didn't see a thing! HAHAHA!"

Will you have to alter the US show much for Donington and the other European dates you're doing this year? "Oh, sure, a little. Playing in Europe you're practically playing in a new country every night, confronting a whole new culture at each show, and you have to adjust the set accordingly because each new audience is a little bit different from the one you played to the night before. My job is to guess how different. Like, you speakada language, boy? Well, yes, we do. But the changes won't be drastic, just appropriate. When you're in a drag race like Donington, and you've got six – count 'em! – natural, fuel-burning, top-line, screaming dragster rock metal bands all on the same bill, and they're all eating the stage up, the crowd is totally geared to that kind of action – I mean, it practically tells you on the invitation how to dress! So the fact of the matter is, you're not gonna be the guy who was too cool to put on the style for the Halloween party, you've got to go out there and fuckin' murder somebody, man! It's that kind of event, you know? And I love it, I'm into it. I've got all the hats that I need stashed right there in my suitcase, and I'm ready."

As you know, this story is for the 200th issue of *Kerrang!*. Would you care to say a few words in the way of a birthday greeting? "Well, *Kerrang!* is the Bible, you know? *Kerrang!* is like Mr Chicken McNugget! Two hundred McNuggets ago it was the only action town, now suddenly here comes Wendy's and Burger King… What I'm saying is, *Kerrang!* was the first and is still the coolest, right down to the name.

"Now you've got Bif Pop magazine, or Metal this, Metal that, you know what I mean? What I like most of all is that *Kerrang!* has always maintained its sense of humour, because it is pretty funny some of the shit that *Kerrang!* somehow always gets to hear about. And there's a sense of honour about it, too. *Kerrang!* has never been afraid to nail somebody. *Kerrang!* is not afraid to complain, because, hell, complaining's more fun, anyway! I know, I do it! HAHAHA! And it's just more human. It's not a fuckin' groupie rag.

"So I'm really proud to be on the cover, man. As long as I don't have to pay for the candles on the cake! HAHAHAHAHA!"

First published in Kerrang! No.200, August 13, 1988

I have interviewed Fish a great many times in several different locations over the years – from London to Los Angeles, via Aylesbury and Edinburgh. But perhaps the best interview we ever did occurred in Berlin in 1985. It was certainly the most prophetic: Marillion, who he had led from obscurity to the heights of the Hammersmith Odeon, now stood perched on the cusp of their first really big, worldwide success – and, somehow, Fish knew it.

In Berlin to record their third album, 'Misplaced Childhood', from which would come their huge hit single, 'Kayleigh', Fish was already telling anyone who would listen that this was going to be "the big one." This despite the presence of a doubting EMI executive who kept boring everyone stupid with talk of 'demographics' and 'market penetration'. Wanker.

At the same time it was clear that Fish seemed to be undergoing some sort of transition in his personal life. He told me of a girl he had met and become "obsessed with" who worked as a hostess at one of the glitzy nightclubs he and the band had begun frequenting during their stay in Berlin. (Indeed, not only would she end up the star of the 'Kayleigh' video but was soon to become his wife.) He was also still quite heavily involved with cocaine; a rock star's accoutrement he would grow evermore fond of as the band's success began to spiral out of control. Not that I minded, of course. It was the rock stars who didn't do drugs that I wished to avoid in those days.

Being the same age, we had a lot in common. I threw in the towel though when he suggested going out to a club as the interview finally wound down at five in the morning. He called me a "lightweight" and, compared to Fish in those days, that's exactly what I was…

Fish, Berlin, May 1985

Five weeks in Suicide City does strange things to a man's head. Berlin is a city of concrete and walls situated smack in the middle of the great East-West divide, its outer limits enclosed by forbidden lands governed by sky-high barbed-wire fences and occupied by soldiers carrying live ammunition guarding God-knows-what from army-turrets surrounded by mine-fields. If you wanna rip it up for a couple of nights in Berlin and shave a couple more years off your life then you can, no problem: the brothels and the clubs and the wide-spread availability of smack and coke guarantee the action. But if you're planning on spending a month to six weeks in this joint, then bring along your oxygen tent because, boy, you're gonna need it. Not even the hand of fate will help if you want to take a drive out to the countryside maybe, or perhaps just get out and visit friends in neighbouring towns and cities: there simply aren't any. You're trapped until an air-ticket tells you otherwise. Hansa Studios, by the Berlin Wall, is where Marillion have been holed-up together these past six weeks recording their all-important third studio album. This is the one they're going to be calling 'Misplaced Childhood' and, as you will no doubt have read in issue 93's news story, it's very definitely a concept album, in the tradition, perhaps, of 'The Lamb Lies Down On Broadway' or, better still, Pink Floyd's 'The Wall', with maybe just a hint of David Bowie's 'Station To Station' masterpiece.

The wild West of Berlin is groaning under the five o'clock shadow of another rainy Monday when myself and photographer Ray Palmer arrive for our scheduled meeting with Marillion. Us and Marillion, we go back a ways. Shit, we actually like these guys: like talking to them, seeing them, even listening to their music once in a while. 'Script For A Jester's Tear', 'Fugazi', 'Real To Reel'… tell me about it. Marillion? They're special, that's all.

In strictest Marillion tradition, 'business' is scheduled for the following day: meaning it's time once again for all good rock and roll boys to comb the hair of the night, exploring the absolute power of positive drinking. And tonight that means a trip to see Frankie Goes To Hollywood play before 6,000 screaming Berliners. Fish, Ian Mosley and I are sitting in the hotel bar before the show lining our stomachs on Blue Label Smirnoff and Black Bush Whisky.

"So what do you think of Berlin?" Fish asks me.

"Nothing. I've been here before," I reply.

"Been here before?" he arches an eyebrow. "We've been here forever... that's what it fucking feels like. We took a couple of days off for Easter and all went home, and for a few days I was on top of the world again. Then I came back here and depression just hits you the second day – bang! Right in the face."

"You wouldn't want to live here then?" I ask.

"Fuck no! How Bowie managed to come here to clean himself up in a place as dreary and insane as this is unbelievable."

Fish is sporting a beard. I can't make up my mind whether it makes him look like the baddie from some James Bond movie or whether I'm sitting at the court of King Arthur. It suits him, and its dramatic appeal is plain, but what about the face makeup when he gets back on the road?

"Oh no, I'll shave it off tomorrow when we do the pictures," he smiles. "I let it grow for a part in this movie called *The Highlander* I was offered, but now the timing has gone all wrong; we'll be touring when they want to start filming, so it doesn't look like it's going to happen."

Film? Movie? BEARD?! But he's gone, long strides and big hunting boots, towards the elevator doors. The following afternoon at Hansa Studios we're all playing Spot The Walking Amnesia Case – I can't remember who won – and then, with precious little warning, the producer's chair at the mixing consul is shoved under my arse and a huddle of hushed grinning Marillion-heads take a deep breath and wait for the tapes to roll. We're gonna hear the single.

Cue: Total Wipe-Out! Stunning, seductive... gimme a Tequila and let me come back to you on that one. 'Kayleigh' may just be the most perfect song Marillion have yet recorded (remember I haven't heard the rest of the album properly yet), their most perfect song on an LP that boasts just two songs, in the words of Fish from the stage of the Hammersmith Odeon last Xmas: "Side one and side two..."

The production on 'Kayleigh', by Chris Kimsey, is little short of superb; built around a beautiful cartwheeling rhythm guitar part, childlike in its simple charm and utterly compelling at the climax, while Fish's lyric is all Alice Through The Whisky Glass imagery, though more understated and refined than we have come to expect and fear from that old 'tongue forged in eloquence'. The voice, too, seems to have finally located the heart and his vocal embraces the whole drama of the song even though the singer remains remote, unreformed, unrepentant.

The other side of the single is not on the album and was written specifically for the 45 here in Berlin: it's called 'Lady Nina' and is named after one of the more infamous Berlin nightclubs the band have read about in their friendly Guide To Berlin Tourist Information leaflets – and it's a bitch! Somewhere in the back of a taxi-cab, ankle deep in yesterday's rubbers, stiletto concealed in her purse, driving through the Turkish Sector on some unfinished business the law wouldn't understand, sits 'Lady Nina'. What Steve Rothery does with his guitar on this track belongs in the Land Of The Unnameable; clawing out the heart of the song and sticking it in his back pocket, while Mosley and the electronic percussion computers erupt and bleed like a volcano between your thighs. The production adds all the champagne touches, the melody pure brandy. When it's over and they've picked me up off the floor, I dry my eyes, take a long swallow of somebody else's cigarette smoke and slump off to a chair in the corner where I sit with my cakehole flapping like a bird in the wind…

Some hours later, Fish is sprawled out on the bed talking on the phone to his ma in Edinburgh. It's the usual Mother Rant: I will, I won't, I did, I don't, shut up ma and I'll see you soon, love ya... On the bedside table sits a large bottle of Black Bush Whisky, an ashtray, a full glass and two mini-speakers attached to a Walkman. Distant 'Fugazi' LP sleeve vibes, ma: Fish as Rock Star, as Poet, Actor, Hedonist and Anti-Hero. Just some of the roles that seem to fascinate the man. Like a child, every time he sees a flame burning he wants to grasp it, hold it and know it. I haven't seen him for months and suddenly I realise that I've missed the bugger with the big mouth and broad shoulders. People like Fish, they're in for the life sentence and should be respected because they are so rare. When he gets off the phone, we pour ourselves some decent measures of that fine Black Bush, I pull the cap from a beer, and sitting there cross-legged on his bed, we let it all come down…

Earlier on today you told me you were going to zap me within the first three minutes of this interview and tell me anything I needed to know. What did you mean by that? "Ah, just get it over and down, get the real heavy stuff over and done with. But it's impossible, you know…"

Why did you come to Berlin to record the album? "There were a couple of reasons, actually. One of them was that a whole lot of producers we asked to do the LP said no because they thought they couldn't make money off it. They said we had no singles on the album and that the format we were working in was so totally alien to anything else coming out nowadays that they didn't want to touch it."

I would have thought that might add to the appeal of the project? "No, no way. A lot of the guys we asked were against a band bringing out a concept album that was like 40-odd minutes long. They were looking at the American market. We carried on searching though, and then we met Chris [Kimsey]. When he came down to see us the first time we were expecting somebody really straight. The guy's done like five Rolling Stones albums and someone like that you expect to be really big time, but Chris isn't like that at all. He believes in heart and feel and… emotion, in all aspects of recording, which we as a band had never concentrated on before. That really appealed to us."

I think because of the more remote aspects of your two previous albums people are always shocked by just how much emotion there is at one of your concerts. It does seem to have been missing, or miscommunicated, on the albums. "Absolutely. We were aware that we've never been able to put the heart that we have live, and the feel and the angst, whatever you want to call it, down on two-inch tape. Every time we've gone into the studio we've always been overly technical because that's what's expected of bands like us. Chris said that he wanted to go for songs on this album. He doesn't want special effects, he doesn't want over-the-top stuff, he wants to hear a song and he wants to feel a song. Up till now I think I've been trapped by the ego-side of recording an album – like, this is for posterity! And I don't like the temporary aspect of listening to albums. For the album to be truly good you must affect people. There's no point in making people go, 'Oh, wow, these guys are really clever', there's no point in that. And I think in the long term it fucked us up because a lot of people who listened to the records were put off going to the gigs."

The lyrics to the two tracks I heard this afternoon really knocked me out. I've always rated you as a lyricist, but I don't think you've come up with anything quite so eloquent or simple before. "That's because I've taken a completely new approach. It got to the point after the 'Fugazi' album where there were people, like in Canada, coming up to me and telling me that I was walking in the shadow of Dylan Thomas and that I was more than a mere lyricist. Because I don't play an instrument I focus on words all the time. The danger is that you can become so involved with words that it ends up like masturbation; you know, the kick you get is all for yourself and that's not the real kick of being a lyricist.

"It might sound arrogant, but the thing a lyricist should do is try and teach. You must try and explain on a sort of street level so that people can understand immediately what you're talking about. Because the things I go through everybody goes through, and I have the ability to put that into words and I should not try to be condescending or pseudo-intellectual, you know, image-image-image, it's your duty to read into this. Bollocks! On this album I finally realised that by working more on imagery I was avoiding a lot of the problems, a lot of the questions and a lot of the answers that I was trying to put across. 'Fugazi' became too wordy from an ego point of view."

'Misplaced Childhood', how personal, or autobiographical, is the story? "This album is very, very personal. The 'Script...' album was about the break-ups and the start of the break-ups; the 'Fugazi' album was the final break-up, but there was no definitive ending; and this album is the analysis, trying to come out of the problems by saying 'yes, that is a limitation; yes, that is a negative aspect of personality'. And I realised that if I sat back on this album and wrote it as poetry, or if I started examining it all inside my own head as I was writing it, I would go nowhere and it would be the fucking same as the last two albums. I've always said in interviews that writing lyrics is like an exorcism for me and this album is the major exorcism."

Why have you been so definite about calling 'Misplaced Childhood' a concept album? You know you could be setting yourself up for a major fall? "'I know I've set myself up as A Lyricist completely. Some of it's very manic, very depressive..."

I like your voice better on this album, it sounds less self-conscious, more emotional. "I think a lot of that's got to do with coming to Berlin. Coming here you've got less contact with the record company, you've got less contact with all the commercial aspects of the music business, so you just go out and do what you fucking want. I've had to come to terms with now, I was becoming too retrospective and my entire romantic life, my personal life, my band life was all based in the past, which is like a complete fuck-up, and I had to pull myself away from that to find my direction again.

"'Misplaced Childhood' isn't so much about an actual childhood, more the simplicities of youth. It's more like someone starting again. You reach a point where your life can get so fucked-up and you try and retrace and you go back and you want to start again, only of course you can't do that. The experiences you have gone through that numb you, that scar you, they are there and you cannot ignore them, the pain is long gone and all they can do is teach you."

Have you ever suffered from an experience that frightened the shit out of you so much that you refused to go any further? "Oh yeah, of course. I think it helps to begin with something like that sometimes. We had the idea for the concept of this album just after we'd finished recording the 'Script...' LP and it was strange that it was never fully realised at the time. I wanted to do an album about, uh, childlike alternatives. The original idea I had for the 'Fugazi' sleeve was to have a kid on the cover and the jester going through the window, and when I told Mark Wilkinson [who does all the Marillion sleeves] he handed me a copy of 'Damian', the Herman Hesse book. And I read it and thought, fucking hell, this is it, this is the album! I didn't have an ending for the album. I knew what I was trying to say but it's like they teach you in school, to have a beginning, a middle and an end. Well, I didn't have the end but I read 'Damian' and that gave me the classic ending."

So how does 'Misplaced Childhood' end? "The guy's looking back on childhood all the time. He looks on his childhood as being the ideal world, the simplicity of then. He can't figure out at which point he stopped being a kid and became an adult and he's wrong because you never stop being a kid while you're still prepared to learn. Adult is always supposed to be synonymous with All-Knowing, Wise, Worldly... you're never that! You're always learning, you're always a child."

Can you still keep your innocence intact? "Your subconscious innocence, yeah."

Or faith, in that you won't slash your wrists when you wake up in the morning, there is another day? "I don't think I had faith when I was a kid. You're still questioning things too much to worry about faith; you're still opening up those dark cupboards and living rooms which you're told never to open because you'll get smacked on the wrists. You're always doing that and learning and finding out for yourself. Nowadays, there is precious little innocence in childhood."

You told me earlier that you would hate to be in the situation of being stuck at home, with no option but to "knob the missus". That you wanted to "see life for what it is". Can you keep that up all the time? "I dunno. When Mark [Kelly, keyboard player] brings his wife Susie and his kid over to my home I think I really want that, I really, really do want that, and I get very jealous of them."

Do you feel it would affect the quality of your writing, a settled home life with a wife and kids? "Yeah, I do. Because of my, um, poetic instincts or whatever you wanna call it, I feel it's part of my job to go out and try and do new things before I come back and talk about them. I've always been attracted to the fringe activities of life, the stuff out on the perimeter."

What happens if close friends abandon you to your fate because of some of these 'fringe activities'? "Close friends don't abandon you. My close friends have never known me any other way; I've always been like this. I have to question the morals of the world I was brought up in."

I know you tend to get bored easily and it seems to be a trait I come across in lots of performers and singers: are the two things linked, are you hung up on excitement? "I don't like repetition and I don't like playing safe. I don't like it when you go on stage and you're guaranteed a good reaction; when you know that you'll walk off stage feeling like a minor deity or something. I don't like that shit. I like to fight, that's why I want to make sure that I always push myself into other avenues."

How far do you want to go with these forbidden experiments of personality? If it was in my power to grant you the gift of pure evil, would you take it to find out what it was like? "No. I still have a mental fuse-wire. Even when I get really, really drunk I never get totally out of order. I don't have blackouts. When I get to that stage where I'm so out of it that Mr. Obnoxious raises his ugly pointed head, I either go straight to sleep or throw up. Believe it or not, I do still possess certain morals."

What laws would you not break? "Well, religion frightens me a wee bit. Black magic and the occult frighten me. I don't like situations which are totally out of my control. I'm not a great gambler, I'm not even a very good gambler, I like to be sure that the odds are very much on my side. The devil and black magic, you don't play with, and hedonists never play with things. Hedonists who play with things end up as suicides or else completely broken people. The point about hedonism is to experience and learn; the human magpie collecting things, collecting experiences. To me that's how people should work. There's no point hiding away; you cannot get it from TV, you've got to go out and collide and spark with people."

I remember speaking to you before Xmas about the new album and you told me then that you were convinced it was going to be mega. Are you still convinced that, despite the advice against calling it a concept album, it will be your biggest commercial success? "I'm confident because it's the first time I've never considered the commercial side. On 'Fugazi', because there was so much pressure that we weren't used to dealing with from inside the business to come up with an album that really sold the band, a record that would give us a degree of established status, I think we had that on our minds when we came to record it. But with this one we've gone in and said fuck it; if you want us, you take us, if not screw you!

"Berlin has had a lot to do with it, too, because you're removed from it all here, which you're not at home any more. We became pure artists here. Somebody said that Berlin is the focussing point of the world, and it's a crazy place: one minute I hate it, the next I wallow in it. If I lived here I'd go crazy, I'd burn. It would kill me, no doubt about that. This place is more intense than New York. In New York you can walk away, you can never walk away here."

You told me you still had one more lyric to write for the album. Which one? "The happy optimistic one!" He bursts out laughing. "Like, 'Sorry man, I haven't got the happy bit together yet, I just can't, you know, relate!' Naw, it's the key lyric but the longer I leave it the more I feel pushed into a corner. It'll happen. But you know what I hate? I hate it when I read somebody saying that they don't want their lyrics to change the world. I don't understand how people can fucking say that: 'I don't want to change the world' I'd love to change the world, of course I fucking want to! And anybody who says they don't should be put up against a wall and fucking shot! Nobody can say they're happy with what's going on around them. I would give my life to change the world. Just say the right words. People have forgotten words, nowadays…"

Changing the subject, what's all this about being in a film? What's going on, man, you gonna be the next John Geilguid or what? "Hahaha! Arise, Sir Fish! Yeah, I've taken on a theatrical agent and she's trying to get me work in films."

Why films? "It's another one of those natural steps. I'm a frontman so I'm involved to some degree in the theatrics we have on stage and I want to extend it, I feel pulled into it. Every song is a minor play, they all tell their stories, and eventually you want to extend it. Like as a lyricist. Right now I'm pissed off with writing lyrics, and I'm not being detrimental to the band, but I want to try and do something more. Sometimes I'll get a line which so inspires me that I really want to do something with it other than condense the whole thing down into a song lyric. It's restricting my natural flow."

Have you ever considered writing a book of prose or poems? "Yeah, I have. Right now we're talking about publishing deals for books and stuff, and I'm really interested in it. The prospect of recording one of those total ego-job solo albums with the greatest musicians in the land would not be as big a kick as I'd get out of putting the words 'THE END' at the bottom of a novel. And it's the same with writing a script or acting in a movie; the kick would be bigger than any solo album."

Do you feel confident that you could carry the lead in a motion picture? "No! I am the most unconfident person you have ever met! I have no confidence in myself at all. I am black. Every extrovert is a classic introvert. Always true, and that's what I am. I can talk very easily. I can find safety in words, and in humour. I used to think I was a really funny guy, but it was a safety valve. Actually I'm a vicious bastard with my tongue. It's a very Scottish thing, being fast with your mouth."

Do you ever wish someone would put a gag in it for you? "Oh yeah, a lot. Sometimes I hate it, the words and the ability to use them to hurt or whatever. I've had girls in my room who with eight words I have killed stone dead."

What about when you're with your band? "It's not my band."

But do you enjoy freaking people out when you're talking to them? You've done it to me. "Hahaha! Yeah, I've been freaking people out since I was a kid. This band's terrible for it; we do it to each other all the time. Ian's brilliant at it. Ian does it to me; he really fucking freaks me out sometimes. Mind you, I love seeing that shock when you turn round and say something and everybody in the room goes 'What?! What did he fucking say?!' I love breaking barriers and busting through walls and just fucking people up with their own bullshit. 'Lady Nina', for Chrissakes! If you say to someone it's about a guy in Berlin who goes out at night to see this hooker, they turn around and go 'You sexist fucking pig!'"

As your career winds on and you begin to take on more and more diverse projects separate from Marillion, how do you react to the responsibility of knowing that the whole Marillion organisation rests on your shoulders too? "I'm aware of the pressure it puts the people around me under. On April 1st we rang up John [Arnison – band manger] and told him, as an April Fool's thing, that I had all sorts of problems with my health. We said that my throat was bleeding, lots of problems. And John and I are very close, and he's like really nice to me on the phone saying 'Don't you worry, you'll get the best treatment, whatever you need we'll have it'. And then he says to someone else, 'And make sure he does the album, make sure he finishes it'. I became aware of it there all right. You wanna hit out!

"Sometimes you just want to walk out on it. Before this album I had moments when I thought, fuck it, I just want to go! It shows on the record. To be starkly honest, I did think about topping myself at one point last year, because I was getting so fucked up with a lot of different things and I just wanted to go away..."

What stopped you? "A couple of things. One that I don't want to go into, to do with my guardian, my short-fuse, a sort of instinct. And the other because it would have upset a lot of people. I love the guys in the band, they're like my best friends, and I thought about how many people it would fuck up if I did. Plus, the whole Lennon, Morrison, Hendrix, Joplin thing. I just knew it would be so sordid, and I want to fight it out, I want to say something. Suicide is such a negative statement, and not one I want to make. Like heroin. Heroin is such negative fucking statement. Like morphine."

As a singer you inspire followers to whom you must resemble something of a guru. Who's your guru? "I don't have one – used to have, but not now. I know it sounds very big-headed, but it's myself. Safe in my own words, learning from my own words..."

First published in Kerrang! No.95, May 30, 1985

It was the day after my 29th birthday and I was sick as a dog – two dogs, in fact. Nevertheless, the record company insisted I get out of bed and make my way to the airport. I was still spewing as the plane took off. It was a shame because I'd been looking forward to this one. Way back in the mists, I had almost become the unsigned Def Leppard's PR. Then, just as I'd shaken hands on the deal with their original management team, the band ditched them and signed with a high-powered New York-based management company.

By the mid-'80s, Leppard was the most glamorous, certainly the richest and most successful British rock band in the world. And yet our paths had not crossed since I'd seen them supporting Sammy Hagar at the Hammersmith Odeon back when I thought I was about to work for them.

Fortunately, the first one I bumped into was Joe Elliott, a bluff Yorkshireman not about to be put off by the smell of sick or a deathly pale face. He welcomed me to the small anonymous club the band was appearing in that night, gave me a seat (very welcome) and a beer (even more welcome) and invited me to join them onstage for the encores that night, doing backing vocals on Alice Cooper's 'Elected'. I wished I'd said yes cos that would have made for a better story. But I wasn't feeling that much better yet and was genuinely worried that I might puke all over the stage, so I declined.

I also met their flamboyant blond guitarist, Steve Clark, that day; someone who was no stranger to the hangover, either. It was, needless to say, the start of a rather unbeautiful friendship which lasted right up to his senseless, drink-related death less than four years later – though there's no hint of that in this story.

Most impressive, in retrospect, were the balls and sheer bloody-mindedness shown by Rick Allen, doing his first major interview since losing his left arm in a horrendous car accident just two-and-a-half years before. I felt like a woozy fake sitting next to him in the dressing room as he rolled cigarettes one-handed and looked straight at you.

I still do.

Joe Elliott & Rick Allen, Tilburg, July 1987

I know you've heard it all before, but any day now Def Leppard are going to release their new album. After two-and-a-half years behind closed doors waiting for the mountain to come to Mohammed, the band have finally finished working on what will probably be the most difficult, time-consuming album they are ever likely to record. Four-and-a-half years after the release of their last album, 'Pyromania', one of the most truly innovative hard rock albums produced so far this ill-starred decade, Def Leppard are at last ready to unveil a new masterpiece. It's called 'Hysteria'; the first single from the album in the UK is called 'Animal'; they're both released some time around the July/August cusp; and though I can tell that you still don't quite believe me, let me tell you I've heard the damn thing, or most of it anyway. I've even seen them playing half-a-dozen of the new numbers live! In short, I've seen the proof, baby. It's been a long time, been a long time, been a long, lonely, lonely time waiting for them to finally do it, and nobody knows it better than they do, but now, to steal a phrase, Def Leppard are back. And very soon we're all going to have to believe it.

To begin at the deep end, 'Hysteria' walks all over 'Pyromania' in much the same way that 'Pyromania' stomped all over 'High 'N' Dry', their previous album. So it took the best part of three years to make. So what? What have you been doing for the last three years that's so goddamned great? Where's your fucking masterpiece? Me, I'd rather put in the time than settle for some half-assed, frog-marched-through-the-studio-doors piece of rubbish, released regular as taking a crap, every nine months.

A full review of the 'Hysteria' album is not possible here. After all, I'm still missing four of the tracks on the tape I've got. However, of the eight cuts I've got my hands on for now, all but one is an up-tempo, two-fisted body swinger, raunchy, swaggering, leatherized. The production by 'Mutt' Lange is quite, quite awesome, as one would expect from one of the most original minds ever to work in the field of hard rock. Breathtaking and intensely dynamic, the production on 'Hysteria' is Lange's most elevated work to date, and that is saying something indeed when you tot up all his successes. I shudder to think how he intends following this one up. Meanwhile, the band, far from being blinded by science, play like angels and everybody turns in magnificent performances. 'Animal' and 'Armageddon It' are quintessential Def Leppard: Steve Clark's and Phil Collen's guitars cranking out one deliciously sleazy riff after another, Rick Savage and Rick Allen's rhythm section building like paddies on bonus time, Joe Elliott crooning like a sheep-killing dog. The rest, with the exception of the lone ballad I've heard so far, 'Love Bites', follow suit. In terms of sheer heaviness, the first single in America, 'Women' stakes the biggest claim: huge choruses that erupt out of the mix underpinned with a guitar riff you could clout people round the head with and, despite its wanton title, a great set of lyrics that avoid slipping into any silly Coverdale-ish aphorisms.

Most impressive, though, are the tracks like 'Rocket', 'Don't Give Me Love & Affection' and 'Hysteria', where, in collusion with Lange's almost other-worldly production embellishments, the band really do start to break the mould. The tone is still unashamedly hard-line rock'n'roll, but the arrangements are so finely wrought, so well-heeled and tastefully delivered, Def Leppard begin to transcend the limited parameters of everyday hard rock, ascending to a more modem musical plain that is going to set the standard for every aspiring superstar rock band for at least the next five years. Quite simply, as of now everybody else is going to have to try and catch up with Def Leppard or they're just going to have to settle for coming second best. When I hear about the new Mötley Crüe album going to number two in the American charts, or how 'Whitesnake 1987' has already entered the Top Three there, or that the Poison album has just racked up another half-million US sales, I sit back and I say, enjoy it while you can boys, because when this new Def Leppard album finally steps out of its cage in a few short weeks from now the game will be over. Because somewhere down that long white line that connects the '70s to the '80s, and bands like Led Zeppelin to Bon Jovi, you will find the inspiration behind a recording like 'Hysteria'. Raucous, but rivettingly melodic; basic swarthy guitar antics enhanced by the latest state-of-the-art studio technology; lead vocals that scream while they burn swathed in lush, multi-tracked vocal harmonies that rush through the room like a burst of fresh air... like broken, dirty fingernails being shaved into a long sharp point... It could take your fucking eye out, some of this stuff. Crammed with monsters and at least eight hit singles! Jesus...

When I finally get into Holland and locate the band – two plane rides, two cabs, too many problems and not enough time – they are sound-checking onstage in a tiny club called the Nooderligt in the small Dutch town of

Tilburg. The next Def Leppard world tour officially kicks off in Dublin on August 27. The Hysteria World Tour, all things going according to plan, is expected to run for the hardest part of two years, beginning with the band's first, full-length British tour since the short end of 1983. There's nothing like making up for lost time, is there? Meanwhile, Leppard have slotted in three warm-up dates here in Holland: two nights at the Nooderligt, followed by a late afternoon appearance before an expected crowd of over 150,000 at the free Park Rock open air-festival in a few days time. Understandably, the band are keen to break in their new set before throwing themselves into the spotlight again in Britain and, in particular, America. In America, 'Pyromania' may have sold six-and-a-half million copies, but in Holland, at last count, the album had sold slightly less than six-and-a-half hundred copies. Nevertheless, Def Leppard's lack of any real fame in Holland has positively worked to their advantage during the three years they have spent here, off and on, painstakingly piecing the new album together at Wisseloord Studios just outside Amsterdam. No distractions, no intrusions, not too many wayward influences, it's been a great benefit in the long term. Now their domestic lack of prestige in Holland has again worked temporarily in their favour. Tilburg is about as close to Nowheresville as one mega-platinum-selling rock band is likely to get. Walk outside the club and ten minutes in any direction will leave you stranded in countryside: the perfect venue for a low-profile band work out. The soundcheck is a long one, but the band look like they're enjoying themselves, stretching like cats through a few bars of 'Rock Of Ages' or 'Tear It Down'. The out-front sound is just that bit too loud. Good. My ears could do with being pinned back by a bit of Def Leppard. It's been a long time, like the man said. And it must be a relief for them to be back onstage, The Album Actually Fucking Finished, and all that.

"Strangely enough, it doesn't really feel that astonishing to be back playing live," says Joe Elliott in the tiny dressing room backstage after soundcheck is over. "It's been nearly a year since we last played live (at the Monsters Of Rock Festival in Germany last August). But the minute we all got up onstage here this afternoon it felt like it was yesterday since we last did this. Having said that though, the minute we do get out on the road every day and start touring properly, it'll probably hit me how much I've actually missed regularly playing live."

The relaxed atmosphere amongst the rest of the band seems to echo

Elliott's sentiments. The stage and the dressing room may be a deal smaller than the band have become used to over the last five or six years of their career, but the occasion looms just as large. This is a gig; Def Leppard are a band that made their reputation early on eating gigs like this for breakfast. None of this is really strange, no matter how long it's been since any of them last stepped into a dressing room. "There's no way this place will be full for us tonight, and it probably only holds about a thousand, maximum," Joe reflects. "But that won't worry us. I can remember playing gigs to about 11 people in the early days! I'm just looking forward to getting onstage and playing some of the new numbers."

When Def Leppard hit the stage at a little after 10pm there's maybe a couple of hundred people there to see them do it. But Def Leppard have always been an exciting and colourful band to watch on stage; handsome and lean and moving around like tigers on Vaseline, the four-man frontline all hang from the lip of the stage and compete for the spotlight. Despite receiving no more than polite applause, the band still make a dazzling entry, Joe Elliott screaming into the mike, "WELCOME TO OUR SHOOOOOWWWWWW!!" The band flying straight into the manic intro to 'Stagefright'.

At the back, face concentrated, hunkered down behind his beautiful new Simmons electronic drum kit, is the man of the moment, Rick Allen, blowing up the kind of storm most drummers with two arms could only dream about. Since the widely-reported car accident in which Rick lost his left arm two-and-a-half years ago, the question nobody liked to ask but everybody was waiting for the answer to was: would Rick really be able to cut it on his own with the band onstage? He did it and did it well at last year's Castle Donington festival; but could he be relied on to keep it up night after night through another gruelling world tour? The answer is, quite simply, yes. Everything Rick used to do with his left hand he now does with his left foot (always an underused appendage for your basic rock drummer; apart from opening and closing the hi-hat a drummer in a rock band doesn't use his left foot for much more than booting the odd roadie up the arse, it seems). Rick's specially-designed Simmons kit is basically two sets of drums combined: one is played by electronic foot pedals, the other using sticks on electronic drum pads. Over the months since his accident, Rick has developed a brilliant left-foot technique that allows him the scope to play complex drum patterns with remarkable ease. The first kit (the 'Top' kit) is five small Simmons electronic drum pads. The 'Bottom' kit is four specially constructed foot-pedals and a Simmons bass-drum pad. None of these drums produce sound, only electronic impulses, or 'triggers', which are sent to a 'Brain' – actually a Simmons SDS7, loaded with a silicon chip containing sampled sounds using a combination of SDS7 Library Samples and samples taken from Rick's own recorded drums. It's this which produces the sounds.

But don't get this thing wrong – these are not goddamned tapes he's using. He only calls on five different sounds, the same five on both kits: bass drum, snare drum, and three tom-toms. Rick still has to beat the hell out of his kit and be able to create the drum patterns himself. That's no robot he's got propped behind the curtain there. It's just another set of drums that you have to learn how to play. It won't make a bad drummer sound good. It won't do a thing until someone shows it how. 'Animal', 'Armageddon It', 'Pour Some Sugar On Me', 'Women', 'Don't Give Me Love & Affection' and 'Hysteria' all get premiered before the lackadaisical Noorderligt crowd. The ones at the back in the Slayer T-shirts are waiting to be impressed, but down the front is where they are mostly, nodding their heads thoughtfully, smatterings of spilt applause greeting the end of each number. Even more familiar Leppard material like 'Rock Rock' and 'Too Late For Love' draws only politely appreciative applause. "It's fair enough, really," said guitarist Phil Collen after the show, "Our music simply isn't that well known enough in Holland for us to expect anything else. I mean, you've got to start somewhere, haven't you?" But when Joe Elliott calls Rick Allen down from behind his kit and says through the mike, "I'd like to introduce you to my mate, Rick…" the crowd finally throw their heads back and cheer. It was the biggest noise they made all night, applauding the talents of this gifted young percussionist whose courage and quiet determination has brought him right back from the brink of tragedy to where he belongs, propping up the beat behind the guitars in Def Leppard…

The afternoon before the band's second show at the Nooderligt, Joe Elliott and I sit catching the breeze on the grass outside my motel room. The night before we had been sipping brandies with Steve Clark and listening to some of Joe's priceless Alice Cooper live tapes on the singer's ghetto-blaster. Now we're both nursing our nerves and slurping from glasses of Coke. With only time to kill I start to unwind with a few questions. The last time Joe Elliott was interviewed, Rick Allen was still at home recovering from the immediate effects of his gruesome accident, and the band were in the Wisseloord Studios with their engineer Nigel Green producing their new album. I ask Joe to fill in some of the gaps for me between then and when Mutt Lange reappeared on the scene some months later.

"Rick's accident happened on New Year's Eve 1984, and we were actually back in the studios in Holland on the second of January '85.1 don't know if you can imagine how we all felt, trying to put a brave face on things. We were in there going around in circles trying to get things done, but all the time at the backs of our minds we were all thinking about Rick, wondering how he was getting on. For the next four months we carried on like that, but we didn't really do a lot. It hasn't happened to me yet, but it must be like if someone close to you dies, then two weeks after it's happened you're back to work, but you're not really there. You go through the motions and you say all the right things, but your thoughts are permanently somewhere else. The day Rick came back to Holland was the day this band came back to life. We'd never even discussed whether or not Rick would stay in the band. That was always going to be Rick's decision. But he just pitched up in the studio and said, 'Don't worry, I'm gonna build this drum kit…' He was brilliant, so positive. It really inspired us to snap out of it."

It would take time, of course, for Rick's special kit to be designed, tested and manufactured, and naturally the drummer had to moderate his technique to fit his new circumstances, but as long as Rick was determined to give it a go, the band backed him all the way. "Nothing ever gets done in a single day," Joe says thoughtfully. "I don't expect the Ford Motor Company stuck out the first model they ever came up with. But it was obvious from Rick's brilliant attitude that it was only a matter of time before he was sitting behind a kit with us again. Then he came in one day and played the whole of [Led Zeppelin's] 'When The Levee Breaks' perfectly right the way through! We knew then we'd turned a big corner. We could start to breathe again."

Rick's accident was by no means the only reason the album took so long to make. From the beginning, the project had been dogged by bad luck and worse timing. First they couldn't get Mutt to produce it for them. After having worked back-to-back on 'Pyromania' and then the Cars' own mega-successful 'Heartbeat City' album, what the ailing producer felt he could not do was run straight back into the studio and begin working on another new album. Mutt needed a break. Badly. "Mutt knew how big a step this next album was for us," says Joe, "and he just couldn't cope with it. At the time, Mutt hadn't been outside a recording studio in something like 17 years, and he felt he was going to crack up if he didn't take a break. Feeling like that, he knew it wouldn't be fair on him or us to pretend he had the energy and enthusiasm for another Def Leppard album at that time. And that's when we got Jim Steinman in and said goodbye to another two months in wasted studio time…"

Erstwhile songwriting partner of Meat Loaf, co-producer of one fairly average Billy Squier album, and the man who gave it all away to Bonnie Tyler, Jim Steinman's problems with Def Leppard have been well-documented in the past. Suffice to say, Steinman did not work out. When the axe fell, the band decided to go it alone with the help of Mutt's regular engineer, Nigel Green. That didn't work out either, though for less spurious reasons. "Nigel is a brilliant engineer; he can get absolutely any sound you want, which is why he works so well when Mutt is producing. But he's not a musician or a singer. Mutt is a brilliant singer and a great musician, there's absolutely nothing he can't play. So there are always ideas and suggestions from Mutt that, unless you're a musician, you'd simply never have in a million years. What we'd been doing with Nigel and on our own certainly sounded as good as anything on 'Pyromania', but it didn't actually sound any better. And it was very important for the survival of this band that whatever we released next had to be better than anything we'd ever done before. And that's when we decided to scrap those sessions too, and start all over again... again!"

Joe says that, by the middle of 1985, he and the rest of the band were starting to feel that they were fated to enjoy a period of mega-bad luck. "We were very aware that we'd enjoyed four or five years of nothing but good luck. Even when our albums were stiffing in England, or the singles were going nowhere, or the reviews were crap, we always seemed to ride it all out, we never let it touch us. We never lost the vibe that each new thing we did was better than the last, that we were truly going somewhere. And then of course it all happened for us with only our third album and we became the big band we always thought we were going to be. Overnight almost, everything went from better to totally brilliant and we could do no wrong. So when one thing after another kept going wrong during the first nine months of recording this album it was almost like we had it coming, you know? In fact…" Joe smiles, his mood lightening, "We were talking about this amongst ourselves the other day, and I'm convinced that all our bad luck started the day Phil and Rick turned vegetarian! Ever since then I swear nothing's gone right!" he laughs.

"To be honest, although all these scrapes affected us very badly when they were happening, and certainly lowered the band's moral for months at a time, looking back I tend to be more philosophical about all those traumas now that we're about to go out on the road again. The thing is we probably had just as many problems in the past, but we were never in the public eye so much before so we didn't have time to sit around and reflect too long about what was going on. Also, it's very hard to get depressed about some problems when you're in a new city every night. But very easy when you're stuck inside the same four walls for three years. It was a bit like sitting in our own shit, sometimes."

By the summer of 1985, however, things took a dramatic turn for the better when Mutt Lange, now fully rested after his long lay-off, returned to the Def Leppard fold and took charge while the band began from scratch again in the studio. A renowned perfectionist, once Mutt got his teeth into a project, especially one as ambitious as the new Def Leppard album, he didn't let go until he was 100 percent satisfied that the job had been done properly. As a result, it was to be another two years before Mutt considered it that way.

The album must have cost a fortune to make, I remark. "'Hysteria' is possibly going to come in as the most expensive rock album ever made," Joe admits. "It will probably have to sell something like two million copies just to break even on the costs. But you know, you have to see these things in perspective. Yes, the album cost a fortune to make, but it is the best thing we've ever done. It would be different if we took all that time and spent all that money and still came out with a piece of shit, but it's not. It's got a magic, the new album that you shouldn't put a price on. And as long as it still only costs a few quid for the fans to buy, then who's lost out? The money was ours to spend and I think we've done it very wisely.

"What else are you supposed to do with money if not spend some of it? It's true we've made a lot of money, a hell of a lot of money. And we've all bought fast cars and big houses and all those things – who wouldn't if they were suddenly rich? That's what it's all for, some of it. But we've also put a lot of it back into the music industry too. We bought a PA, which has been used by everybody from Dio to Duran Duran, and we put a large part of it back into making the best possible album we were capable of, and I think it was worth every penny."

Nevertheless, in the past, Def Leppard have suffered a staggering amount of criticism for being, it seems to me, rich and famous, of all things. And not just at the practised hands of the UK press, but even from the mouths of fans... you know, the flash bastards syndrome. Are Def Leppard flash bastards, Joe?

He leans back in his seat and laughs. "Look, let's get this one straight for the record. It's not as though we won the pools, all that money didn't just fall from the sky. It happened because a lot of people liked our records enough to buy them. Anyway, it's not as though we're that rich. Compared to a lot of bands that I could name, but won't, we haven't even begun fulfilling our earning potential. I can think of plenty of other rock musicians who have all got the big mansion and the big cars and the servants and the perpetual hangers-on and treat everybody that works for them like complete cunts… they always end up getting the 'good blokes' profiles in the music press.

"I think because in the beginning when we were first being interviewed by the press we were so young and naive we'd end up sounding a bit too cold and certain in some of the interviews that appeared around that time. Like, if someone asked what we thought of the new AC/DC album and we turned round and said something like, 'Oh, it's OK. Good not great', which actually happened when 'Back In Black' was number one in the American charts, we'd end up getting crucified for 'slagging AC/DC off!' The letters would start arriving: 'Who the hell do Def-Leppard think they are?'" He purses his lips in disapproval. "Things like that and the whole debate over whether we'd Paid Our Dues, man! Three albums! Boom-boom-boom! Six million sales! People couldn't handle it… Well, we've paid some dues since then. The last three years have seen to that. I mean, tell me about it!"

The world, of course, has not stood still while Def Leppard have been off the road. Strange to relate, when 'Pyromania' was released in March 1983 no such things as Bon Jovi or Ratt albums existed; Mel Galley was still in Whitesnake and the 'Slide It In' album hadn't even had its first mix rejected yet. David Lee Roth was still at home trying to write lyrics to a new thing Eddie Van Halen had put together called 'Jump'; even Mötley Crüe were still playing the clubs in LA… What's it been like staying quiet in the studio while history was being made by all the other bands, Joe?

"I'd never even heard of Bon Jovi the last time we released an album..." He shakes his head, not quite taking it in. "The first Bon Jovi record I ever really listened to was 'You Give Love A Bad Name'. We were in Britain last summer and I turned on the radio and there it was... I was thought, fucking hell! Rock music on Radio One shock! This is good news! And lo and behold, they've become like the band we should have become... And it's a fair comparison, I think. Bon Jovi on their last album are sort of like we were on 'Pyromania'. They're 24-years-old, it's their third album, a new producer and so forth... I say good luck to them. I love it that I can hear a Bon Jovi record on the radio. Obviously, it just made me want to get out there and do things too, but I still bought their album! Whenever their singles come on the radio or the TV I still turn the volume up full blast. I'm a fan, I like them! I think it's fair to say as well, and they'd probably admit it too, that they've stolen things from us. But so what? We stole from Thin Lizzy and UFO, and now somebody will come along and steal from Bon Jovi. That's just the way it works."

There's no doubting that the success in America of 'Pyromania' (and the huge US hit single it spawned, 'Photograph') opened a lot of doors for most of the newer bands that have emerged in the wake of Leppard's phenomenal success there. Just when hard rock and heavy metal were getting the bum's rush again from the bourgeois American media, 'Pyromania' came along and sold so many records it was two years before it finally dropped out of the charts. Only Michael Jackson's 'Thriller' (the biggest selling album of all time, don't forget) kept 'Pyromania' from the number one spot in America – a position no British rock band since Led Zeppelin had been in. Suddenly hard rock was hip again. But does Joe Elliott feel that, as some have suggested, the more recent successes of bands like Bon Jovi and Mötley Crüe have stolen any of Def Leppard's thunder?

"No, I don't go for all that stuff about Ratt, or whoever else, stealing our audience. It's bullshit. Look at the US charts at the moment – Bon Jovi have just sold nine million albums, Mötley Crüe are at number two, Whitesnake are in the Top Five, Ozzy's just been in the Top 10. So have Poison... Kids don't just buy one band's albums and not others. The same kids who bought the Bon Jovi album have probably gone out and bought the Poison album and the Whitesnake album, too. In that respect, nobody has stolen anything from anyone. There's plenty of room for everyone – as long as they've got something to offer.

"It's true though," he agrees when prompted, "that a lot of bands either rode in on the back of 'Pyromania', or took it as a blueprint for what they wanted to do themselves. I think we set a standard there. It's staggering just how many bands it did influence. And I don't mean just big American bands. I remember meeting Kim McAuliffe from Girlschool in London after their 'Play Dirty' album came out, and she came up to me and said, 'I'd just like to say I'm sorry'. I said, 'What for?' She said, 'I feel I should apologise because we've just totally ripped your 'Pyromania' album off!' I just stood there bemused. I'd never even heard the Girlschool album she was on about. But I went out and bought a copy of 'Play Dirty' – it's that album that Noddy Holder and Jimmy Lea from Slade produced for them – and played it, and I couldn't believe it! I swear, there's one track on there, if you took the lead vocals off you could sing 'Rock Of Ages' over it! The drum sound, the guitars, it was all straight off 'Pyromania'. I had to laugh. I mean, you have to take it as a kind of backhanded compliment, really. But at least Kim wasn't afraid to admit the influence, which was nice..."

Joe downs another cold glass of Coke. It soothes his throat, he says, after burning it on the brandy with me and Steve Clark the night before. I proffer the theory that the band's long lay-off may, eventually, prove to be a real advantage in certain respects. For example, the last Def Leppard album may have sold over six million copies in America but, truth to tell, it didn't really sell doodly-squat anywhere else. However, the fact of their enormous success in America, where by the end of 1983 Leppard had achieved almost legendary status on a par with any of the old '70s giants, coupled with the unprecedented amount of time they've taken in order to mastermind a worthy follow-up, has, in itself, reinforced the image of the band with a new and deeper credibility. You may not have bought their last album, but you sure as hell know who they are by now. You may never consider yourself a Def Leppard fan, but I bet you'd like to know exactly what these fuckers have been up to all this time. If you're 16-years-old right now, you were eleven-and-a-half, still wearing short trousers to school and a probable Beano fan when 'Pyromania' first came out. Surely you will want to find out what all the fuss is about?

"Yeah, I've thought about that too," says Joe. "The plus side in Britain, for example, is that a 21-year-old kid who remembers us from '83 and wasn't a fan probably won't be a fan now, either. If he remembers us slagging off his favourite band, he's still gonna hate us. But if his 18-year-old brother, who was 12 or 13 when we were out on the road playing 'Pyromania', hears the new album and likes it, he's not gonna give a shit about any of the old prejudices that have dogged us in the past. He'll be too busy discovering Def Leppard on his own terms to listen to stupid old arguments that go back to his infancy. Kids aren't interested in history; they're into what's happening now."

The conversation drifts back and forth a while. We touch on the band's decision to appear on the bill at last year's Castle Donington festival. Joe says Leppard played Donington and the two Monsters Of Rock festivals in Germany for no special reason other than "we were absolutely bored playing to four studio walls."

The most fun the band had though, he says, was on the five warm-up dates they played in Ireland the week before the festivals began. "Honestly, it was brilliant," he chuckles. "We did one gig in Limerick in this tiny place, and we'd only sold about 185 tickets come the night of the gig. So we went around to all the local pubs giving the tickets away to anybody who fancied coming along. In the end, we had about 350 people in there, although I'm sure half of them had never heard of us."

It was also while they were out flexing their muscles on those five low-profile dates in Ireland, in 1986, that Rick Allen, appearing live with the band for the first time since the car accident that robbed him of his left arm, first tackled the unenviable task of playing an entire Def Leppard set without the aid of an auxiliary drummer onstage. Former drummer with Judie Tzuke, and now a permanent fixture with Status Quo, Jeff Rich accompanied Rick on the first few dates, then, for a variety of obscure reasons, couldn't make one gig. It took a lot of nerve but Rick said he'd like to have a crack at it on his own. "We tried Rick on his own at this tiny club in Ireland, only a small crowd, and it worked really well. There were a couple of cock-ups, but basically he did brilliantly. From that point Jeff Rich was history and we were back to being a five-man group."

That must have come as great relief, Rick proving he could handle the gig on his own? "Yeah, it did. But it wasn't entirely unexpected. Rick had been coming along so fast with his new technique that we thought he'd probably be ready to have a serious crack at going it alone at some point. It just happened a year or so sooner than we expected."

Looking toward the immediate future, Joe tells me that the band's next world tour will almost certainly be their longest and most ambitious yet. Right now, Def Leppard are scheduled to start the ball rolling on August 27, in Dublin, then creep across the water for their first decent stretch of UK dates since 1983. At the end September they return to America where they unveil their most stunning stage show yet. (I don't have too many details to hand at present, but I can tell you that it involves a circular stage placed in the centre of each arena they alight on. "It'll be a completely bare stage except for the band," Joe tells me. "Even the amps will be mounted underneath the stage. And we're going to have giant catwalks so we can literally walk out into the auditorium and say hello to people!")

They'll carry on like that for maybe nine months, then plan to return in mid-'88 for an extended European tour. They will then return to America for another six months. All this should carry Def Leppard safely through to the New Year, 1989, when there is a strong possibility they will tour Japan. What is this thing you have about touring, Joe? I mean, we're talking about the best part of the next two years out on the road! You're not doing this out of guilt for being away so long, are you?

"No, don't be daft," he smiles. "We're doing it because if there's one thing that's detestable it's when bands make it big in America and immediately settle for doing 20-date tours of the place in the biggest, most ridiculous places. You know, pack 'em in quick, grab the money and bugger off home. We want to play everywhere we played last time, only this time we want to play two nights where we last did one, three nights where we last did two, and on and on. We want to come back looking, sounding, and playing like we're four times the band we were in 1983! And we haven't done anything wrong taking our time about it, either. It was the best thing we ever did, taking three years off from the road.

"And the word is spreading, too," he assures me, running a hand through his long yellow locks. "Even in England people are starting to get a buzz about us going out on the road again. This time we're doing two nights at the Hammersmith Odeon, which I know ain't much for a lot of probably less successful British rock bands to do, but for us it's a first! We've only ever been able to sell the place out for one night at a time before now..."

Soundcheck time approaches, and besides, I haven't spoken to the man of the moment yet, Rick Allen. I throw a last one Joe's way, which he handles with characteristic aplomb. I ask him how he would like Def Leppard to be remembered when their time is over and people like me start saying things about them like 'Remember when…?' Just like they do these days about Led Zeppelin…

"I'd like us to be remembered as a legendary band," he shrugs, eyes crinkling. "I mean, that's not how I perceive the band right now. To me, a genuinely legendary band would have to be Led Zeppelin, and I couldn't possibly think of Def Leppard in the same way. But I'd take it as the highest compliment we ever had if in years to come that's the way the new generation of rock fans looked back on us. But the only way we'll achieve that is if we never give in and release a dog of an album, and then if we do split up stay that way. Iron Maiden's manager, Rod Smallwood, made a very shrewd observation once when he said to me that the day Deep Purple ceased to be a legend was the day they reformed. And he was right! I promise you, there will never be any of that with Def Leppard. We'll just go away quietly and not tell anyone we've split up!" One last throaty chuckle and he's gone, soundcheck bound.

A couple of hours before Def Leppard take to the stage for their second, and last, night at the tiny Nooderligt club in Tilburg, me and Rick Allen and a couple of brown bottles of beer hunker down in a comer of the upstairs production office and out of the goodness of our hearts throw down these words on to the tape. I begin by asking Rick how soon it was after his accident he made up his mind to try and carry on as the drummer in the band?

"About two weeks," he says. "What happened was, I'd lost my left arm, and I'd busted up my right pretty badly as well. So to begin with my right arm was more or less strapped to my side. To help me sit up straight in bed and move around a bit and make myself comfortable, the nurses placed a hard block of foam in the bottom of the bed so that I could push against it with my feet. Well, it was just in the perfect position for me to tap away on it with my feet. Out of sheer boredom I used to lie there tapping my feet against this thing, and I started thinking, hang on a minute, I can use this. This has possibilities... So I got this friend of mine down and he looked at what I was doing and he agreed that the idea of some kind of foot pedal that would at least enable me to get a snare sound with my left foot could probably be worked out and designed. Within a matter of days this guy returned to the hospital with what turned out to be the prototype for the pedals I'm using onstage now.

"The other thing I got into doing, don't laugh, was sitting in my wheelchair and banging on the footplates, getting a rhythm going. And to be honest, what I'm doing now onstage isn't much different..."

Rick Allen may have lost an arm, but he hasn't lost his sense of humour. "Because the rest of the band were so much behind me as regards, like, you're still in the band, Rick, all that occupied my time while I was in hospital was working out what I was gonna do when I got out. It was great to be able to think positively about the situation, it really helped a lot in the beginning. Because of that, because I had this tremendous urge to get out and actually start again, I was out of there inside a month!"

With an iron will, and displaying remarkable courage, Rick Allen was back in the studios in Holland with the rest of the band within six weeks of his accident. It wasn't easy, he says, making a sudden reappearance. Not at first, anyway. "I don't think any of us quite knew what to say. It was strange for all of us, to begin with. I think the rest of the band were waiting to see if I was going to crack up or something. Nobody was sure yet how I was going to handle it. But they gave me their support, totally, from the word go. I mean, if they'd have said, 'Sorry Rick, we can't really carry on this way', I'd have stepped down gracefully, you know, fine, no problem. But that was never the case at all, they all left it up to me to decide – and that was the spur I needed to try and work things out as a drummer again."

The technical details for Rick's new specially designed electronic kit were worked out over a period of a few short months. Meanwhile, in the studio, Rick relied mainly on a Fairlight computer to achieve the drum sounds you can hear on 'Hysteria'. Outside of the studio, he worked overtime on refining a startling new technique that would enable him to return to the stage the next time Leppard played as a legitimate live drummer. Showing the same heart that dragged him from a hospital bed back into a recording studio inside the space of six short weeks, within a year of his return to the band Rick decided he was ready to put his balls on the line and try out some of his big ideas on a stage.

I ask Rick how he felt in the dressing room, before he went on for that first gig alone? "I never, ever drank before I went onstage, but that first night in Ireland using the new electronic kit, even with Jeff Rich beside me on the stage, I was so jittery I downed the best part of a half-a-bottle of brandy before we went on. And then the minute I got onstage I was straight!

I mean, I was just so frightened! And I made a few silly mistakes, a few obvious errors; my timing was a bit off and I kept thinking of things before I was supposed to play them, and then rushing things. Because Jeff Rich was there, though, I didn't have to panic too much. And then over the space of those first few gigs, I started getting it together again. Suddenly I felt a lot calmer and I was doing all right.

"There's an old Irish joke that goes, 'When you see a guy with a short leg you can be sure the other one's always longer!'" He laughs. "It's only a daft joke but there's a grain of truth in there. Losing an arm might have been the worst thing that could ever happen to me. But it happened, and that's that. In the meantime, I feel like the rest of me has grown much, much stronger as a result. Maybe it's just nature's way of compensating for the loss of one part of me, I don't know, but within the space of those first few gigs in Ireland everything started coming together so quickly I think I surprised everybody, myself included. Peter [Mensch, Leppard's manager] had been saying all along that I should try playing live on my own, but I really needed those gigs with Jeff to take some of the pressure off while I got used to the idea of being onstage again, and the new way of playing.

"Then, the second-from-last gig, Jeff had flown out for a couple of days work with Status Quo in Germany, and he was supposed to take a flight back to where we were in Ireland on the afternoon of this particular gig. Something happened – he missed the flight, or the plane was delayed – but soundcheck time came and Jeff still wasn't back. We carried on without him, but when it was time for us to go onstage and he still wasn't back, and nobody knew whether to go on or not without him, with just me by myself. In the end, we decided to do it anyway and hope that Jeff would show up soon. We went on as a five-piece, which I must admit felt great, and then we just ploughed into the set and I got on with the drums on my own for about the first six numbers! It was good, too. Nothing too fancy, but I was definitely holding my own. And then Jeff finally arrived and jumped up onstage and the two of us finished the set together."

Impressed by his solo performance, the following night, their last in Ireland before readying themselves for their appearance at Donington a few days later, the rest of the band encouraged Rick to have a go at the whole set atone. He'd got this far on sheer guts and determination; maybe his new-found technique would carry him the rest of the way...

"I did the gig on my own and Jeff stood out by the mixing desk listening for any obvious mistakes, trying to spot if I wasn't holding my end up on each number, ready to step in and help me if it looked like I couldn't handle it. Well, I got through the entire gig, and afterwards Jeff came backstage and shook my hand and said, 'Well, it looks like I'm out of a job then!' It was a nice moment…"

Leppard's appearance on last year's Donington bill was an understandably special occasion: Leppard's first in England in three years; Rick's second on his own. "When we went on we knew there would still be some people out there who probably thought we had a second drummer hidden somewhere underneath the stage," he jokes. "I was really nervous. I think we all were. But we started off OK, the set started building and I just got into the gig. And the longer we played the more I could sense that people had stopped staring at me and were just getting into it, too. And then Joe started talking to the crowd in-between numbers, and then he said something like, I'd like to introduce you to my mate, Rick Allen!' And the place went mad! I've never seen so many hands go up in the air! I just sat there behind the drums and burst into tears..."

He pauses, looking into the middle-distance. "What we need to do right now is get out on the road, go everywhere we can, and prove to the world that Def Leppard are still a great live band," he says eventually. "Since Donington, we've finished the new album and I've had another 12 months to improve on my ability and my technique, and now we're as ready as we're ever going to be. We've been away a long time, but we've got nothing to hide behind. And now we're coming back to prove it."

Heroic last words from a heroic young man indeed. Later that night, during the show I crouched down in the darkness behind Rick's drum riser and watched the boy work. I looked on bleary-eyed as he romped through a blistering 'Rock Of Ages', his right arm doing what it always did while his bare feet rained down hard and with precision on the pedals. Can he still rock? Is Argentinean tennis star Gabriella Sabatini a horn-ball? Do fish fuck in water? See for yourself in September, then you tell me...

That Def Leppard had to work their asses off to get this small Dutch gathering going is one thing. They got their encores. A wonderfully anthemic 'Photograph', a wired and weird roll through Alice Cooper's 'Elected', which at least kept the grinning fool from *Kerrang!* happy, and a thoroughly bad-minded romp through the most popular number of the night, 'Wasted', all were included as I recall. But ultimately, Leppard weren't out to seriously wow a new and wall-eyed audience. They went out to oil their gears. And at the end of the second night it seemed safe to say they had their machine ticking over nicely.

The road beckons. This cat's finally outta the bag. You, me, the band, we're all sick of waiting. Well, we don't have to any more…

First published in Kerrang! Nos.150-151, July 9, 1987

I had always looked on Mötley Crüe as something of a joke – and a very bad joke at that. They may have looked the part – if the time the part happened to be in was 1984 and the place Los Angeles – but musically they had never recorded anything that ever remotely turned me on. (That changed later when they released the 'Dr. Feelgood' album but even that felt somewhat ersatz and over-sugared.) This, surely, was rock for people who had never seen Adam Ant or heard of the New York Dolls. Or kissed a girl. The only sane response seemed to be laughter. When, however, they called off some UK dates in January 1988 because – according to official sources – they feared snow on the Wembley Arena roof would drag the ceiling down on top of them, the hilarity turned to disgust. They didn't really expect their fans to believe that, did they?

Apparently they did. Meanwhile, word was already creeping out: the real reason the Wembley shows had been pulled, I was told off the record, was that the band's recent tours of America and Japan had degenerated into such a nightmare of drug overdoses, guns, fights and walk-outs, the road crew had nearly mutinied at one point, threatening to quit if the band didn't get their act together. Hence the cancellation of the rest of the tour, including those Wembley dates.

As we now know from the band's thrillingly explicit 2001 autobiography, The Dirt, *it was pretty much all true. In fact, the reality was even worse than we suspected back then. Poor old Mick Mars. I almost felt sorry for him as he floundered around on the phone to me, doing his best to keep a lid on things as I probed him for "the truth".*

Not for the first time, Mars was left with egg on his face. Maybe that's why it's always been so white…

Mick Mars, London, February 1988

The story so far: just a week before it was due to begin, Mötley Crüe announced the sudden cancellation of what was to have been their first British and European tour for two years. Officially, as reported in issue 171, the cancellation was made because of the band's 'exhaustive and non-stop schedule in 1987'. That's what the official press handout said, anyway. Unofficially, however, the stories continue to pour in: from the sublime to the ridiculous, we must have heard (and printed a good few) of them all. From the alleged drugs overdose Nikki Sixx nearly died from before Christmas, to being told that the real reason the band had cancelled was because they thought the weight of their lighting-rig would put too much strain on the various arena ceilings in Britain and Europe, which would be at breaking point anyway due to all the snow we have in this part of the world around this time of year.

Jee-zus! And those are just the more plausible stories we've been listening to. Ultimately, though, what this all boils down to is that no-one in Britain actually believes a word the band are saying any more. The British Mötley Crüe fans smell a rat. That you shouldn't believe every goddamned thing you read or hear about a band, that goes without saying. But something is obviously wrong here. Tired and exhausted Mötley Crüe may well be, but snow on the roof? Naw… if Mötley Crüe couldn't get it up for a couple of weeks in Britain, it wasn't just because they were knackered, it was because something had gone wrong with the machine…

When the shit hit the fan here in Britain about the 'real' reasons behind the last-minute cancellation of the Crue tour, we got in contact with the band's UK record company and asked them to try and get someone from the band to do a quick phone interview, because in Britain right now, the Crue's reputation is shot. It's in tiny pieces on the ground. We needed to talk to one of them now. The record company said they would try.

Originally, I was going to speak to singer Vince Neil. Then Vince cancelled, we made it for another day, then Vince cancelled again. "He must have got the days mixed up," said a spokeswoman for the band in Los Angeles. A pig flew by my window. I growled at her and told her that Mötley Crüe already looked like Goddamned fools in *Kerrang!* without any more help from anybody. The only thing left for them to do in order to really kill off the band's reputation in this country, I said, would be to fuck me around right now and blow the only chance they've got to tell their side of the story. She sounded suitably concerned and promised she'd get back to me. It was 8.30 pm on a Monday night. *Kerrang!* should have been passed for press by now and the deadline couldn't stand being broken one more time. It was now or never, as Elvis used to sing.

10.00 pm. The phone rings. I answer it. It's Mick Mars. "You wanna talk about cancelling the tour, right?" he asks. You bet. "Go ahead…"

I begin where the rumours begin here in London: that the Crue tour of America last year started getting out of hand when Guns N' Roses joined on as the opening act. "We were doing so many dates, the whole thing was just really exhausting," he says. "I don't recall things getting too out of hand, though. No more than usual on one of our tours."

What about the Nikki Sixx drugs OD story? It's said that it occurred right after that tour ended. "I heard about that too, and I just started laughing! It's total shit… just another one of those dumb stories that get put out about us. Honestly, man, stories like that about us go out all the time. Did you hear the latest one about how I'm supposed to be getting married? I mean, COME ON! No way…"

So Nikki Sixx definitely did not suffer a drugs overdose? "No! None of that happened! Nikki didn't die either... I heard that one, too! It's just dumb shit."

OK. Moving on to your Japanese tour, which immediately preceded the scheduled British shows, it's here that the stories really start to pick up. It's whispered that it was while the band were weaving their way around the land of the rising yen that the personalities really started to get out of control, a factor said to have contributed greatly to their eventual decision to blow out the UK and European dates. What's the truth here?

"The truth here is nothing like what you might have heard. The simple truth is, we were totally and utterly wasted! Done in; seriously fucking tired! We realised after the Japanese tour that to come to Europe would have been a big mistake. If you ever see one of our shows then you'll know we only ever give a hundred percent. We wouldn't have been able to do that if we'd come to England straight after the tour of Japan. We were terminally exhausted. You wouldn't have liked us if you'd seen us, it would have been a big disappointment."

There was a story that had you pulling guns on people backstage in Japan.

"No, no, no… We bought some toy guns while we were out there to keep ourselves amused, we were firing them at each other all the time. But they weren't real guns… they look pretty real, I guess, but they're toys – bought 'em in a store!"

What about the scenes we had described of various band members beating up a party of women they had picked up while you were out there? "What? That's the first time I've heard that one… Shit, no! We got a little drunk on the bullet-train, that was about as far out as we got. The rest is total shit!"

What's the truth behind that plaster cast that Vince now carries on his hand and arm? "I'm not absolutely sure how he did it, but he cut himself on some broken glass…"

We heard that he did it in a fit of temper backstage one night – that he jammed his fist into a glass jar of mustard and smashed it against the dressing room wall. "No, no, no! He cut his hand all right, but not in a fit of temper or because he had his hand in a jar of mustard… Where do these stories come from?"

Actually, some of the most ludicrous stories seem to come from the band's official sources, I tell him. For example, the absurd we-can't-play-because-of-all-the-snow-on-the-roof story that appeared in the very last issue of *Kerrang!*.

"You got that from an official source!" he cries, barely able to control himself. I read him the whole thing out, word for word, over the phone. "That is the most COMPLETE and UTTER BULLSHIT I'VE EVER HEARD!! I can't believe that came from someone who works for us! You're kidding me! I'm not even going to bother denying it… I mean, nobody believes that, do they?"

One thing I'm not sure whether to believe or not is the latest story hot off the underground wire: that all of Mötley Crüe – Mick Mars included – are about to undergo detoxification at an expensive Californian clinic before returning to the rehearsal studio to begin work on the next Crüe album. I ask Mick for his opinion.

"Well, we're certainly cutting down on all the heavy drinking right now. Next time we go out on tour we don't wanna burn ourselves out so fast. On the recent tour I have to admit that we were in danger towards the end of getting a little bit too out of control, but nothing like as bad as some of those stories say it was. The only way you could properly understand what we have been through as a band this last year is if you'd been there with us. I know it sounds kind of lame, but you'd have to have experienced what we've been through yourself to truly understand how deeply exhausted we are right now. We did the smartest thing by cancelling the tour…"

By way of an official apology, Mick Mars says that the very next Mötley Crüe world tour will kick-off with dates in Britain and Europe. "Believe me, nobody is more disappointed and upset about what's happened than us. But it's like I say – if we had turned up, you would have been more disappointed than if you had to wait a few months until you could really see us at our best. Next time we go out on the road, we start in Britain. That's the deal."

With recording on the next Mötley Crüe album not scheduled to begin in earnest until July, the likelihood of a tour in the UK by the band occurring much before next Christmas is slim indeed. I wonder how many genuine Crüe fans out there will be convinced enough of the band's integrity to wait that long? Because something is still wrong here, somewhere. The credibility gap remains. Mick Mars didn't laugh off a single one of the questions I asked him. He sounded like he was giving evidence. He sounded tired. Only I still don't know why. Not really.

Maybe he doesn't either…

First published in Kerrang! No.173, February 6, 1988

Still largely unknown outside hip circles, it was a good time to meet the Red Hot Chili Peppers. Barely famous, let alone rich yet, Anthony Kiedis arrived at my hotel room unaccompanied by PR or management flunky. He looked a little lost, actually, gazing out at the swimming pool as he tucked into the omelette I had bought him. Bumming cigarettes off me, after the interview he drove us to the photo-session at Ross Halfin's studio in an old jalopy that juddered and spluttered as he pushed the speedometer up past 70 mph.

Recently off all drugs and alcohol, he was doing his best to stay "clean and serene," which had the knock-on effect of keeping me sober that day, too. I couldn't compete with his muscles, though. Even though I was something of a gym-rat myself at the time, Kiedis looked like he'd been training for the weightlifting event at the Olympics. "I was the buffest junky you ever saw," he joked when I mentioned it. And like a lot of ex-druggies and drinkers his only real pleasure now was sex. He told me he'd recently hooked up with an 18-year-old model he'd met in Japan and that she "demanded sex at least five times a day."

I didn't know if he was joking or not but sensed there was always at least one grain of truth in anything he might say. I was also surprised to discover he was a Charles Bukowski fan. In those days I still thought I was the only one who'd ever heard of him. When I showed him a new copy of Celine's Journey To The End Of The Night *that I'd just bought, though, he admitted he was impressed. "Wow," he said, looking at the cover photo of a man clearly on the edge of despair, "he even looks kinda like Bukowski."*

I decided to give him the book. I'd be able to have a drink after he'd gone, he would only have the book to read. (And the model to fuck but he made that sound like a chore.) He gave me a CD of a group called the Digital Underground. I decided he was the nicest, most down-to-earth and – just possibly – most honest – American rock star I'd met in a long time. Possibly ever...

Anthony Kiedis, Los Angeles, June 1990

I'm sorry, ladies, but when he appears in the doorway, immediately I'm struck by how small he is. Onstage with the Red Hot Chili Peppers, Anthony Kiedis looks like one of those classical Greek statues; large, muscle-bound, big willy dangling. In person, however, the singer with the original 'hardcore, bone-crunching, psychedelic, sex-funk band from heaven' looks much more manageable. Five feet eight maybe, long straight tea-coloured hair, younger looking than his 27 years; dressed in shorts (natch), T-shirt and sneakers. Still with the big muscular arms though. As for the willy? Well, he never showed it to me, which is a shame. Maybe if he had, I might have sued him and made some money out of it. He explains how a similar situation came about...

"It was backstage after a show and I was changing and there was a girl there. We were all joking and laughing together and when she left, no one was under the impression that she was perturbed by my nudity in the dressing room."

Within 24 hours, however, the girl, a student at the George Mason University, in Virginia, had sworn out a complaint and Kiedis was tried and convicted on misdemeanour charges of 'sexual battery' and 'indecent exposure'. He was fined $1,000 on each count. He paid the fine for indecent exposure, but is appealing against the sexual battery charge. She claimed Kiedis had dangled his dick in her face. Had he?

"No," he says sharply. "I'm not that type of person. I'm a very fun-loving, friendly person. The fact that I was found guilty of misdemeanours and given a nominal fine pretty much indicated to my attorney and to hers that it was a pile of shit."

Unlike the singing voice, which has rapped, yapped and crowed its way through four albums with the Red Hot Chili Peppers, the speaking voice is even-tempered, almost monotonous, or would be if what he had to say wasn't so interesting. We meet on another typically red hot day in Los Angeles. Actually, I'm lying. It was pissing with rain, chucking it down. I just liked the line.

"I love the rain," Kiedis tells me, glancing out the window of my hotel room. "It's very important to Los Angeles; the air pollution is so deadly here that without the rain we would die. So, you know, we're very lucky to have rain today."

We digress to discuss the environment. Kiedis says it needs all the help it can get. I don't argue. We sit there looking thoughtful. Then the conversation steers itself back onto safer ground: more sex crimes. In March, performing during MTV's Spring-break party in Daytona Beach, Florida, bassist and – along with Kiedis – co-founder of the Red Hot Chili Peppers, Michael 'Flea' Balzary, and drummer, Chad Smith, were arrested by beach rangers after they had leapt off the stage to much commotion and Flea allegedly threw a young woman over his shoulder while Smith spanked her. Both face charges for battery, with Flea facing additional charges of 'disorderly conduct' and 'solicitation to commit an unnatural and lascivious act'. Kiedis remains tight-lipped on the subject. It's clear he thinks the whole thing has been blown out of all proportion. Maybe if it had been solely a Red Hot Chili Peppers gig instead of a variety show, the girl would have understood, maybe even demanded it…

"Most people who come to our shows understand that there's a humorous element to what we do and not necessarily intended to offend anyone," Kiedis says straight-faced. "The First Amendment of the American Constitution gives you the freedom of speech and the freedom, you know, to do what you will from the stage."

Tell it to the PMRC, I tell him. Or the Governor of the state of Minnesota who is trying to introduce an over-21 law for all major-league concerts in the state, whether the venue is selling alcohol or not. "That's a terrible concept," says Kiedis, shaking his head. "I hope they fail miserably. Creativity has always been threatened by certain right wing factions of society. But they've never succeeded and I don't see why they should now."

Nevertheless, the last Chilis' album, 'Mother's Milk', came complete with 'Explicit Language' stickers plastered on its sleeve. "That doesn't bother me at all," he says. "Our lyrics are very explicit, whether it's about sex or friendship, or love for life in general. If they wanna inform the buying public that it is explicit, I have no problems with that."

However, when a certain large chain of American stores wanted to buy 50,000 copies of the album, they balked when they saw the sleeve (the naked upper torso of a young woman cradling the four miniature figures of the band in her slender arms). The band's US record company, Capitol, got round the problem by redesigning the sleeve to make the bodies bigger, in order to obscure more of 'Mother's' breasts. 50,000 records later, Kiedis says he is comfortable with the decision and denies any implications of selling out. Yuk! Horrid words.

"The art of the Red Hot Chili Peppers is first and foremost that of our music, and we never change our music as a compromise for anybody's desires or tastes. That we should have to enlarge ourselves on the record is really not that big a deal. It's what's inside that counts," he points out pragmatically. "These things are so arbitrary, anyway. Nobody kicked up any fuss over our T-shirts..."

The two most famous being the legendary socks-on-cocks number, and the less well known woman-masturbating shirt. "It's a drawing of Madonna masturbating, and she's dreaming of the Red Hot Chili Peppers," Kiedis explains with a straight face. It's not known if Madonna herself has actually seen it. "I think if she saw it, she'd want one, that's the type of girl she is. I mean, I don't think she's ever denied masturbating. Or denied masturbating to the Red Hot Chili Peppers, for that matter..."

What about the serious side of the Red Hot Chili Peppers, though? All play and no work makes Jack a dull jerk... Does it concern Kiedis that some people might not be able to see past the silly faces in their photos, the smutty T-shirts, the whole zany, kinky, mama-we's-all-crazy jive? That some people might not take the Red Hot Chili Peppers seriously at all?

"But that's like people going to see Jimi Hendrix play and coming away from the concert with nothing more to say than, 'Wow, that guy can play with his teeth!'" he says. "This is show business, and we are here to entertain. We like to entertain people. The visual value of it is there, but there's a lot more to it than that. People who are truly interested or concerned will find that out eventually."

On the other hand, of course, some people take the Red Hot Chili Peppers almost too seriously. To the point of actually wanting to be them. No, I'm not talking about Faith No More: just their singer, Mike Patton. I ask Kiedis straight for his opinion on the matter: did Mike Patton rip you off hook, line and sinker, or what? "Yeah," he says, no hesitation. "My drummer says he's gonna kidnap him and shave his hair off and saw off one of his feet. Just so he'll be forced to find a style of his own."

Is this genuine bitterness here, or just another joke? "It used to really bother me. I thought, what a drag if people get the idea that I'm actually ripping him off! Especially in the UK where Faith No More are much better known than us. In America, it's a different story, people are aware of the profound influence we had on them. But after it stewed in my stomach for a while, I just decided to accept it. He is just a kid. Besides, without his left foot he's going to have to change..."

In America they have just received a Gold record for 'Mother's Milk'. It is only now, though, that the Chilis' have started to make any serious inroads into the British or European markets. This month they return to the UK for a clutch of dates and TV appearances. How important is it for the band to be a success this side of the ocean they named after a record company?

"Everywhere we go in the world we try our hardest and we play our hardest every night we play. That's basically what we have to offer Britain. The way the industry's set up over there, the only way to get across is go over there and play. It's to expose what you have to offer to the entire world."

Does he actually like it, though, in Ye Olde Country? "To be blatantly honest, England is not our favourite place to go," he admits without guilt. "It isn't because we're not as well-known as we are in America: it's the weather we don't like, and it's very far away, and the food's not very good – they tend to overcook the vegetables."

He adopts a teasing, bitter English accent: "You know, steak and kidney pie is not really me favourite... I think that sooner or later, though, it's inevitable that we will conquer England, as well as Scotland, Ireland and the rest of the world."

This without a hint of an exclamation mark in his voice. "It's very much like the long-term process of making love to somebody: you start off with the foreplay, you kiss them and you suck their neck and you titillate their sensory areas with your fingertips, with the first couple of records. Maybe you start giving them head with the third record, then you finally slip it in for the fourth. That's essentially what we've done with our career up to this point. 'Mother's Milk' was incredibly well received in America. Basically, we're still involved in the foreplay section with the rest of the world, since they didn't really get our first two records."

Sex… it all comes back to sex with this guy. Almost as soon as we met, Kiedis told me he was on a "sex diet". And he had the love-bites – one either side of the jugular – to prove it. "I've got a new girlfriend. She's 18 years old and demands rigorous sexual activity several times a day."

For those of us who need to know, Kiedis' sex diet consists of "no fattening foods, lots of protein, and a lot of exercise before and after you eat. Basically, you just can't afford to have an ounce of fat because a sexual diet is for performance. But it's also for aesthetics: she's a model and she's quite perfect in her physical structure."

So is this lurve, Anthony? "Love is a word taken much too seriously sometimes," he says enigmatically. "People are afraid to say they love somebody, but the fact is I do love her. I'm not gonna marry her and I'm not gonna dedicate my whole life to her, because I need to devote time to myself and to my music. But she understands. I just broke up with the girl that I lived with for two years. To get out of the frying pan and to go straight into the fire would be stupid right now. We've decided we're gonna be blatantly honest about all our feelings, at risk of hurting each other. But I do love her and she loves me. She's the biggest sexual genius I've encountered in the last 10 years..."

He strikes a post-coital pose and lights a cigarette. Excluding sex, smoking is his one remaining vice. "My guitar player [John Frusciante] is such an avid smoker, and he really loves the quality it gives my voice, the raspiness. But he's the kind of guy who was heartbroken to find out that John Waters, his favourite film-maker, had quit smoking at the age of 44."

Once upon a time, of course, smoking a cigarette was the least of Kiedis' problems. Heroin abuse, alcoholism, both had threatened to take him over for much of the band's seven-year career. Then his guitarist, friend and co-conspirator in the twilight world of drug addiction, Hillel Slovak, died. "Like me, Hillel had the disease of drug addiction," Kiedis says, not flinching. "He didn't die of an overdose; he died from having a disease. No one wanted to accept that this young man with so much to offer was just gone, you know, wiped out in a second. But in a strange way, we found strength from that. It forced me to make a choice. I could either join Hillel or I could try and finish my life.

"I've been completely off all alcohol and drugs for 21 months now. I mean, completely. I don't drink or use anymore. But I don't do it by myself. Hillel tried to do it by himself and he died. I do it with the help of other addicts that have cleaned up. That's the only way I know how to deal with it."

A new Red Hot Chili Peppers single, 'Taste The Pain', the third to be taken from last year's excellent 'Mother's Milk' collection, is released by EMI to tie in with the UK shows. A new video, directed by Alex Winter (the weedy, blonde guy in the movie, *Bill & Ted's Excellent Adventure*), has already been shot, and features, says Kiedis with obvious satisfaction, "some very twisted images of pain and brutal reality. It's impossible to describe. There's a sense of surrealism to it all as well."

When he's not devouring his new girlfriend, Kiedis says he likes to spend his spare time reading (Bukowski is a big favourite, as is Capote, Hesse, Bach); listening to music ('Sex Packets' by the Digital Underground is a current favourite, he tells me). But mostly, he insists, he has sex. Well, it's a hobby, I suppose...

While still discussing his sex diet and all the exercise involved, I eye his bulging arm muscles (like Popeye) and enquire how often Kiedis lifts weights? "No, no weights," he deadpans. I look surprised. "Where did you get those big arms from then?" I asked. "Sex," he replies. "No way!" I laugh. What does he do, carry them around over his head before he gets them into bed? At last, he allows himself a small chuckle, amused by my puffing and blowing, my envy and disbelief.

"The only exercise I ever get, unless I force myself to do push-ups, is sex and being on stage. Stage is the cardiovascular scenario, you know, an hour and a half running around every night. That's a perfect exercise. And sex. You'd be surprised. I mean, you're holding yourself above a girl for any length of time, you know, utilising your pelvis, or whatever. Don't you feel pumped up after you've had sex?" he asks me, face a perfect mask of sincerity.

Outside it's stopped raining...

First published in Kerrang! No.292, June 2, 1990

An air stewardess once told me that the nicest people on the plane were always the ones in First Class. "They've made it and have nothing to prove," she explained. The people in Economy were usually nice too but there were always a few trouble makers. While the ones in Business Class – caught quite literally in the middle between First and Economy – were almost always the worst. "The ones who haven't quite made it but still demand all your attention," as she put it, "the know-alls and wannabes."

I have found the same can often be said for rock stars. Put simply, the bigger the star, the easier they are to deal with. This is certainly true of Jimmy Page. An artist with nothing left to prove – except perhaps to himself – he has always been remarkably free of attitude whenever I have spoken with him. A gentleman in every sense, I have always struggled to put the guy I know next to the dark-eyed evil-doer we have all read about in other books.

And yet, as he would be the first to admit, that doesn't mean he has always been a saint. As you can see from this interview, he freely acknowledges that much of the life he lived in Led Zeppelin was, in his words, "quite hedonistic", and that he and the group actually fed off that dark energy, using it to inform their creativity and their personal appeal. Perhaps surprisingly, however, to those that only know Zeppelin from the books, Jimmy remains utterly unrepentant, describing his years in Zeppelin as some of the "happiest of my life."

That said, Jimmy has always been somewhat shy of divulging his true feelings about Zeppelin, over and above acknowledging how "proud" he is of their musical achievements. Of all the many interviews I would do with him over the years, this was the first time that he really opened up about it. The first time I realised, in fact, how much he still missed those days and what he would give to actually put the group back together. If only Robert Plant felt the same way too…

Jimmy Page, Berkshire, October 1990

A word to the wise guy. This month has seen the release of the first legitimate Led Zeppelin 'product' for over a decade. First was the triple-album 'Remasters'. Now this week comes the real McCoy: 'Remasters Boxed': a 54-track, six album / four cassette and/or four-CD collection of some of the finest moments from arguably the most legendary rock band of all time. The tracks for both were officially selected by the three remaining band members – Jimmy Page, Robert Plant and John Paul Jones – then compiled and re-mastered from the original studio tapes by Page.

The story of Led Zeppelin has, of course, been well-documented over the years; the tales of road madness and Red Snappers, cocaine and mind-games, always with the suggestion of something darker lurking in the background, are as well-known and often repeated as a favourite dirty joke. But never has the case for Led Zeppelin been put so forthrightly, so imaginatively, or so poignantly as it is throughput the duration of this collection. A good time then to talk to the man responsible not just for the re-mastering, but who wrote, played on, produced and directed – both musically and artistically – every important move Zeppelin ever made. A good time then to talk to Jimmy Page.

We meet up at the house in Berkshire Jimmy lives in these days along with his pretty blonde wife, Patricia, and their two-and-a-half-year-old son, James Patrick. Now in his mid-40s, on the day we met Jimmy was looking fit, well, tanned even – about as un-Zeppelin as you can get, in fact. And, in case you're wondering, our preferred choice of beverage throughout the interview was tea…

To start with, whose idea was it to put this box-set together? "I don't know who had the original idea. It came from Atlantic Records and it was just put to us. I, for one, was very keen to do it because, primarily, the CDs that have come out of the Zeppelin material in the past didn't sound as good to me as they should. I had nothing to do with them. When we made the records I'd always gone through everything, producing, mixing, right down to checking the test pressings. I always saw it right through to the end. The way they re-mastered those original CDs though, there wasn't much to it and there were a few things which annoyed me – like the cough that was cut out at the end of 'In My Time Of Dying'. It wasn't until I started working on it in the studio

I realised how into it I really was, on every level."

How did you pick the tracks? Did you actually get together in a room with John Paul Jones and Robert Plant and discuss it? "No. We just all made a list of the ones we wanted. Given the time and the situation, I think, Jones just sent through a list, I don't think Robert even did that. It came to the point where I sent a proposed running order out to the chaps and they seemed happy with it. That was it. There was also a couple of extra numbers included that weren't on any of the original Zeppelin albums. One of them, 'Hey, Hey, What Can I Do' was the B-side of 'The Immigrant Song' single. And there are a couple of tracks salvaged from the vaults of the good old BBC: [Robert Johnson's] 'Travelling Riverside Blues', from a Top Gear session, I think it was. A John Peel thing, anyway. And another one from those sessions, 'White Summer' / 'Black Mountainside'."

How long ago would that be? "Oh, that's right from the early days! Late '60s, early '70s. And there are the two Bonham tracks – 'Moby Dick' and 'Bonzo's Montreux' – I didn't want to leave one or the other off, so I had a crack at joining the two up with a Fairlight. It starts with the 'Moby Dick' riff, then it cuts into the solo part of 'Bonzo's Montreux', and then the riff comes back in again. It works great, actually. I think John would have been quite happy with it."

Looking through the running order it occurred to me that there are very few rock bands anybody would want to wade through 54 tracks for, and yet everyone's a winner here. "Yes, it's sort of surprising to me, too. I was going through the albums taking things off this one and that one and leaving a lot behind. At the end of the day, with 54 numbers there, I hadn't realised we'd written that many good songs. And there was still a lot left."

Before you started this project, did you often dig out the old Zep albums and have a blast while you were on your own at home? "Oh, yeah. Every day! I like a little blast every now and then," he says crinkling his eyes.

Once you'd chosen the tracks, how long did it take to re-master them? "It must have been about five days. I'd have to check, because I was punchy after the first three. I got off the plane in New York and went straight to the studio to begin working. During that process, though, I certainly lived my life over again. It was quite incredible, really. I'd be listening to a track and start thinking about where it was done and under what circumstances, and funny little anecdotes about it. Sometimes a really joyous feeling, sometimes a little sad. Nevertheless, it was evident what a brilliant textbook Zeppelin was. Especially in the different areas we approached. We went boldly where few men have been before, let's put it that way."

And where few have been since, in your opinion? "Yeah, maybe. Cos we had a licence to do it. It was all album-oriented material. It wasn't about having to come up with something to fit the singles market."

It seems like you've deliberately rearranged the original running order of the tracks to add a further element of surprise. For instance, it comes as a real jolt to the system not to hear 'Livin' Lovin' Maid' come belting out of the speakers straight after 'Heartbreaker"... "Yeah. I think the good thing about that is it sheds new light on those tracks. It's the same picture in a different frame. Like 'The Song Remains The Same' from 'Houses Of The Holy' now goes into 'Ten Years Gone' from 'Physical Graffiti' instead of 'Rain Song'. But it works great!"

You mentioned that working on the box-set brought back a lot of memories. Can you give me a for instance? "The sessions we recorded at Headley Grange immediately spring to mind. We had three or four different spells there. They were really good times for us, very productive because we were living in and we came up with a lot of material we definitely wouldn't have done otherwise. I remember one night I came downstairs and Jonesy's mandolin was lying there. He always had loads of different instruments lying around. I'd never played a mandolin before but I picked it up and started messing around with it, and I came up with all of 'The Battle Of Evermore' [from the untitled fourth Zep album]. That would never have happened if we'd just been in a normal studio situation."

Do you miss that kind of creative camaraderie; four guys in a band just hanging out together and making music? "Ah, well... in the writing sense I do, yes. In those days there was a purpose behind it. I knew exactly who I was writing for. If I was writing something I was hearing Robert singing it, and you knew you were going forward all the time."

What ingredients defined the Led Zeppelin sound for you? "Well, I think that the first album had so many firsts on it, as far as the content goes. Even though we were heavily involved in a sort of progressive blues thing, one of the most important parts was the acoustic input. Things like 'Babe I'm Gonna Leave You', which had the flamenco-type bits in it. The drama of it, I don't think had been touched by anybody before. With the acoustic input you had this sort of embryo, which was good."

It was always very exotic-sounding music, I thought. "It was very passionate, that's for sure."

Other guitarists have commented in the past on how strange and unpredictable many of your guitar chords are on certain Zeppelin songs. 'Rain Song', for instance, is said to be a particularly tricky one to learn. The guitar doesn't appear to follow any 'normal' rock progression. "That comes from the tuning. I was constantly fooling around with tunings on the acoustic. Sometimes they'd progress onto the electric. Like 'Dancing Days', things like that. But a lot of the acoustic numbers had different tunings. 'White Summer' [originally Jimmy's acoustic showcase with the Yardbirds], that was a standard folk tuning. 'Friends' is a different kind of tuning again."

Did that interest in experimenting with tuning come from your well-known fondness for Oriental music? "Mmm... It's like, 'Black Mountainside', 'White Summer', I call that my CIA – Celtic, Indian and Arabic. It's got all those influences in it. I was always interested in ethnic music. Still am."

When you first put Led Zeppelin together, did you have a clear idea of what you wanted the band to do, how you wanted it to be? "Yeah, definitely. I'd come from the Yardbirds, which was a guitar-oriented band, and there were lots of areas which they used to call free-form but was just straight improvisation. By the time Zeppelin was getting together I'd already come up with such a mountain of riffs and ideas, because every night we went on there were new things developing."

How do you feel when people say Zeppelin was modelled on the group formed by your brief sparring partner in the Yardbirds, Jeff Beck? "Well, it wasn't. It wasn't modelled on Jeff's band at all. For a start, Jeff had a keyboard player in his band, he was attempting an entirely different thing. The only unfortunate similarity was that we both did a version of [Willy Dixon's] 'You Shook Me'. I didn't know Jeff had recorded it too until our album was already done. You know, we had very similar roots but we were trying for a completely different thing, in my opinion."

What about the overtly mystical slant of much of Zeppelin's lyrics: was that a sign of the times, or are you just like that, anyway? "I was like that at school. I was always interested in alternative religions. These days it's alternative medicines, isn't it?" he kids. "But, yes, I was always interested in mysticism, Eastern tradition, Western tradition. I used to read a lot about it so consequently it became an influence."

As Zeppelin began to grow bigger and bigger, did you feel you were tapping into something greater, some form of energy more profound than 'good time rock'n'roll'? "Yeah, but I'm reluctant to get into it because it just sounds pretentious. But, yeah, obviously, you can tell that from the live things. It was almost a trance state sometimes, but it just sounds, you know..." He looks away.

"That was what was so exciting about it, though, certainly. Once we'd recorded the numbers and then started playing them live we were pushing them more and more, making the numbers work for us. Like on the live soundtrack to [the movie] *The Song Remains The Same*, you hear all this energy roaring through it. That energy and intensity that there's no escape from."

When you were at the height of your power in Zeppelin, were you ever afraid, as you stood on stage, that things were in real danger of getting out of hand, beyond your control? "No. The only thing that became apparent was that there were more and more people wanting to see us. It just kept increasing right till the very end. If it ever did start to get like that some nights, if it was getting too rowdy, we used to stop the concert and get them to cool down. If you didn't do that and allowed it to fester, it could get… Well, someone could get hurt. We wanted people to go home happy rather than with a few bruises – or worse."

Did you remain matey with the three other members of Zeppelin right through to when John Bonham died and the band broke up? "Yeah, I think so."

What about towards the end when it's said you used to walk offstage and immediately disappear into your own world, away from the others? "Well, I'm a very private person, and still am, so maybe people played that up into something else."

Do you feel you're still living down the image that continues to linger from those days – the bad man with the guitar in one hand and the bag of tricks in the other? "Well, there's no smoke without fire. I guess I'm a pretty complex person."

You once told me you had what you called an acoustic side and an electric side to your personality. Can you expound on that a little for me? "It's true. But there's light and shade to everyone, I would presume. I mean, I'm obviously a different person offstage to what I am on."

You were always very flamboyant – what about the famous suit with all the symbols woven into it. Was that your own creation? "Yeah. I came across this person who wanted to make me some stage clothes and I said, 'Try this!'. It was incredible. It had dragons going up the side and the astrological symbols and stuff. It's a work of art that suit."

Did the astrological symbols have a specific meaning? "Yeah, like my sun rising sign…"

Are you very into astrology? "I'm interested in astrology, yeah," he smiles self-deprecatingly.

You're a Capricorn. What characterises a Capricorn? "Stubbornness, but reliability, I'm sure."

On stage you had the fantastic costumes, yet off stage you seemed to guard your privacy jealously. "I tried to get… Because of the whole spectacle and energy of the shows, you couldn't live your life like that. You had to reach some balance in between. You know, coming back from a tour instead of setting up a 200 Watt stack, I'd pick up an acoustic."

Can you describe for me a little of what it was like to be on the road with Led Zeppelin in those days? "Well, you know..." He pauses, lights a cigarette… "Most of it was so cocooned. We used to leave the stage, jump into the cars and get whisked off to the aeroplane, which would fly us to the next gig. Our feet never really touched the ground."

The aeroplane in question – the notorious Starship – couldn't have held much more than a couple dozen passengers and yet the amount of people who have since claimed to have ridden on it with you would be enough to fill a Jumbo… "Yeah, right. But we never actually let too many people on the plane."

And for those of you who did actually ride on the plane, what was the truth? Were the after-show parties really as wild as some of the scenes that have since been described in endless books and articles? "Oh, yeah, there was always a lot of theatre. There always is on rock'n'roll tours, though I think we might have pioneered a lot of it. In fact, I know we did!" he chortles.

When you see bands like the Who and the Rolling Stones, much older bands than Zeppelin, getting back together and doing great things, doesn't it make you want to do it, too: reform Led Zeppelin? I mean, could you see it? "I'm sure there's a lot of people who would like to see it. Me being one of them. The telling thing about the Stones was that even with Mick and

Keith's differences, at the end of the day they owned up to the fact that the band was bigger than both of them. Whereas with us, we've all collaborated through the years. I played on Robert's album. He played on mine. Jonesy and I collaborated on the 'Death Wish II' soundtrack album. So I don't think it's impossible that we could do something in the future."

Does it worry you though, that the moment might be gone and that Zeppelin couldn't be revived? "I've never doubted for a minute that if Robert and I sat down and started writing that we could come up with some really good stuff. We've already got 10 years of music to prove what we can do."

It's been a decade since Zeppelin broke up, which is almost as long as the group was together. And yet in a way the band is bigger now than it ever was. "Absolutely, no doubt about it."

How does your lifestyle compare now with your years in Zeppelin? "Well, I was never unhappy in those days, let me tell you, and I'm certainly not unhappy now. The only difference is I'm not doing so much touring as I used to. Which is something I intend to rectify when I finish working on my next solo album."

You've certainly clocked up the old guest appearances this year. Bon Jovi at Hammersmith; Robert at Knebworth; Aerosmith at Donington and the Marquee… "Yeah, I'll be giving jamming a bad name soon."

When you joined Aerosmith at the Marquee, that was the first time I ever saw Joe Perry smile on stage. "That was great. They're such a good band to play with as well, let me tell you. They really know what it's all about, all right."

I never saw so many musicians in the audience. "Yeah, we'll have to have some more of it, eh Mick? Hopefully, when I get my new band together next year."

You've got a young son now: Patrick. Will he be musical, do you think? "Yeah, sure. He's coming from a musical family, so if he wants to, sure. I'd like to see him enjoying the guitar like I do. At the moment though his hands are too small to get round a guitar, even a small custom-built one. But as soon as I think they're big enough…"

Let's go back and talk about your earliest experiences as a musician. How did you come to form Led Zep? Did it happen suddenly, or was it just part of a natural development? "Well, I'd been in a band when I left school. One thing led to another and I ended up going to art college. But nevertheless I was still playing guitar. By then I was playing in the interval band at the Marquee, supporting Cyril Davies. I was sort of plucked out of that to do a session. Someone just came up and said, 'Would you like to play on a record?'"

It's rumoured that you played on just about everything in those days, from 'Walk Tall' by Val Doonican to 'You Really Got Me' by the Kinks. What actually was the first session you ever played on? "The very first session I did was 'Diamonds' by Jet Harris and Tony Meehan [Number One in the UK in 1963]. Do you remember that? That was the first thing I did. The A-side was all right, but the other side meant me reading music and I hadn't got a clue about all that, so I wasn't seen again for a while. Then when I was in the interval band at the Marquee I got to play on this other record and it crept into the bottom of the charts. After that the phone started ringing more frequently; my art studies sort of stopped and I carried on with the studio work. At that time the Beatles and the Stones were just beginning to happen and the studio producers needed a young guitarist who knew what was going on. Then that started to progress into other things and I'd be doing folk sessions and jazz sessions and film music..."

It must have been great training for what came later. "Yeah, it was really, really good for that, because I had to get to know all these different techniques. It was good discipline, too. The studio discipline was essential for later days."

Was it during this period – the early to mid '60s – that you developed your interest in ethnic music? "I was always interested in ethnic music. I had a sitar in those days that I'd had imported from Bombay. I didn't even know how to tune it. Fortunately, listening to Ravi Shankar, I learned how to do it."

This was before George Harrison and the Beatles got their hands on one? "It was certainly before they were using them, as far as I know."

Although you soon became known for you prowess and versatility as a session guitarist, it wasn't until you joined the Yardbirds in 1966 that the wider public became acquainted with the name Jimmy Page. How did the Yardbirds thing originally come about? "I replaced Paul Samwell-Smith, the bass player, to begin with, and then I took over on guitar as well with Jeff [Beck], which was something that we'd always wanted to do anyway. Then Jeff sort of had a flare-up on tour and left the band."

His own freak-out or a freak-out at you? "No, no, his own thing. The whole Yardbirds thing became fragmented after that. What the manager did was to take the two acts as an overall package to producer Mickie Most, who was starting his own label, RAK – Jeff Beck, his solo thing, and us, the Yardbirds. But the material we were doing was all wrong. I wanted to try a different approach and they seemed to want to do it on their own."

And so you set out to form your own band? "Yes. Keith Relf, the founder member, was really disillusioned towards the end. I can understand why. But I had all these ideas that I wanted to explore with a band, especially the acoustic stuff. So I knew from the kick-off what I wanted the backbone of the outfit to be."

What about the improvisational aspects of Led Zeppelin: was that another area you deliberately set out to explore from the start? "Oh yes, right from the very first live performances there were these stretched-out improvisations."

Which is, perhaps, what gave Zeppelin their edge live – not being able to predict what was going to happen next? "Yes, absolutely. There was always that energy, which just seemed to grow and grow. It could be almost trance-like some nights."

In some of the audience shots from the *Song Remains The Same* movie there are some incredibly beautiful, sophisticated young women and some very intense-looking young men in the audience. Led Zeppelin didn't just attract screaming teenagers and long-hairs… "I hadn't thought about that, but you're right. It was like the Rolling Stones' crowd, there was a real cross-section of people into us. It went right through the age groups. That was what made it so great."

You once told me you had a large collection of vintage live Zeppelin recordings spanning the group's career. Weren't you tempted to use any of that on this new box-set? "I think that the live stuff would be better in a collection of its own. In fact, before [the posthumously released final Zeppelin album] 'Coda' I'd decided to make a chronological album with the live tapes, cos we had tapes going right back to the Albert Hall in 1970, right through to Knebworth [Zeppelin's last British gig in August 1979]."

Why didn't you do it in the end? "It wasn't done because there wasn't enough interest between the band members. Whether any of that stuff will surface in the future or not…" He shrugs.

Of course, Led Zeppelin's reputation was solidly founded on the fact that it was a determinedly albums-orientated band. Hit singles were never a consideration. Do you think if the band was around now you'd be pressured into releasing singles? "It's just a totally different ball game now, because in those days there was the music 'business', there wasn't the record 'industry' – the corporate industry where every band is viewed purely as an investment and there's the whole package that goes with that. We certainly wouldn't have been able to explore the areas that we did and feel no pressure. Because we weren't putting out singles we didn't have to worry thinking about what was going to be the follow-up single when we were recording the next album. All we concentrated on was trying to make a statement of where we all were. That's why all the albums arc so different, I think."

Success came very quickly for Zeppelin. According to *Rolling Stone* magazine, during its first year of release 'Led Zeppelin II' sold over five million copies in America alone. Were you taken aback at how quickly the band took off? "I wasn't even aware of it, really, to be honest with you. That's the truth. We knew the albums were doing better each time. 'Zep III' probably didn't do as well as 'Zep II' but we knew that there was a bigger audience out there each time."

To the point where you stopped having anybody else on the bill opening for you. "That happened purely because the set we had when we first went out playing just increased as our catalogue grew. We had real difficulty dropping any of the older numbers cos we enjoyed doing them so much! So the set just started to get longer and longer until it got to about three hours long, sometimes three and-a-half, and there just wasn't time to have anyone else on the bill!"

In September it was the 10th anniversary of the death of John Bonham. Are you aware of that date when it comes around each year? "The time of the year, yeah, sure."

One of the great rock'n'roll tragedies. "Musically, that's for sure..."

For you personally, too? "Yeah, definitely. It was a real blow at the time."

Did John's death sour your memories of the band? "No. I was basically numb for a while afterwards. As I'm sure one is, it's quite natural."

What do you remember as John's most important contributions to the band? "Just his whole input. People always underrated John's input into the songs. Everybody always knew he was a phenomenal drummer; what they missed was how much he had to do with the writing of the songs. A lot of those songs simply wouldn't have been written or come out how they did, if it had been anyone other than John playing in the band."

He also had a pretty fearsome reputation. "He was a great leveller to have in the band. At group meetings, if people were waffling on he'd just say, 'Ya what?' When anyone used to get a little too far out, John would always be there to pull them right back down to earth."

Obviously this box-set is very much your own work: of the three surviving members of the band, you were the one who sat down and did all the hard work. "As well as all the hard work in the early days! It's true. I was thinking in the studio when I was re-mastering the tracks, 'My God, the amount of time I've put into this over the years!' It really was… It was my life, you know?"

If it means so much to you, isn't it somehow wrong to just let the story end there – with Bonzo's accidental death in 1980? Don't you almost have a duty to get Led Zeppelin back together at some stage? "We've all kept in touch, we've collaborated here and there on each other's albums, so I don't think it's completely beyond the realms of possibility that we could all do something in the future. It would be the logical conclusion."

If Zeppelin were to get back together, would you do like the Stones did and record a new album first? "I don't know about an album, as such. As I say, I'm sure we'll collaborate in some shape or form in the future. But it's premature to say when or how, really. At this point in time, this year Robert's out on tour, and when I've not been working on the box-set I've been writing my next solo album, which I hope to begin recording quite soon."

You're intent on pursuing a solo career then, for the time being? "You bet your life I am! I've only had one solo album out so far, and I'm determined to have a second. Which will be better than the first, of course…"

Robert has talked vaguely of the possibility of there being a new Zeppelin film being put together, made up of footage from the band's private collection. Is that true? "The truth is that we were searching through old footage to see what there was. We started to look through the outtakes from *The Song Remains The Same*, which wasn't really the best place to look. We have got some unused footage lying around, but sadly not as much as other bands probably would have. We haven't got as much footage as we have live tapes. In that respect, it's probably a good thing that *The Song Remains The Same* came out, otherwise there wouldn't be any documentary evidence at all of what was happening. That's the truth of it."

Do you see much of Jason Bonham these days? "I haven't seen Jason since his wedding."

Have you seen his drum kit with the Zeppelin album sleeve designs painted on it? "Yeah. I think it's got a bit over-the-top, all that. He's forgetting who he is. He shouldn't keep leaning on us. I think he's been totally ill-advised by his manager. The whole thing's questionable, to say the least."

But almost everybody wants to be Led Zeppelin these days, don't they? Did you hear the track 'Judgement Day' from the last Whitesnake album, by any chance? "No. Why?"

It's 'Kashmir' all over again. When I asked David Coverdale about it he just said, 'It has nothing whatsoever to do with woolly jumpers'. "I think that's silly. The fact is, 'Kashmir', that track especially, is totally original. We may have built stuff around old blues numbers but the riffs were always totally new. Something like 'Nobody's Fault But Mine', for instance, doesn't bear the slightest resemblance to the original. That's one thing about Zeppelin – the riffs and what we could do to them were always totally new ground. Always..."

You looked like you were having a gas on stage with Robert at Knebworth this year. Does the 'spirit of Led Zeppelin' still move you when the two of you get on a stage together? "We were having a really good time that day at Knebworth. We'd had a rehearsal before we did it and that was great fun."

Is it a relief to be able to launch into something like, say, 'Rock And Roll'? "Oh yeah. It's really good playing all the old numbers. Especially 'Wearing And Tearing', cos we never actually played that live with Zep, apart from recording it. It's a really tricky number because it's got some silly sequencing, and verses and choruses with odd bits in the middle. It really was on a wing and prayer that we went on with that at Knebworth. We were back to living dangerously again."

It's plain you miss touring regularly. "Oh Lord, yes. But as I say, I intend to rectify that as soon as I can, and the way to rectify that is to get my solo album finished, and I'm well on the way to doing that."

And until then? "I don't know. Another cup of tea, I think. Shall I put the kettle on?"

First published in Kerrang! Nos.313-315, October 27, 1990

After it was published this story quite quickly became known as the one where I was 'locked in a cupboard'. What was even stranger to me back then was just how long the piece was talked about afterwards – literally, for years. Flattering though that is for any writer, the reasons it became so well-known to Kerrang! *readers had little to do with how well (or not) the story was actually written. In retrospect, it was simply because that, for once, rather than broadly praise the subject of one of its features,* Kerrang! *had actually allowed one of its writers to put the boot in. While this was a fairly regular occurrence in the reviews' section, it was rare enough within the features' pages – let alone in one of its cover stories, which this was – that it immediately became one of the most talked-about stories I ever did for the magazine.*

What was less well-known was the fact that I ran into Poison again just a couple of weeks after its publication. I was in LA hanging out with Slash from Guns N' Roses when we got wind of the fact that there was a Poison party on in town that night. Slash had once, very briefly, been in the band, but now professed to hate them. Partly, he explained, because they had "turned into a bunch of posers". But mainly, he said, because "that asshole" CC De Ville had recently taken to wearing a top hat onstage – the top hat, by then, being a Slash trademark, of course.

Given our mutual antipathy towards the band, I saw no reason why we would want to go to their party. Slash had other ideas, however, and a couple of hours later, much the worse for wear, I found myself face-to-face with Bret Michaels.

"I don't know whether to be nice to you or not," Bret pouted.

"I don't know whether to be nice to you or not," I parroted.

"I think we already know how you feel, dude," Bret countered.

It was a fair point. I burst out laughing. "Let's have a drink and forget about it," I said.

And to his credit, that's exactly what we did. As a result, I would go on to pen more features on Poison, including the last thing I ever did for the magazine, which made the cover in October 1991. But of course nobody ever remembers those…

Poison, New York, May 1988

With very tired eyes, Ross Halfin looks at me and asks the 64,000 dollar question: "Do you have the slightest idea what's going on here?" It's 8.15pm. Ross and I are standing alone, chair-less and cheerless, unable to escape, in a large empty room backstage at the Nassau Coliseum in New York. In the distance, we can hear Poison onstage, rattling their jewellery for all it's worth, 15 minutes into a tight, strictly-no-encores, 40-minute opening spot for David Lee Roth. Ross should be in the photographers' pit shooting the show; I should be out there scribbling half-arsed little notes and reviewing the damn thing. It is, after all, what Ross and I do best, which is why Poison's record company, Capitol Records, spent all that money flying us out here in the first place. At least, in our mutual madness, that's what we'd assumed...

Well, not according to the band, baby. What me and Ross should be doing is standing in this goddamned room, pulling our plonkers and counting the bricks in the walls. Escape is impossible. Two hours we've already been trapped in this room, and it will be two more before we finally get the hell out of here, and the weirdness is compounded by the fact that neither of us understands why any of this should be happening. And yet here we are and here it is. Three doors out of the room; two of them guarded by men who are not interested in our stories, only interested in our passes, of which we have none because nobody will give us any; the third door, leading to Poison's dressing room, slammed and locked shut to us.

"Mickey," Ross groans, "What's going on? I don't understand it. If they don't want us around, why don't they just tell us to fuck off? Why have they stuck us in a fucking room and left us here to stew? I'm dreaming, aren't I? Go on, tell me I'm dreaming..."

Five pm precisely, as requested, we had turned up at the gates of the Nassau Coliseum. Backstage passes were to be collected; a pre-show photo-session was to have taken place; there was business to be taken care of; some rock and rolling to be done; a show to see; who knows, maybe even destiny to write. Kidz, as far as Halfin and I were concerned, for the next 24 hours we were going to make *Kerrang!* Poison's oyster! And then the shit started...

"Sorry boys, no Halfin or Wall down here on my list," drawled the sweet old uniform on the backstage gate, just like something out of a B-movie. "I'll try calling the production office for you, though."

He calls, he tries. Nothing. He has to repeat our names four or five times before whoever he's talking to on the other end of the line is able to tell him for sure that there are no passes back there for any Halfin or Wall. "Sorry boys…"

OK. A mistake, a mix up, we've seen this movie too. The band haven't arrived themselves yet, we are told, so we decide to sit it out and wait. An hour and a half later we're still waiting outside. It's cold, we can't come in, but it's an hour's drive back to where we're staying and there's no car to take us there, and anyway, what the fuck, this can't go on for much longer. The band will get here, there'll be apologies and smiles, we'll get what we can done, cover the show, bang bang, yeah yeah… Where the fuck are our passes?

At last someone arrives to take us through. A roadie; young, hair, solemn. "I've come to take you guys in…"

We ask him if he has any passes for us. "I don't know anything about any passes. I was just told to take you guys through."

We get taken to Poison's dressing room where another roadie tells us we cannot stay. "You'll have to wait in the corridor outside." Only then yet another roadie tells us we cannot wait there either because we don't have any passes. "You'll have to wait in here."

'Here' turns out to be the room Halfin and I will not leave again for another three and-a-half hours. Adjacent to the band's dressing room, The Room You Cannot Leave is a derelict space cluttered with empty abandoned bookshelves and a couple of bare tables. Two roadies shift the bookshelves in order to make some space for us to stand in. Then they leave us to it. We stand there looking at each other, Ross and I, sharing this horrible sinking feeling…

At 7.15 pm, Poison arrive. Not with a bang, but with a whisper. Standing in the room next to theirs, going out of our minds with boredom, we hear them at it. It's obvious they don't know we're in here. Rikki Rockett, Poison's drummer, suddenly sidles into our bit with an 'I wonder what's in here?' look on his face. What's in here are two very uncomfortable Limeys left with no pass, no class, and no arse, in a windowless room fortunate enough to at least boast a toilet, saving us the indignation of having to piss on the floor like chained dogs.

"Hi guys, how're ya doing?" Rikki smiles uncertainly. Ross and I can't help staring at him as though he was a person from another world. "OK… see ya later," he says, disappearing into the dressing room. A minute later

Poison's bass player, Bobby Dall, appears in the doorway connecting our two very different rooms, clutching a sandwich, again with no more curiosity than a mouse. "I wonder what's in this old room…?"

By now the vibe Ross and I are filling this room with is very bad and Dall seems to pick up on it straight away. He just looks at us for about three seconds, throws us a barely perceptible nod, and turns on his heel back into the dressing room. Two minutes later the band's personal security man walks in, says nothing, just yanks the door connecting us to the dressing room closed with a thud and locks it, checks the lock is good, then leaves, job done.

With 15 minutes to go until Poison take to the stage, Ross and I have been waiting around, inside and out, for nearly three hours. We're starting to lose it, giggling inanely at each other like inmates in a nut house, singing Poison songs under our breath like 'Talk Bullshit To Me', 'I Won't Forget This' and 'Nothing Like A Good Time', and we're sweating and starting to stink, the weirdness of it all starting to seep through our clothes.

Scotty Ross, Poison's tour manager, walks in. "Hey guys, the band got held up getting here and now everything's in a panic…" he begins. We ask Scotty for our passes. The rest can wait. "The passes I have won't get you anywhere," he tells us. "It's not worth having them. But don't worry, I'll take you both out to watch the show from the mixing desk."

"The mixing desk?" interrupts Ross, appalled. "That's no good for me…"

"Well, you can stay here and set up your stuff for some shots after the show?" Scotty suggests remarkably calmly, considering the impact his words are having on Ross, whose eyes are almost popping out of his head. Scotty leaves. Everybody except us that comes into this room manages to leave within 30 seconds! What's wrong with us?

By the time Scotty Ross returned to take me out of that filthy goddamned room and actually to see some of the Poison show, it was 8.22 pm exactly. I know, because I made a point of looking at my watch when he walked in the room – just for the record, as they say. "Hey guys, I'm sorry!" he begins again. "I didn't forget about you, I was just busy getting all the photographers organised in the pit…"

This is the last straw, the final insult, the banal cherry on the whole rancid, ridiculous cake. I'm frightened Ross is going to explode. "Anyway Mick, I'll take you out to see the show now."

At best, there is less than 15 minutes left of the Poison set, and frankly my dears, I no longer give a fuck. "Frankly Scotty," I begin, "I didn't come here to see the last 15 minutes of the show, I'm supposed to see the whole thing. And I have to say that with no pass I have no confidence whatsoever that once my 15 minutes are up I will be able to get back here."

I'm still trying to be polite. I don't know if Scotty understands me fully or not but I'm trying to tell him this whole stupid thing is a shambles and a disgrace and wondering what he proposes to do about it.

"OK," he says, completely unruffled. "You'll be ready to go with your shots when I get them in here after the show?" he asks Ross, but Ross isn't listening anymore. "OK... fine. Good, good," mumbles Scotty. He leaves and I help Ross set up his gear. We work in silence, the distant drone of Poison still echoing far off down a corridor we will never see. We hum along, thin sticky grins marking our faces like scars. I think we're beginning to like it in here. Another couple of hours of this and we'll be completely habituated and then we'll never want to leave this room again...

And it had all started so nicely as well. Only the day before our Nightmare at Nassau, I had met with singer Bret Michaels and drummer Rikki Rockett in a room at their hotel in New York, and for half an hour while we chatted for the benefit of my tape-recorder, we seemed to have something going. We joked and talked about the new Poison album, 'Open Up And Say... Ahh!', and when I asked them if it was true that the success of their debut, 'Look What The Cat Dragged In' (three million sales in the US alone last year), had turned them all into temperamental, ego-tripping thugs – as had been told to me more than once during the weeks prior to our meeting – they sat there and tried to convince me with their laughter that nothing could be further from the truth.

"Listen, the only thing about us that's changed is that now we get a little more freedom to enjoy ourselves," says Michaels, the baby-blues twinkling. "Before we were successful I was out to prove to everyone that I was like – this is the way Bret is: I drink too much, I smoke too much, I party too much, I fuck too much. Now I've learned how to enjoy it more than trying to prove it. After the show tonight, if I feel like going to my room alone and writing a song, I'll do it. Before, I thought I .had to get drunk and fucked before I did anything else. Now I can sit back and let people decide whether they like me for what I really am, or whether they like me because of some kind of facade I'm trying to create."

Michaels smiles so sweetly as he says this, so sincerely, I almost believe him. He wants me to write that Poison have, contrary to all rumour, actually matured as a result of their staggering and unpredicted success last year; that the brat-pack LA trash image that still clings to them like last night's mascara is unwarranted and unfair; that all these boys wanna do is have FUN! I've heard all this stuff before, of course, from countless other bands in Poison's present second-album-make-or-break position. But then I've been around a lot longer than Poison have, so I decide to cut them a little slack and wait to see with my own eyes what this shit-stick called success has or has not done for them.

The following night, an hour after Poison have left the stage, still stuck in my favourite room, a line of girls walk in dressed in nothing except after-show backstage passes. Outside in the auditorium, as pass-less and clueless as Halfin and I, are 16 Heads Of Department from the British and European offices of Capitol Records, all flown in Business Class specifically to see the show then go back afterwards and tell Poison how hard they are all going to work at making the band as big throughout the rest of the world as they are presently in America. None of them, though, can get back to meet the band. I'm told the next morning that the Capitol execs gave it an hour of waiting around being hustled by deaf, dumb an' blind kid security guards before giving up the ghost and skulking back to their hotels. Lucky buggers! At least they didn't end up getting the full Cell Block Number Nine treatment.

Is this what Bret Michaels means, then, when he talks about life being "just a popularity contest"? Now that they've sold three million albums you can hate them all you like because they simply don't give two shits about anybody else anymore? Hey, it's only a question…

Back to the previous afternoon with Bret and Rikki: I ask them if it's a pain in the arse being recognised in the street? "If people come up to you in the street and they like your band, it's never a pain in the ass to stop and say hi to somebody who recognises you," Bret tells me. "The only time it's a pain is when they stop you and they hate your guts! You know what I mean?" he smiles.

"It's weird though when we walk into a club here in New York, or in LA," says Rikki. "Sometimes it's like walking into an old Rod Serling movie where the whole room starts moving in slow motion. You can feel all the eyes swivel round like beams of light that just land on you!" he laughs.

"I remember on my birthday being taken to this club in LA called the Cathouse," says Bret. "And the place was full of people that all seemed to know me and want to party with me, and for the first couple of hours I was loving every minute of it!" he exclaims, wide-eyed. "Then I said to myself, wait a second here, I've just got to get my bearings. I remember sitting at the bar, in the end, like an old man, just drinking by myself, looking straight down at the bar, face grey, you know what I mean? Fame's great, man, but sometimes you just need to be left alone for a while and given some space to remember who you are..."

I know just what Bret means. Actually, me and Ross could recommend this very nice room we know... Lots of space... nobody to bother you or come near you for hours...

Poison's second album, 'Open Up And Say... Ahh!', has just been released. I never read the music press so I don't know what everybody else is saying about it, but here in *Kerrang!* Poison's album has already met with loud yawns and disappointed grunts of derision. Geoff Barton it was that put the glitterized moon-boot in. A long-time fan of Poison's since the days before those three million American units had been shifted, and a world-renowned and completely remorseless devotee of glam, Geoff's main complaint was that the new Poison album lacked all the sordid bite and puppy energy of their debut. 'You never quite know where Poison are flouting their stilettos: on their heels or in their hands' is how the gist of it ran, I believe. For Geoff, first time out Poison carried their stilettos in their hip pockets; second time around though, they moved like they had 'em jammed up their arseholes.

For myself, listening to the new Poison album is much like listening to the last Poison album – dumb, tacky, glitzed-up to the eyeballs, as sparkling as fake diamonds and twice as cheap. But with one crucial difference: no 'Cry Tough', no 'I Want Action', no 'I Won't Forget You' and no 'Talk Dirty To Me'. No obvious hit singles whatsoever this time, in fact. The first single released from the new album, 'Nothing But A Good Time', is the most obvious candidate for Hit City USA (which is presumably why they released it first), but though it comprises the predictable Poison mix of second-hand guitar riffs and sugar-plum, pop-metal choruses, it's about as memorable as old whassisname...

'Love On The Rocks', 'Look But You Can't Touch', 'Every Rose Has Its Thorn': all, I would guess, are destined to become singles at some stage this year, though how many become hits – and make no mistake, that's what Poison thrive on – I will leave Capitol Records to gamble their money on. Recorded in a week and a half in 1986, and paid for in peanuts and dreams, 'Look What The Cat Dragged In' is the Poison album with all the wit, the laissez-faire charm and conceit. 'Open Up And Say… Ahh!', recorded over a three-month period around the end of '87, beginning of '88, with a dollar-rich budget and famed LA producer, Tom Werman, backing them, fails to capture the stinging adolescent verve of its predecessor: tracks like 'Tearin' Down The Walls', 'Your Mama Don't Dance' or 'Bad To Be Good' (all of which sound just like their titles suggest) have all the cosmetic appeal of earlier Poison ravers like 'Talk Dirty To Me' or 'No. 1 Bad Boy', all the cheap flash and frills, but none of the real straight-to-the-viscera hooks. Most of all, they lack visible charm and identity. Poison never did sound very deep, but here they're as shallow and forgettable as a lip-glossed pout.

The pressure was on for Poison to deliver the goods second time around. No question. Maybe that's what spoiled the album. I had asked them: how much of the pressure they were under to come up with a credible (not to mention commercial) follow-up to their first mega-hit album came out in their work in the studio? "Sure, we felt the pressure, a lot of pressure," said Bret Michaels. "I still feel like that. You know, first time around, it was like when you've got nothing, you've got nothing to lose. This time round we have everything to lose. But we work good as a band under pressure. We know that people are waiting to see if Poison's going to fail or if we're going to succeed this year. We're that kind of band – it might all go up in smoke at any moment! We hope not, but we don't really know. And that kind of gives everything we do that edge and it's what keeps us excited. You know, the thing with us, we're the kind of band that was voted the best and worst band in every magazine going last year!" He suddenly bursts out laughing. "Best new band and worst new band, you know what I mean? At least they have an opinion on us, good or bad, right or wrong, they all want to see what happens next."

What happens though if there are no hit singles this time? "I don't think we're a band that lives or dies by hit singles," says Michaels. "If we lost the crowd that only come to our shows to hear the singles this band wouldn't die. I think we have a much larger core audience there that know Poison are first and foremost a rock band, not a bunch of pop stars. At the same time, 'pop' means popular, and if you're popular you must be doing something people like, and that's all right with me too…"

"Also," Rikki interjects, "we didn't become successful last year because radio played us. It happened because the fans were calling up all the radio stations and asking them to play our records. The people that first got into us did it by coming to see us play, and that's where we really score."

"A lot of people have told us that they never gave us a second thought until they saw us play live," says Bret. "Poison is a band that was built for and grew up on a stage. And if you wanna know what makes this whole thing tick for us, then you make sure you're there tomorrow night and see for yourself!"

"Yeah," drawls Rikki, "We'll have a couple of beers and have a good time…"

Uh-huh...

At 9.30 PM, four-and-a-half hours after we first arrived at the gig and three since we were taken to The Room Of A Thousand Yawns, Poison at last troop in to have their pictures taken by Ross. They shuffle in – Bret, Rikki, bassist Bobby Dall and guitarist CC DeVille – nonplussed and nonchalant, faces like wax. I stare at them and wonder who they all are. Ross gets five minutes of group shots in the shower, and a couple of minutes with each of them individually, except for when it comes to Bobby Dall's turn he refuses, snapping at Ross: "We don't do individuals!"

"Well, this should look great for a cover story, shouldn't it!" cries Ross, utterly exasperated. "One group shot in the shower, no live shots and no individuals. Is that what you want?"

Without missing a beat, Dall says OK to individuals. "But I guess you know how much I'm enjoying doing this," he says out of the side of his lipsticked mouth. Two minutes and half a roll of film into it in the shower with Ross, Dall says, "I think you have enough pictures now," and strides off, not a backward glance.

"That's what I like, working with real professionals," spits Ross.

In another corner of the room Bret Michaels suddenly approaches and asks me into the dressing room to speak with me. I follow him into Poison's dressing room and he asks if I'd like a drink or anything. It's the first time if five hours of arriving at this hell-hole that anybody has bothered to ask whether either Ross and I were at all hungry or thirsty, dead or alive, fags or putzzes, gimps or fans, men or dogs…

"No, thanks," I tell him.

We sit down and Bret asks why I didn't see the show. I tell him. He acts like he's just been told the world really is round and starts shoving the blame back and forth – the fuck-ups getting there late, the lack of passes, the this, the that… I didn't have time for it then and I don't have time for it now. I leave Poison's dressing room and return to the room of my dreams to help Ross load up his gear. All of Poison are also in the room chatting to their guests. We manage to ignore them and they manage to ignore us without too much embarrassment. When Ross and I are finally shown the way out the door only Bret Michaels notices us leaving.

"Hey, you guys, I'm really sorry about all this, you know what I mean?"

Actually, I'm not sure that I do. It's been a real pressure talking dirty with you, boys. Fix me up a nice empty room for a few hours and we'll do it again real soon…

First published in Kerrang! No.188, May 21, 1988

I can't remember how I managed to wangle this one – an all-expenses paid trip to Rio – though I'm fairly sure it had something to do with my old mate Ross Halfin's ability to talk even the most sour-faced editors into anything. I still couldn't quite believe it was happening even when we got off the plane and got our first peak of the chicks on the beach – sheer heart attack, and that was just the trannies! It wasn't until I woke up the first morning to find a very pissed-off Ross banging on my hotel room door that the reality of the situation finally began to sink in.

"How come you got a bloody room by the pool and I didn't?" he thundered. I had no idea. Sod's law, I supposed – from Ross's point of view, anyway. Undeterred, he simply moved himself in as my room became the official Kerrang! *HQ for the next 10 days. And what a 10-days they turned out to be. Reading this piece again, I'm amazed the magazine allowed us to get away with it. It was still a fortnightly publication back then and so the story – originally run in three parts – took six weeks to eventually reach its somewhat vague conclusion. Yet it went down a storm with the readers – and quite a few of the other writers, some of whom then made it their mission to try and later concoct their own versions, resulting in one very memorable piece on Bon Jovi (before they were famous) from Dave Dickson that didn't even mention the words 'Bon' or 'Jovi' until the second part had been published. This, needless to say, did not go down so well with the readers or editors.*

Nevertheless, Rock In Rio had set a precedent: the first of what would be several outlandish trips aboard for Ross and me over the next six years – and a quite unfeasible amount of features that would run to two or three parts. What follows was just Part One but you'll get the gist…

Rock In Rio, Rio De Janeiro, February 1985

In this world there are three ways you can fly: first class, club class and cunt class. Ross Halfin, who has just been voted one of the world's Top Rock photographers by the readers of *Creem* magazine (all unfortunate halfwits to a man), has his arse plonked squarely in a first class, access-all-alcohol, $2,000-seat. To his right is Rod Stewart and entourage. Rod is looking incredible for a guy who in a matter of hours – at the stop-over in Lisbon, on the stroke of midnight, London time – will be celebrating his 40th birthday. He's sporting an LA tan and LA blond locks swept up in traditional Stewart cock-sparrow style. Every picture tells a story and Rod's eyes, his face, even his nose, are a perfect picture – old rock money built on three ancient Stones guitar riffs and a Dylan love song from Bob's younger days. Seated on Halfin's left are the boys from AC/DC, who over the years have acquired the unhappy habit of completely ignoring the existence of any living thing outside their own familiar sphere. Very little of any cogent value lies outside their own sightless cosmology of band managers, roadies, bodyguards and immediate family members. Malcolm Young nods a 'hi' to Ross, and Ross offers a copy of the new *Kerrang!* to drummer Simon Wright. Simon sneers into Ross' face and declines. Ah… us and AC/DC, we don't get on any more…

It goes without saying that The Kid has his half-starved arse parked in the pig-sty humorously referred to as economy class, along with the Rod Stewart Band, several dozen reptiles from Filth Street (the *Daily Mirror*, *The Sun*, the *Daily Express*, *The Observer*; everybody wants a holiday in the sun!), a gaggle of competition winners on a Trip Of A Lifetime, and a couple of hundred for-real passengers with only one question they want answered. So tell me, my old doughnut, are you going to the Rock In Rio festival? Yes, we thought so…

All over Xmas and New Year my name has been JAMMY BASTARD to my friends. What my girlfriend was calling me I didn't know how to spell. Yeah, I was Southbound on some Varig Airlines skyway, climbing through the Heavens to Rio De Janeiro, Brazil. And no-one is going to let me forget it. 13 hours, including a 45 minute stop-over in Lisbon, from London to Rio, and all the snow, all the January hassle of a London blanketed in a macabre cloak of black afternoon sky and white treacherous roads would now be history for the next week. Ahead lay, we'd been assured, temperatures in the

'90s, the largest, most prestigious rock festival to be staged anywhere on the Earth this year, and, according to the *Daily Star*: '24 HOUR ORGIES' and 'SEX AND SUN AS ROCK MUSICIANS LAY WASTE TO RIO'!

As it turns out, Rio de Janeiro is three-and-a-half lanes of traffic populated by Brazilian psychopaths who feel confident enough to drive a taxi without once resorting to clumsy indicators or old-fashioned concepts like keeping their eyes on the road.

"Keep your fucking hands on the wheel, you stupid homo foreigner!" screams Ross into the ear of our driver, who has just narrowly missed hitting two old women and a dog. "Si, si, Senor," grins our friend. ""ESTOSTANOVACALLIMARRI ALBERO COMPLIMENTO!" he cries, winding down the window and gobbing hideously into the kerb. "Oh Gawd, just shut up and get us to the hotel in one piece you horrible, stupid..." Ross Halfin is not a man to be easily impressed, and, so far, what with the three-hour delay going through the antiquated Brazilian immigration, and now the raging onslaught of being subjected to the most dangerous man in Brazil taking the wheel for our round trip to the hotel, Rio is doing nothing constructive for his indigestion. "A fart for all the people who never gave a fart for me," he sneers before letting go one of his most evil smelling emissions.

"Welcome to the Rio Palace Hotel, Senor," hisses the oily desk-clerk into Halfin's beetroot boat race. "Push off Fernando, just gimme my room keys while I've still got a temper left to keep..." And Ross is off, bell boys laid to waste as the great man slings his giant hook in the direction of the elevators.

The Rio Palace Hotel is situated on the lap of Copacabana Beach in a security-guarded spot as uptown as Rio De Janeiro can offer the casual stinko-riche US tourist out on a middle-aged prowl. It's the best that bread can buy and much of my time is going to be spent by the kidney-shaped pool while sinking a suitably large, ice-cold jug of the finest local Sangria. That, and watching the browned and bulging torso of Halfin waddling in and out of the sun, calling a spade a spade, day in day out for the next seven days. That, and wrestling with the languid, sunburn-slow way in which the Brazilians conduct their business...

My first co-ordinated movement, after dropping off my baggage, is to take a walk down poolside, there to find women, mostly American, mostly on the wrong side of 30, stretched out on plastic floral mattresses, bikini tops discarded. It's all too much for my nerves so I plough gamely into the first six-pack of the afternoon. There is a Whitesnake press conference scheduled for 2.00 pm, with one for Iron Maiden to follow at 3.00 pm. But plans are already askew. George Benson, who was scheduled for 1.00 pm, has turned up an hour late, and the 'Snake boys are left to wander around aimlessly during the interim. Meanwhile, outside the hotel, hundreds and hundreds of chanting, cheering, hysterical Brazilians push dark, toothy-white faces up against the glass doors and screech menacingly every time a limo pulls up outside. Fame and success and glamour and MONEY and a comfortable ticket on the first flight out of the country are the chief attractions these European rock stars hold for the ticket buying beat-on-the-street types here in Rio. In a country where you either exist completely on the poverty line, or else are extravagantly rich, 90 per cent of the people walking the Avenida Atlantica alongside Copacabana Beach are making a living from thieving, begging, mugging, prostitution, and all manner of high turnover petty crime. One of the roadies working for Whitesnake was taking in the sun on the beach one day, his head resting on a travel bag, when two kids simply lifted his bonce gently off the bag and snatched it away (the bag that is), making off down the beach like Carl Lewis with his arse on fire. The guy gave chase, but when he finally caught up with them they turned round and beat the living shit out of him, before proceeding to empty out the entire contents of the bag in front of him, right there on the pearly white sand. The remaining 10 per cent of the resident population make their money from carving slices of flesh off the backs of the 90 per cent. That's the way it is, Brazilian style…

Back at the Rio Palace, when the Whitesnake press conference finally begins the first thing I notice is how well everybody is looking. Coverdale appears to be in the absolute pink of good health. Within 24 hours John Sykes will have his face plastered across the news pages of all the national Brazilian papers with a banner proclaiming him to be the major sex symbol of the festival. Even Neil Murray is looking decidedly clear of eye, while Cozy Powell gives the appearance of a British mercenary about to burst his taut skin like an over-grilled sausage – brown, brawny, and superfit. The questions are coming slowly and painfully...

"ELTOBRAVO CONNIDENDA QUEL CUMILULU?" asks the man from the paper *O Globo*. The interpreter inclines his head towards the microphone and repeats the question, in English. "He wants to know what you think about Deep Purple reforming?" he croaks through a cloud of cigarillo smoke. Coverdale looks bored and flips the guy off with some distant instant remark. Quite right too, for asking such a predictable question, I said to myself, and hurriedly crossed that one off the list I wanted to kick around with David at a later date. Ten minutes of my time is all the deal is worth so I snake off back to the pool where I fall into conversation with a nice, jolly Texan chap who's in Rio on his honeymoon. His newly wed is down with the shits back at his hotel, so here he is killing time and sinking beers under the Crimplene blue sky. He tells me where I can buy all the Moet Chandon champagne I want for £6 a bottle, so I thank him and take myself back upstairs where the Iron Maiden press conference is about to kick off.

As I saunter through the door Bruce Dickinson is doing his best to explain the true and lasting nature of Eddie. "He's just a phantom really," he suggests. "He started life as the band's logo, for records and stuff, and just developed from there."

"Si, si," interrupts the interpreter. "But they want to know who is Eddie?"

After the conference is over, Cozy Powell decides to jog along the beach back to the Copacabana Palace Hotel where Whitesnake are staying. David Coverdale is already being chauffeured back, while Neil Murray, John Sykes, Steve Harris and Maiden drummer Nicko McBrain, along with a few hardened rock hacks like myself, repair to the poolside bar for further light refreshments. The festival doesn't begin until tomorrow night and there's nothing to do but drink and wait, drink and... On the way back to my room, I bump into Maiden manager Rod Smallwood who is in his usual jocular form. The word, says Rod confidentially, is that all the security guards operating out at the festival site are really undercover policemen keeping their beady eyes open for any hint of drug taking amongst the European rock fraternity. "And that includes the likes of you!" he says, jabbing a finger in my direction. "The thing is, if they catch you red-handed having anything whatsoever to do with drugs they'll arrest you on the spot and they don't stand bail on those sort of charges here. So be warned! Anyone caught indulging by the local constabulary is liable to be left behind." I'm not really listening, though. I'm too stoned...

So what's it all about? Why suddenly, straight out of left field, is there this extraordinarily super-hyped event, Rock In Rio? I mean, when it comes right down to it, so what? There are dozens of rock festivals the world over taking place every year; better organised, more experienced and a hell of a lot closer to home than Rio De Janeiro. With the exception of Queen, who have performed in Brazil precisely once before in their lives, in Sao Paulo three years ago, nobody else on the bill – which includes Whitesnake, Iron Maiden, Rod Stewart, AC/ DC, The Scorpions, Ozzy Osbourne, Nina Hagen and Yes – has ever cared to step onto a Brazilian stage before now. But in London and New York the popular message to the media right now is that there is a vast market for rock music, not just in Brazil, but also in neighbouring countries like Venezuela, even Argentina (where Rod Stewart has already planned a visit). The people of South America, it seems, are just waiting for a little live encouragement before leaping thongs first into a rock music major overkill. There's bucks to be made from these schmucks and suddenly everybody wants in.

So, yeah, sure. But the most basic research will uncover the fact that over 75 per cent of the record buying market in Brazil is much more fascinated with plain old mellow MOR. The biggest names in popular music amongst the hippest factions of Brazilian youth culture are George Benson, Al Jarreau and, mightiest of all, James Taylor.

Nevertheless, we are here and we are, like it or not, getting ready to rock. Certainly, sitting at home in London watching the snow fall outside my bedroom window, Rock In Rio seemed like a grand thing to be happening in the world. Nursing a heavy hangover the morning of the second day, however, with Rock In Rio coming at me from all sides, I'm starting to wonder. *O Globo* is running daily front page stories and the damn thing doesn't even start until tonight; radio is rampant with the whole deal; and on day-time TV videos of all the bands appearing tonight are being rotated like a spit. First there's Queen, then Iron Maiden; and then it says 'Whitesnake – 'Love Ain't No Stranger' on the screen but what they're showing is a clip of Ronnie James Dio crowing his head off. Dark clouds crept into the corners of the morning sky...

In fact, Rock In Rio is the brainchild of Roberto Medina, who is the president of an advertising agency called Artplan. He is the man responsible for enticing Frank Sinatra down to Brazil a few years back for a gig in front of an estimated audience of 140,000, then roped in all his clients for sponsorship and made a mint out of the whole deal. He is, to all intents and purposes, a sharp-eyed entrepreneur who does a lot of good business out of arranging these 'media events'. He paid for the building of the site – the Barra da Tijuca – situated next door to Rio's Formula 1 motor-race track the Autodrome. Erected on what was formerly swampland, it has been furnished with state-of-the-art sound and lights by Gerry Stickle, the expert production technician who does a lot of work with Queen. Medina's initial outlay, therefore, came to a cool $11.5 million! That means that over the ten-day period the festival is scheduled to run for, with tickets selling for between five and seven dollars apiece, Artplan will need maybe 280,000 people there every day to even begin looking at any real profit. Take into consideration the salaries of the hundreds of interpreters working round the clock, the roadies, the security, the bands, the this, the that, and any way you looked at it the money wasn't going to be coming from ticket sales. Indeed, when the festival was over I was told that Artplan had lost over $5 million on that side of the deal, but that the business the several sponsors involved were doing proved so phenomenal it was worth the hit. Top of the list was a beer company called Malt 99, then came Wranglers, McDonalds, the usual crowd…

Now I'm told the plan is to follow up Rock In Rio with annual events. The site has been officially rented from the government for the next four years, and after that the likelihood is that it will be torn down. So the magic of knowing you're going to Rio disperses pretty quickly once you're actually sitting there using their toilets and drinking their beer. Everything feels kind of languid and one-off. Everybody seems to dig the place – a drop of sun, sea and sin is hardly the roughest week on the agenda – but nobody really cares if they ever see it again after a while.

By lunchtime during the sweltering afternoon of the second day, word has it that, with only one major road leading to and from the site, the through traffic promises to be a nightmare and delays of up to three hours are being predicted on a journey that should normally take no more than half-an-hour or so. Whitesnake are scheduled to appear on stage at 9.30 pm. Even so, Ross and I are advised to leave for the site no later than 4.30 pm! Just to be on the safe side. While all the bands – today that means Whitesnake, Iron Maiden and Queen – are being transported by helicopter no later than 6.00pm, which will bring them into the site by 6.30pm. I hitch a ride with Dwayne Welch, EM International PR exec and son of Shadows' drummer Bruce Welch. Contrary to information, we reach the gig within 40 minutes, arriving at much the same time as the bands. This gives us the next four hours to kill, lucky us. "Definitely time for a spot of sightseeing," I say to myself. And by flashing one of the six different passes I already possess before the eyes of the security, suddenly I'm out with the late afternoon crowd.

So here we are finally: Rock In Rio, Friday night, and only four hours left to go. I am standing in an area 250,000 square metres in size. The Barra da Tijuca site is trimmed off to the north by large dark hills and a deep, still, blue sky. The actual stage is huge, large enough to hold two bands and all their equipment and props, back to back. At the end of one set the revolving stage simply spins round to bring the next band into view. As a result, the changeovers throughout the festival were always fast and clean, exceptions occurring only when artistic petulance reared its conceited, artistically, uh, sensitive head from time to time.

The sound and lights all belong to Queen. The lightshow is competent and generous, professional in every respect if slightly less than completely dazzling in scope and imagination. The out-front sound, however, is superb. Apart from the gigantic army of statuesque amplifiers and speakers perched either side of the stage, approximately 100 metres from the front are placed two further towers of power that will throw the sound, as crystal clear as the foul waters of Brazil are polluted with germs and poisons, an even greater distance. However, with the festival capable of containing 300,000 people, the absence of two large video screens to help you navigate the pelvic gyrations of David Coverdale or the head-butting athleticism of Bruce Dickinson (total Neanderthal, baby!) is a strange omission to an otherwise largely impressive set-up. There's a Press Room, replete with typewriters and Telex-machines; a shopping centre with over 30 shops, beer gardens, fast food restaurants; a telephone centre; a mini-hospital for the severely intoxicated; an information centre for the overly anal; even toilets and – gulp! – showers. I was told that there were also, in fact, two 'video-centres' which were both transmitting the live shows and stringing all the boring press guff simultaneously, but I never managed to locate them personally. I dunno, must have been something I didn't eat…

As I wander backstage again I spot Freddie Mercury standing there at the gates signing autographs. He's got a superb, quite ridiculous cowboy hat on his head and, my oh my, but isn't he short! I'd always imagined our Freddie to be a lanky matador in shades. In reality he looks more like the villainous cousin of Manolito from *The High Chaparral* the far side of one two many

Enchiladas; broad Captain Kirk torso and gaucho Groucho moustache! So he is human...

In his dressing room, David Coverdale is working out before the show; Cozy Powell, Nicko McBrain, John Sykes and Neil Murray are all wandering amiably around, not quite sure what to do with themselves until show-time. Sneaking out onto the stage, however, craftily disguised behind his portable video camera, is Steve Harris. "I wanted to get the crowd on video just so I could show it to people when we get home," he tells me. But he's recognised within minutes and the crowd start to go crazy. He looks at me, surprised. "I knew we'd sold a few albums over here, but I had no idea they all knew what we bleeding look like..."

For the final hour before Whitesnake arrive onstage to begin the festival proper I'm holed-up in the beer-locker in Iron Maiden's dressing room. Rod Smallwood is laying down on the couch pondering the life expectancy of the average Marlboro, Adrian Smith is quietly plink-plonking away on his guitar, Bruce Dickinson is squaring up to his mirror reflection, fencing blade gripped in his right hand, repeatedly en guarde, en guarde, en guarde, and tour manager Tony Wiggens is swarming in and out of the door with the urgent calm of a man fully equipped emotionally to deal with at least 12 nervous breakdowns and 550 niggly problems, while still finding time to deal with important stuff like getting the drunken slob from *Kerrang!* a bottle opener. Oh well, tick-tock-fuck-the-clock...

"LADEEZAN' A-GENTLEMEN... PLISS WELCUM FROMMA LONDON, INNLAND... WHITESNAKE!" Cue instant, immediate, quite unexpected hysteria. Coverdale shakes his tail under the nose of the crowd, John Sykes rattles his long blond locks while ripping out the monster riff to 'Slow 'N' Easy' and Neil Murray and Cozy Powell lock horns like rowdy stags and suddenly the 150,000-strong audience are full of at least 149,999 smiling upturned faces, relieved as much as anything that the whole shebang is finally off the ground.

The one solitary screwed-up and pissed-off face belongs to Ross Halfin. "BLOODY JOHN SYKES!" he screams. "He had me THROWN OFF the stage! They haven't even built the bloody photographers' pit yet so there's no way you can shoot live pictures that mean a shit. Iron Maiden had to fight tooth and nail to get the security to allow me onstage for their set, then I go through the same routine with Whitesnake and 30 seconds before they come on I'm told I have to get off the stage and get off NOW! AND WHY? Because BLOODY JOHN SYKES said he'd REFUSE to play while I was there. BLOODY JOHN SYKES!!"

Ross is not having a fun time at all. Poor old doughnut. Meantime, Whitesnake are battling hard to keep the enthusiasm for their set high. They haven't played live for seven weeks and are still rusty. Through 'Love Ain't No Stranger' and 'Ain't No Love In The Heart Of The City', Coverdale's voice cracks at the edges. Cozy Powell's drum solo is cut from the show, and it's clear that a short, sharp shot in the ass is what Whitesnake are out to give Rock In Rio; and, despite the disappointment Coverdale expresses over his croaky larynx after the show, that's exactly what they do. With Mel Galley now out of the picture for good and the keyboards – handled well by ex-Magnum/Alaska man Richard Bailey – tucked inconspicuously behind curtains side-stage, the rambling, bluesy Whitesnake of just a year ago is gone and gone for good. This line-up is stripped and ready for some heavy MTV-type Stateside action. With obvious exceptions like Bobby 'Blue' Bland's aforementioned 'Ain't No Love…', which, no matter how emotively interpreted by Coverdale, will always sound forced and white and very '70 to me, the direction the Whitesnake set is following these days has much more to do with the super-chrome, rear-wheel drive of upfront rockers like 'Slide It In' and 'Slow 'N' Easy', the best numbers of the night. Coverdale ends the set with his usual "We wish you well, God bless and good night!" And the crowd sighs deeply...

If the response to Whitesnake had been one of unrestrained awe, the reaction Iron Maiden drew from the heart of the vast beast was exultant. 'Aces High' comes roaring out of the speakers with the mega-tonnage of a hub-capped, diamond-starred Sherman tank, the frontline of Dave Murray, Bruce Dickinson, Steve Harris and Adrian Smith hanging over the cliff-face of the outer-stage limits like condemned marionettes suspended by the throats from invisible steel wire. The impact is still on the 'up' when Bruce announces '2 Minutes To Midnight' in semi-fluent Portuguese and the crowd goes even wilder. 'The Trooper' and 'Revelations' follow, and Bruce is climbing the rafters, taunting the crowd to raise their arms and punch chest-deep holes in the star-tinged stratosphere. "Scream for me, RIO DE JANEIRO!" he screams. "SCREEAAMM FOR MEEE!!" Here and there, Union Jacks are sprinkled throughout the crowd, but not to be out-done the

Brazilians take up the ferocious chant of "IRRON MAYYDEN! IRROON MAAYYDEENN!!" With emphasis on those rolled rrrs...

The 'Rime Of The Ancient Mariner', replete with taped creaky hull atmospherics, totally freaks everybody out, slaying the audience completely when the band come trooping back for the snarling finale. But the suspension of disbelief isn't truly complete until, halfway through 'Powerslave', the 12-foot tall figure of Eddie bounds on stage to cries of utter astonishment from the Brazilians who know that these English rock groups are, you know, a leetle crazee, but hadn't bargained on the appearance of the surreal rogue-phantom, headbanging his savage way across the footlights. Eddie is the ultimate symbol of Iron Maiden's superiority, and the glazed, phantasmagorical image of Eddie insanely poised, arms flailing behind the huddled figure of Adrian Smith, is something they were still yakking about on the streets of Rio long after the group had left the country to continue their marathon trek across America.

Because they have actually played here before, Queen are without a doubt the best known international rock act on the bill. So when the stage-lights ignite and the taped intro creams from the speakers it's enough to push large sections of the loco public right over the edge. Freddie Mercury senses all this, and with one mighty puff of his broad chest throws his head back and coos like a lovebird nestled on her eggs; prancing and pirouetting, chain-smoking and joking with the crowd, winning their confidence and admiration with every regal flick of the wrist. Guitarist Brian May, bassist John Deacon and drummer Roger Taylor maintain the same super-tight musical backdrop that has been their live trademark throughout their careers, and the set is largely the same as the show the band were touting around the UK last year. The 'Seven Seas Of Rhye', 'Now I'm Here' medley is still a feature, as are 'Tie Your Mother Down', 'Somebody To Love' and 'Love Of My Life'. It's all the hits and more... 'Killer Queen', 'Radio Ga Ga' (which, just like the video, has the crowd all clapping right on cue, a quite surreal sight), 'Another One Bites The Dust'... the only real moment of serious METAL MAYHEM occurs on 'Hammer To Fall', which sees May and co. playing with the slow-handed, sophisticated aplomb of true early-'70s veterans: mean, moochy and meticulously magnificent. The only pain in the nose is when Freddie and Brian climb up on two stools and make like Frank Sinatra and Dean Martin after a night on the piss for 'Is This The World We Created?', a pure acoustic wimp-out for all the James Taylor junkies in the audience. It's enough to bring a cold tear to my glass eye.

The big fun begins with the encores, though. After the anticipated volcanic eruption of applause, the band bounce back on stage for 'I Want To Break Free' with Freddie sporting the same dark black wig he sports in the video. He looks like a Meard Street tart taking the Monday morning bus home from Soho: faggy, draggy and all shagged out. But the funniest part(s) are the enormous pair of falsies he's wearing! Huge bristols that so excite the lapsed Catholics in the audience that they start to hurl stones and gravel. There's even some that attempt a quick heave-ho over the security-infested stage perimeter, only to be met by devastating blows from the wooden truncheons of the guards. Knuckles are being viciously rapped by long pieces of hardwood, and there's still a ton of gravel flying through the air when the band return for their second encore, 'It's A Hard Life'. This time Freddie's got his blond number two wig on, but, wily old mistress that he is, he also has a huge Union Jack flag which, when reversed, metamorphoses into the Brazilian national flag. The crowd go suitably ape-shit and a semblance of good order is restored…

First published in Kerrang! Nos. 88-90, February, 1985

Like a lot of rock bands that became stars in the 1980s, I had known Metallica since before they were famous. So while it definitely felt weird watching them make it so big in the '90s, one thing I felt sure of was that their drummer and chief spokesman, Lars Ulrich, would not change much. He would become a lot richer, of course, but I still envisaged him, like Steve Harris of Iron Maiden, keeping his wits about him and being able to tell the fools and the fakers from the old friends that had helped him along the way.

Certainly that was the attitude I still had at the time of this interview. What I hadn't anticipated was that the self-titled album they were then recording – now known as the 'Black' album – would sell so many millions of copies it would turn Metallica into the Bon Jovi of the thrash generation: not just bigger and more famous than bands like Maiden, but, alongside Guns N' Roses, the biggest, most famous rock band on the planet. (That is, until Nirvana came along – a fact which Lars plainly resented when I later spoke to him about it. But that's another story…)

The point is that, as a result of all this, the Lars Ulrich I used to know – as represented by this interview – was not going to be around for much longer. The unbelievable money – as one mutual friend put it, "The fountain in his courtyard is bigger than my house" – the colossal fame, the self-confessed drug problems, all would conspire to turn the Lars I once knew into someone I didn't know at all. Where once he would phone and ask to crash on my floor if he was in town, now he flew into London incognito to buy his antiques and art.

Frankly, who can blame him? If I'd been blown away by that kind of zillion-dollar deal at his age I'd have probably been worse. A lot worse. Anyway, this piece captures him on the cusp of that massive lifestyle change. Back when he still lived amongst mortals and was forced to take drum lessons by the producer. I didn't realise it then, not fully, but Lars knew what he was doing. He certainly achieved what he set out to do, and how many musicians out there can say that?

Lars Ulrich, Los Angeles, April 1991

I catch up with Lars Ulrich on a grey and chilly afternoon in North Hollywood. He's in the recreation room at One On One studios, where Metallica have been holed-up these past six months, recording their new, as yet untitled, album with neo-legendary producer Bob Rock. Neither Kirk Hammett's saw-toothed guitar nor Jason Newsted's belly-rumbling bass are required at the studio today. But James Hetfield is seated in the next room – studio one – guitar cradled on his lap, patiently laying down the ponderous melody that makes up the cyclical guitar part to a song called 'The Unforgiven'. Lars chomps on a hastily slapped together cheese-and-pickle sandwich and shows off the amenities: pinball machine, video game, pool table, punchbag... Punchbag?!? "For fucking tension!" Lars exclaims, crumbs sputtering from his lips. "You know that shit; you're in a studio and you're trying to get something down and you can't get it down right and you just need to hurt something. Then you receive the bill for it next week. You can hurt that and not have to pay for it." James has been using it a lot lately, apparently. "But now that Jason has started doing his bass he uses it a lot too!" he chortles loudly.

Cut to a side room further down the corridor. MTV is murmuring from a screen in one corner and – nine-line phone positioned on a table by his side – Lars settles his whip-thin body down into an armchair and fixes me with that piercing, squinting stare he reserves for such occasions. "So what do you want to know?" he spitballs in his graceless Danish-American drawl. Well, there's a lot of things about the new album that I'm curious about, I tell him. Firstly, the idea of you working with Bob Rock. When I think of the name Bob Rock, I immediately think of very different bands to Metallica; more commercially-minded outfits like, say, Mötley Crüe or The Cult. "I think that's the main thing I've been asked about. Everybody asks me about Bob Rock."

Let me be more specific then. People choose Bob Rock to get hit records. "Yeah, that's a fair comment," he nods his head solemnly. "But I look at it a little differently. Last Summer when we started writing this shit we were just thinking we'd do what we usually do, be safe and predictable and record the album like we always do. But we'd never really liked the mixing on '...Justice', 'Master...' or '...Lightning'. So we were thinking, who can we get in to do the mixing? We felt it was time to make a record with a huge, big, fat low-end and the best sounding record like that in the last couple of years – not songs, but sound – was the last Motley Crue album. We really liked the really big fat sound on 'Dr Feelgood' [produced by Bob Rock]. So we told our manager, 'Call this guy and see if he wants to mix the record'. He came back and said not only did Bob want to mix the record, but he saw us live when we played Vancouver, and really liked us and would like to produce the album. Of course, we said, 'We're Metallica, no one produces us! No one fucks with our shit and tells us what to do!' But slowly, over the next few days, we thought maybe we should let our guard down and at least talk to the guy. Like, if the guy's name really is Bob Rock, (it is), how bad can he be?"

James and Lars flew to Canada last Summer to meet the producer at his home in Vancouver. "We're sitting there saying, 'Well, Bob, we think that we've made some good albums but this is three years later and we want to make a record that is really bouncy, really lively; just has a lot of groove to it'. We told him that live we have this great vibe and that's what we wanted to do in the studio. It's really funny cos he turned around and said, 'When I saw you guys live and then heard your record I thought that you hadn't come close to capturing what you do in a live situation'. He basically said the same thing as we had and from then on we thought that maybe we shouldn't be so stubborn and maybe see where the fuck this would bring us."

The only snag was Rock's notorious reluctance to record anywhere outside of his own Little Mountain studios in Vancouver; home of the hits for Poison, Bon Jovi, Mötley Crüe, The Cult, Aerosmith, David Lee Roth and so many others it hurts my wallet even to think about it. "We really didn't want to do it in Vancouver – everyone comes to him. For a while I didn't think it was going to work out. Bob's got a big family and he wasn't that keen on coming to LA. Then when we played him the stuff I could see his eyes light up. We'd built a little eight-track studio in my house and made some rough demos; just me on drums and James, not really everybody, just really rough. Bob was like, 'Wow, this could be the 'Kashmir' of the '90s!' He's saying all this stuff and me and James are looking at him thinking, he's listening to one guitar and one set of drums and a vocal melody that goes na-na-na-na-na…? Anyway, as soon as he heard the stuff things started livening up. We brought him here to One On One studio, and in this very room, on that machine over there, I played him the next two or three songs we'd been working on. It was like, boom! From there it was pretty much a done deal."

And the band's reaction to the results of their, on the surface at least, offbeat new studio relationship? Thus far, it would seem, judging by Lars' pixie face, nothing short of elation. "The way I look at it is that Bob Rock brought out the best that Mötley Crüe had to offer and made the best Mötley Crüe record. The same with The Cult or Bon Jovi. If you listen to 'Slippery When Wet', he made the best Bon Jovi album, he brought out the best that Bon Jovi had to offer at that time. Looking back on our last four albums, they were great records, I'm not going to say anything bad about them. But we never thought that we'd done one where you think, there it is. That one album is it. You're never gonna be able to make a record like that but as close as you can get to that one album, this is fucking it. The new stuff that we've been writing is like a breath of fresh air. We're just really excited in a way that I don't think we've been excited before. Bob says he thinks it shows we've got a lot of soul, or… what's another word for soul?" Depth? Emotion? "Yeah, we have a lot of emotions that we don't let out easily, cos we're very guarded as people. He says that he could see through that right away. He says that one of his things on this album was to try and let us take down our guard and let out the shit that's in there."

Do you think that it was also because the time was right for you as people? Perhaps you were waiting for someone to say, 'Okay, let's drop this big bad Metallica attitude for a second and find out who you really are…' "Yeah, but I also think it's a combination of us getting pretty bored with the direction of the last three albums. They were all different from each other, but they were all going in the same direction. You know, long songs, longer songs, even longer songs. Progressive, more progressive, even more progressive… It was time to take a sharp turn. The only way to do that would be to write one long song to fill the whole album or write songs that were shorter than we had done before. And that's what we did. I don't need to tell you again how I feel about being pigeonholed with the whole thrash metal thing. But the new shit's just got a whole new vibe and feel that I never knew Metallica were capable of. Before when we've gone into a recording studio we've always frozen up and tried to be too perfect. It's like, five minutes after I could play drums, Metallica were going, and the shit just rollercoastered. Suddenly we're making demos, then we're touring, making our first record after only being together a year-and-a-half... all of a sudden it was like, well, we have a record out but we really can't play. So I had to take drum lessons and Kirk's doing his Joe Satriani trip…" (Kirk takes regular guitar lessons from the San Francisco-based guitar ace.) "I think we spent a lot of years trying to prove to ourselves and to everyone out there that we can play our instruments – you know, listen to this big drum fill I'm doing, and Kirk's playing all these wild things that are really difficult… When we were first starting out in 1981 the two big bands in America that year were the Rolling Stones and AC/DC. I clearly remember sitting at James's house going: 'The worst drummers in the world are Charlie Watts and Phil Rudd! Listen to them, they don't do any drum fills, they're not doing anything. Listen to that, it's horrible! Give me Ian Paice and Neil Peart'. So for the next eight years I'm doing Ian Paice and Neil Peart things, proving to the world that I can play. Now it's like my two favourite drummers at the moment are Charlie Watts and Phil Rudd. At the end of the last tour, 'Seek And Destroy' had practically become my favourite song in the set. It had so much bounce and groove I could really just sit there and play it without worrying about when the next quadruple-backwards-sidewards paradiddle came in. About halfway through the '...Justice' tour I was sitting there playing these nine-minute songs thinking, 'Why am I sitting here worrying about how perfect these nine-minute songs have to be when we play stuff like 'Seek And Destroy' or 'For Whom The Bell Tolls' and they have such a great fucking vibe?'"

So is that why you would occasionally record songs like Budgie's 'Breadfan', or the covers on the 'Garage Days Re-revisited' EP? That was 'fun', but your own songs were 'serious'? Now it's more integrated, rolled into one? "Yeah, that's probably true. Yeah, that's a very good way of putting it. We were finally able to let that happen. I never really thought of it like that. I guess there was this thing lingering inside of us that wanted to do things like that, but when it came time to sitting down and making the record..." He shrugs his shoulders fitfully. "If you look back on the albums, next to the song titles, the times are always listed. I used to be really proud of it. In the past we'd do a rough version of a song and I'd go home and time it and go, 'It's only seven-and-a-half minutes!' I'd think, 'Fuck, we've got to put another couple of riffs in there'. Now I'm not bothered either way."

But wasn't that always Metallica's forté: jamming in as many riffs as you could snap your neck to? "I guess the point I'm trying to get across is, I used to be really concerned with the timing and lengths of a song when we were writing them. But this time I didn't even want to think about it. There is one six-minute song – 'Friend Of Misery'. It wasn't written on purpose, though. It was the last song we wrote and we did the usual to-the-point verse and chorus and came up with a cool thing in the middle which is a bit longer. Most of the tracks are about four minutes, though."

With 12 tracks already slated for the finished album, is this going to be your 'Hysteria'? The big seller loaded with hits? The record company must be rubbing their hands in glee at the prospect of so many potential hit singles. "They are!" he snickers. "I'm sure we're gonna get a lot of people saying we're selling out, but I've heard that shit from 'Ride The Lightning' on. People were already going, Boo! Sell out! Even back then…"

Isn't it a self-made cross though; refusing to do videos: the whole underground you-don't-tell-us-what-to-do-cos-we're-Metallica kind of thing? "I really don't look at it like a cross. Everybody should know by now that we get really bored easily with things we do. We move between this really serious album to a stupid cover version EP. You know, serious videos, goofy videos. We're a band of extremes and we keep changing, keep following our instincts in whatever direction our heads takes us."

Okay, but have their heads taken them to a point where we're gonna see four or five singles (plus videos) pulled from this album? "It's much too early to say. One side of me wants to sit there and defend it – just cos they're short songs doesn't mean they're any more accessible. Then the other side says, I don't give a fuck. I know what these sound like'."

So what do they sound like? Lars played me very brief, very rough snippets of three tracks: 'Sad But True', 'The Unforgiven' and 'Don't Tread On Me'. The first thing that hits is that, Bob Rock or not, half the length maybe, this is still Metallica. Fearful as a widow's wail, stark as a new moon; it could be no other. "They all have these big fat guitar riffs," says Lars with relish. "But instead of after the second chorus steering into another fucking universe, they stay in the same one then go back into the chorus. Then we go to another universe on the next song. Whatever people want to think of that, they can. But for me that's how I look at it."

Which song was it Bob Rock said could be 'the 'Kashmir' for the '90s'? "Aarrgghhh! I asked for that one, didn't I? It's 'Sad But True', but I'd like it to go on record that I don't agree with that, ha! It's just one of those songs that has one of these monstrous guitar riffs that you latch on to right away and the drums kinda cruise in the background and just lay down a solid thing. It's about how different personalities in your mind make you do different things – and how some of those things clash and how they fight to have control over you. From the mind of James Hetfield, you know? Don't ask me..."

What about 'The Unforgiven', the track they were currently working on. What was that about? "It's about how a lot of people go through their life without taking any initiative. A lot of people just follow in the footsteps of others. Their whole life is planned out for them, and there's certain people doing the planning and certain people doing the following."

One I didn't get to hear but liked the title of, 'The God That Failed", Lars says, "is about this thing that's going on in America. This kind of religion thing where they don't believe in medicine. So if their kids get some heavy illness it's like, 'Please God, heal this sick child', and three days later the child is dead. It's stirring up a lot of shit over here because the courts are going after these people now and nailing them with murder. But it's not necessarily against or for. It just tells a story..."

Lars says his favourite song is always "the one we're working on today" but that he has a peculiar affection for the next song they begin working on after they complete 'The Unforgiven' – another strangely-titled artefact called 'Enter Sandman'. "That song has been on the fucking song titles list for the last six years," he smiles coyly. "The way it works is James and I sit with a big list of song titles and throw them at each other. We might pick one that will work with a specific guitar part. Others that don't catch straight away, we just leave on there. I'd always looked at 'Enter Sandman' and thought, what the fuck does that mean? Me being brought up in Denmark and not knowing about a lot of this shit, I didn't get it. Then James clued me in. Apparently the Sandman is like this children's villain – the Sandman who comes and rubs sand in your eyes if you don't go to sleep at night. So it's a fable and then Metallica turn it into..."

Freddy Krueger? "Nooo... James has just given it a nice twist. Hahaha! But it's this classic example of having something lingering around. People might say is that cos you can't come up with something new? No, not at all. Six years ago I looked at 'Enter Sandman' and thought, 'Naw, let's write 'Metal Militia"... Metal all the way, you know?" He squinted his eyes, then chuckled self-consciously. "Six years ago, yeah…"

First published in Kerrang! No.335, April 6, 1991

Apart from his extraordinary guitar playing, probably the two big things Ritchie Blackmore was known for back then were a) his antipathy towards most music journalists, in particular British music journalists, and b) his spectacular wind-ups, of anyone and everyone, including his own band. No-one was safe. So when he chose to turn the occasion of what was supposed to be a five-minute phone interview for a news story to announce the newly reformed Deep Purple's British comeback show at Knebworth, into an excuse to have me fly halfway around the world to meet him face-to-face, I suspected he was indulging both passions: putting me to a great deal of trouble in order to wind-up a member of the British press.

When, as you will see, he then gave me the run-around, claiming to have waited for me in a bar he had not actually told me he would be in, I was convinced I was on a typical Blackmore goose-chase. Even if I did manage to pin him down for an interview, I had been warned to expect the worst. "He hates cunts like you," a roadie friend told me confidently. What did he mean, like 'me'? "You know, smart-arses."

I didn't feel so very smart though sitting on the plane from London over to New York. Given just 24-hours notice, I'd barely had time to buy a new cassette-tape and change my kegs let alone come up with questions clever enough to pique the interest of The Man In Black.

Fortunately, Blackmore turned out to be nothing like I had expected. The air of mystery was all a sham, as he told me himself. There wasn't anything he was afraid to talk about; it was just that most of the questions he tended to get asked were so boring. Most journalists were like sheep: easily startled.

I tried not to bleat too much and even though I didn't quite manage it he seemed to appreciate the effort…

Ritchie Blackmore, New York, June 1985

New York City: the Warwick Hotel over on West 54th Street. It's 2.30 in the morning and in room 1110 the telephone is ringing. A sleepless hand reaches out and grabs the receiver, lifting it tight to a sleeping head. "Yeah?" the word crawls out of my gob like a snake from a sandpit. On the other end of the wire is Bruce Payne, manager of Deep Purple. "What happened?" he barks down the line. "Ritchie waited in the bar for you for two hours! And you didn't show! What happened?"

"Whaddayamean Ritchie waited in the bar for two hours? I get straight off the plane and make it over to the hotel in double quick fashion. I don't even know for certain if there's going to be a room reserved for me, I don't know when, where or how I'm supposed to be getting together with Ritchie, so what do I do? It's Friday in New York, do I go out on the razz and hit the clubs? Do I crawl on my hands and knees into the bar and launch myself ass-first into a bottle, any bottle? Do I fuck! I sit in my hotel room and wait. I need instructions, I need orders and I am a good boy and so I wait and nothing do I hear, no more do I know until this very phone call... Shit, so what do I do now? Can I talk to Ritchie tomorrow? Is he pissed off? Has the whole deal been shot down in flames and am I about to be the proud receiver of a *Kerrang!*-sized boot up my ass?"

Two long seconds of silence... "No, you wait and sit tight until I ring you back in the morning," says Bruce, sensing that my nerves are raw and my head's on backwards. The phone dies slowly in my hands.

The following pm the phone starts up again and this time I'm ready.

"Do you play soccer?"

"Uh, well, yeah," I say.

"OK, good. This is what you do. Ritchie says he came to you last night so now it's your turn to go to him. The thing is, Ritchie is playing football this afternoon so he suggests you have a game too and then get the interview together. What do you say? You'll have to take a train out to Long Island and we'll worry about getting you to the airport afterwards."

Bruce's voice is all smiles. The deal struck, I spend the next 45 minutes limbering up round the fixtures and fittings in my room, psyching myself up into classic Bryan Robson animal-magic pose. If it's football they want, I am going to make damn sure I can shoot with both feet. But an hour into the training programme the phone is doing its ring-thing again.

It's Bruce. "There's been a change of plan," he announces and, oh no, I can feel my mood of doom and gloom in June returning. But the voice inside my head tells me to stay cool and I listen patiently. "We're gonna send a car over to pick you up and take you to a restaurant in Long Island at six where you'll have dinner with Ritchie and you can do the interview then, while you're having your meal. What do you say?"

I say I'm disconnecting this damn phone from the wall before you change your mind again. Some time later I'm leaning into a fine Bloody Mary at a table reserved for Mr Blackmore and his guests. Out the window I can see Ritchie Blackmore and his friends walking up the drive towards the eatery and my stomach turns over like a Ferris-wheel in a force nine gale. I don't get nervous as a rule – too long in the tooth and knob for that sort of kiddie kick – but hell, this is Ritchie Blackmore! The Man In Black! The One That Never Talks! And what am I but a short-arsed scribbler from Soho? And so I remove my nose from the red juice and stand to attention when the man walks in the room and finally we meet.

I needn't have worried. Contrary to all the preconceived ideas everybody and their milkman threw at me when they knew I was making the trip to meet Ritchie Blackmore, in person he's warm, friendly and very good company indeed. The first thing he does is break all the rules by smiling, and so as we both sit down and I grin back at him it's time to cut the bullshit and do what I came to do... talk.

Do you see the forthcoming Knebworth Fayre show as an important gig for the band? "Nah... I'm off to see U2 myself that day." A wry smile creases the corners of the mouth. (It had just been announced that U2 would be playing Milton Keynes Bowl the same day as Purple headlined Knebworth.)

Why just the one UK date, though? "We took a kind of vote. Some of the band wanted to do more gigs and some wanted to do one big one. But it's so difficult when you've got a big production to break even when you play England, which is why not too many bands go there. I wanted to do a few gigs – one in Scotland, one in Birmingham, two in London, something like that, but I was overruled by... someone," he deadpans. "I can just see people saying now, 'Oh the halls aren't big enough to hold Ritchie's head!' I know if it was down to Ian Gillan the band would do every club and hall in Britain, but I don't know, politics come into play and all kinds of things and it's ended up this way… We're gonna kick off the European tour by playing a small club date in Sweden actually."

When was the last time you played in a club? "Oh, Christ... Well, I play in a club here in Long Island a lot, a place called Sparks; it's a heavy metal club. I get into a lot of fights over the football table though," he chuckles.

It's been a good 12 months since the announcement that Deep Purple had reformed. At the time there must have been a great many personal expectations within the band for the coming album and world tour; have you fulfilled a lot of those expectations? "Funnily enough, yes. I didn't have too many expectations, I thought 'Sod it, let's do it!' I was sick of all the rumours and Roger [Glover] said 'I'm with you!' I couldn't believe the business we did and the amount of records we sold. We had to double up everywhere we went – Australia, Germany, America – and I was worried about filling out one show in each city. In fact, we ended up doing two sold-out nights everywhere.

"It's nice to know that so many people wanted to come along to the shows. Deep down inside I'm a very cynical person and I always think no-one's going to show up, no-one's interested. That's why I shy away from interviews because I can be very negative and I don't want to represent the band in a negative way. I thought it would happen in America. The Americans do tend to stick by their bands, their Black Sabbaths. It takes a hell of a lot longer to make it over here than in England, but once you have made it they don't forget you."

When you came to choose the material for the show, how did you reach a decision on what to play and what to throw away? "What we did is, I sat down and thought, well, what's going to show me off as a brilliant guitar player, and then I told the rest of them what we would be playing!"

It's nice to see Blackmore sparring humorously with his own The Man And His Dark Moods image. All the same I press the point. "I'm so used to manipulating a band, as with Rainbow, that I tend to be very domineering with my thoughts. So I said: 'I think this is a good repertoire', and Roger looked at it and thought it was good, but wanted to add another number, I think it was 'Mary Long'…"

Oh, do you play 'Mary Long' then? "No. We don't, see what I mean? And Jon [Lord] was happy to go along with the set because I think Jon was just very nervous about the whole thing anyway and not particularly into the repertoire, more just how it was all going to sound after so many years."

Would you like to break into the singles market again? You had a lot of hits in the Seventies. "Yeah, but it's always worked very strangely for us. 'Woman From Tokyo' was a big hit here in America, but I don't think it was even released in England. Whereas 'Black Night' was a big hit in Britain and did nothing here. 'Smoke On The Water', meanwhile, was only a hit on its third release here in America; I mean, it got to like Number Two but it took three goes to do it. That just goes to show that you have to keep going with something you have faith in."

Before the very first reunion gig in Australia, did you or any of the band lose any sleep? "I don't know. I don't make it my habit to sleep with the rest of the band if I can help it. I think it has been known for some of them to sleep together, though. I have heard rumours about the management and the bass player sleeping together."

Only if it's been a good gig though, right? He snorts derisively. "Yeah, right… No, actually, for that first gig I just got drunk, whiskey comes in very handy I find. I usually have a level I drink down to before a gig. It's kind of below the label by about an inch."

When I drink whiskey it turns me into a raving lunatic, which is OK if you happen to be John Wayne, but can get you into trouble if you're not, you know? "Well, when I drink whiskey it doesn't turn me into John Wayne. I turn into Oliver Reed! And then I usually punch someone and run, let everybody else get on with it."

After you've played a particularly exciting gig, how do you relax? "I try and drink as much water as possible because I'm usually so drunk at that point. I drink all through a gig, and afterwards it feels like my body is saying no more! I end up feeling so guilty that I've drunk so much that I walk around guzzling water and pretending I'm perfectly healthy… I think I'm actually quite a shy person and to be on a stage you have to project and that only really comes out when I'm drunk. That's why I do it."

Doesn't that waste you, though, on a long tour? "Yeah, it does. The travelling doesn't get to me or the playing, it's the drinking. It's a stimulant which can keep you up most of the night so you might end up taking a sleeping tablet or something, but it's a problem everybody has I think. When we have a day off I never go to the bar, just try and keep the system clean for 24 hours."

Are you into taking vitamins or stuff like that? "Yeah, I am. It gets ridiculous, though. I started off taking multi-vitamins, then I thought, I need more C, then I thought, well, I'm a nervous wreck so I started taking extra B. Then the real games began because I started thinking my muscles were tense or tired so I started taking more E. Then I found I was lacking potassium from some doctor who told me I needed it, so I took that every other day. I used to have a lot of back problems. I got injured in one of the games of football I played which developed into a muscle-spasm which set off all my other muscles and in the end I couldn't play [guitar]. I was tingling all along my arm. This was just before the last European tour with Rainbow and I didn't think I was going to make it. Every time I put the guitar strap on I pinched a nerve and I couldn't move my fingers properly without pain. I had a masseur on the road with me all the time to massage the muscles and it was always touch and go whether I was going to make the date. During the day my hand kept seizing up."

Didn't that freak you out? "Yeah, I started getting really worried. It turned out I had an arthritic joint in the back of the neck. They X-rayed it and told me I had degenerative arthritis. I was immediately panicking, I thought that was it, I was dying, it was all over. But the doctor told me to relax and said that I didn't have any more arthritis than any other normal 39-year-old man. Degenerative arthritis doesn't mean it's getting steadily worse and worse, it's just that as you get older you naturally get more bouts of it. It's not rheumatoid arthritis which is the real crippler. So I went to a physiotherapist and started doing all the exercises and now I wear a copper bracelet every time I play. That and the potassium are the minerals you should always have. My mother always wears a copper bracelet, she had rheumatism, and there's always an element of truth in ancient folk-lore, so I thought I'd wear one too. Over the last two years – touch wood! – everything's been OK."

Have you recorded any of the live dates on this tour? "Some of the Australian dates were videoed, I think, which we used as our second video. When it comes to making videos, though, we're a lazy lot; nobody will dress up as an actor or anything ridiculous like that... The video they used for 'Perfect Strangers' was a part of a documentary some people were making. I haven't even seen it yet. If I see myself I get totally self-conscious and turn it off. I haven't seen any of them. I heard there was a part in the 'Perfect Strangers' video where you can see me smiling and I tried to get that cut out...

"We just can't be bothered with videos. I'm a musician, you know? I make a record and then I'm on the road; this video business makes me crazy! There's enough to do to sell a record as it is – to think up the songs, to record them and produce them and then get the record out, and play, and then to be asked to make these stupid videos gets me crazy. I hate them! I hate MTV! I don't know if you've seen it at all but it's awful! You get people like Michael Jackson going completely overboard, spending a million making a video…" He shudders.

If someone left the band now, or there was a recurrence of the Ian Gillan departure of '73, would Purple carry on as it did back then? "I don't think so, no. I think everybody's amazed at each other's talents at the moment. We're still in that mood. I'll watch the band when I'm offstage and Jon is taking a solo or something. I think they're all amazing, I really do. The way Ian Gillan sings – he's got such a big voice. He ends up shaking the place every night with the sheer power of his voice…"

And there's still that camaraderie? "Yes. Ian comes up to me after some of the gigs and says, 'You're my hero!' Little weird things like that go on all the time, so the band is really into each other on stage. I suppose there still could come a time when politics might again get between us, but when we're on stage we really click because we all respect each other very much. And I love the way Ian introduces songs. Like with 'Perfect Strangers'. When we were in Japan he used to say 'This next song is about a football team back in England who used to live down the road from me in Hounslow'. And everybody's going 'What? What's he saying? Did he mention cocaine?!' And then he'd go there was this football team and they were from a place called Perfect Street, and this is called the 'Perfect Street Rangers'! Everybody was totally lost and I'd be cracking up at the side of the stage, you know? The Japanese didn't know whether to laugh or send away for pictures of the Perfect Street Rangers!"

Do you plan to carry on with Deep Purple to the total exclusion of doing anything else solo? "I don't know, every now and again I'll think about that. But I feel that, although Rainbow did some good stuff, it didn't ever have the identity that Purple has. Sometimes with Purple I'll hear the end product and maybe think it should have been more like this or that, but it's always very popular with the masses. With Rainbow I had everything more or less how I wanted it, but it didn't appeal as much to the masses so there's obviously something I'm not tapping into. I don't feel that I was wrong – I had to do something on my own – but the popularity of Rainbow compared to Purple shows me that I'm not right all the time. That's part of the chemistry and magic of Purple."

The last two years have seen a lot of reformations what with Yes, yourselves, now ELP, and Ozzy and Sabbath doing the Live Aid gig... "Yeah, and now Mountain's back together. They're supporting us on our European dates... You're right, it's amazing how these groups have all come back. Grand Funk Railroad, Three Dog Night... Yes were the first, but we didn't get back together because Yes did. It took us ten years to do it... if people want to go and see those bands, why not?"

The conversation drifts off to more general stuff then out of nowhere he suddenly says: "This is gonna sound weird, but I really liked the last Whitesnake LP, 'Slide It In'. I liked the video to their single, very good song, should have been a hit, but it wasn't. I can't think of the title, though, I wouldn't know it, someone told me what it was. But it's very refreshing. People are always saying 'What do you think of David Coverdale?' and I try and remove myself from that and it doesn't influence me. I just see the band Whitesnake as being a good band with a good singer. What I might do to him if he turns up backstage at any concerts is a whole different thing, that's personal! But I'm not that stupid that I would let it corrupt my way of thinking if I hear something. I can say 'That is good: don't like the guy, but I thought the album was very good'. Meanwhile, Madonna is Number One which makes you realise just how bad things are. I get these moods where I put the whole business down. I love music and I love playing guitar, being on stage, but the industry gets me crazy."

Do you think it's got worse in the business since you started out as a musician? "Yeah, I think so. In '68 when we first started... people were into whether the band were any good or not. They weren't into the novel approach. Now if the guy dresses up as a girl, or the girl dresses up as a guy, that seems to do a lot for their careers. I don't know, I could go on and on. It disgusts me, most of it. People have said I'm jealous, but I'm not jealous. I've got my audience and I do very well in this business but it does bother me to see good musicians put out of work by these fucking freaks. Your Boy Georges and people like that! That novelty gimmick approach. It's ridiculous. I think we're all doomed, basically."

He's serious but the bitterness is sweetened by another unexpected smile, and a soft shrug of the shoulder. "And I think England will probably go first," he chuckles.

Mentioning England, could you ever see yourself living there again? "It's my favourite country, along with Germany. Yet I find myself not moving from here in Long Island. I've noticed when I go back to London that the unemployment thing has got so bad that if you have a little bit of money and you can afford to buy a round of drinks people start in on you, saying 'It's alright for you, but some of us have to work for a living'. That's their favourite saying: 'It's alright for some'. There's that kind of chip on the shoulder. But that's true of me as well: I have a chip on my shoulder, but I don't know quite what about. I'll find something. And the English are lazy. I'm lazy! Basically, we all just want to go to the pub and play darts. But then again the English, the British, have so much creativity. For some reason we seem to come out with the most amazing things: the medicine side, the music side... The biggest strides that are made in music come from England.

"They have big people over here, but they don't seem to last, they don't seem to make a mark on history. I always put America down when I'm here and when I'm back in England I walk around saying 'Typical! The bastards!' It's like a Basil Fawlty thing the way they look at you and talk to you..."

Are there any new British rock bands that have sprung up since the '70s who have impressed you? I'm thinking specifically of Iron Maiden, Def Leppard, that generation, you know? "Maiden have got a great football team. We still owe them a game. They beat us 5-4 the last time we played, but I'll get them! Steve Harris is a good footballer, got a goal on the volley straight from a comer. That impressed me."

Steve Harris told me that he thought you were a good footballer but that you could be a bit lazy; wait till you got the ball then use it. "Yeah, that's right. That's very true, especially in that game. It's my biggest fault; I can't always be bothered with running back. I don't work the field. If I've got the ball I'm alright, but I'm not gonna run up and down. That's very true.

"Def Leppard have a very fresh sound, I can see why people over here like them. They're very fresh, almost like a Beatles thing. It's still a little bit rough, but it's got glamour in it and they look right. America went berserk for Def Leppard the year before last. It was nice to see Van Halen knocked off their perch. They're a little bit smug; they think they've got it all sewn up. Ian Paice is a big fan of Leppard's you know?"

What about Mötley Crüe and Rätt? "It's all been done 15 years ago. They don't have that spark of creativity. It's all copying, bits of Van Halen, bits of this, bits of that, I can see everything in them."

What about The Firm? "I've seen a few videos, but I haven't seen them play live. I think it's good that they're doing something. Paul Rodgers is a good singer."

Did you ever rate Page as a guitarist? "I've said it before. He's a strange guitar player. He's not the type of guy you can say is brilliant – no musical theory – but he has a way of writing good riffs, things like 'Kashmir' and some of the other Zeppelin stuff. His riffs were great. He's not a player I would attack. He puts down a very coloured construction to a song; he's a very colourful player of the guitar. It's pleasing to hear because I don't feel I have to be on my toes all the time and fence with somebody. He's not the latest gunslinger in town, you know? You can get so fast that it gets silly, but Jimmy's not like that. There are a lot of guys doing that now, though, going berserk on the fret-board and I feel like telling them to settle down, say something, what is all this? It's like quoting Shakespeare at 100 miles per hour. It's like having sex for five minutes listening to some of these guys."

You're right. I bet they're not even good in bed. "Well, I wouldn't know about that, thank you. I think this is where we came in…"

First published in Kerrang! Nos.96-97, June 13, 1985

Unlike Live Aid in 1985, which, despite my inbuilt cynicism, I can't help but look back on as some sort of achievement, the Moscow Music Peace festival, held four years later and barely remarked on outside rock circles, is something it's hard not to regard as something of a sham. A puny, self-serving spectacle by comparison to the Live Aid event it was meant to echo, the whole thing was so obviously a get-out-of-jail card for Doc McGhee (who, at that time, managed all the acts on the bill bar Ozzy Osbourne), rather than an honest-to-goodness attempt to raise money for the various drug charities it purported to support, that it was almost impossible to report on the whole thing with straight face. So I didn't. I took the piss and this time rightly so. The Make A Difference Foundation may have been a perfectly wonderful organisation run by pure-hearted rock'n'roll philanthropists. I just remember all the bands bitching and fighting about where they were going to be on the bill.

As for Moscow, I hear they have a MacDonald's there now but that the queues for the few food and clothing stores are just as long as ever. God help them. I have been to India and Brazil but I've never seen poverty like the kind I witnessed in Russia; the kind that starves you mentally as well as physically. Coming home after a week in that grey place, Ealing Broadway on a Saturday afternoon looked like Santa's grotto it sparkled and shone so much.

Moscow Music Peace Festival, September 1989

It all began when a man named Ward approached me in the bar of the Soho Brasserie in London and began babbling excitedly about Russia, punching the air with his fist on certain key phrases like "Media event!", "History in the making!" and, most ominous of all, "Once in a lifetime experience!" That did it. The shutters came down. I have accepted enough offers of a 'Once in a lifetime experience' to know to steer well clear of anyone, blind or stupid enough to offer me another one now. Nevertheless, something about his manner endeared Ward to me. He was 30-ish, dressed in a crumpled suit and worried tie, and he looked like he hadn't slept in several days. He spoke in rapid bursts, like quick-fire speech bubbles, and he had the wild red eyes of the True Believer.

He began to throw a few names around – Bon Jovi, Ozzy Osbourne, Mötley Crüe, the Scorpions. Then he stirred in a few ripe images – Moscow gripped by such a fearful heat everyone that can flees the city: Red Square at night beneath the shadow of the Kremlin: the vast and imposing Lenin Stadium getting ready to Make A Difference...

I had to admit, it sounded like my kind of scene. Jon Bon Jovi in the back of a Russian-made Zil limousine waxing lyrical about Nelson Mandela, Bob Geldof and the impossibility of obtaining a cold beer in Moscow; Ozzy in Red Square in the pissing rain, philosophical as ever: "If I was living here full time, I'd probably be dead of alcoholism, or sniffing car tyres – anything to get out of it. I can understand why there's such an alcohol problem here. There's nothing else to do!"; the Scorpions hamming it up onstage at the Lenin Stadium with a turbo-charged version of 'Back In The USSR'... I could see it all splayed out before me like a giant map.

Ward kept the drinks coming and eventually a deal was struck: I was contracted to present a 30-minute documentary film for Sky Television, who were broadcasting highlights of the second of the two scheduled concerts, attempting to explain the purpose of the event and exploring some of the reasons for holding it in the first place.

This was to be Total Coverage From Every Angle, a veritable blitzkrieg of prolonged media gibberish centred on this deal called the Moscow Music Peace Festival. Ten days later I was drinking vodka in Moscow. Well, it's like Ozzy says: there simply is nothing else to do...

I don't know what images the name Moscow conjures up in your mind, but I suppose the archetype must be of a large, grey, unhappy citadel full of cold stares and food-queues. The reality of the situation, however, is much worse than that. The first thing you learn when you settle down to spend your first night in Moscow is that There Is No Food. At least, nothing actually edible. There are restaurants, of course, but mostly they are closed. Usually for 'cleaning'. Which seems to take place approximately six nights out of seven. When you do find a restaurant open it's a take it or leave it deal: you can have the worst Chicken Kiev you ever tasted in your life, or you can go drive a tractor.

Learning to survive on the road means learning to eat anything. Fussy eaters are the first to throw in the towel. As a result, over the years I have, at various trying moments, found myself: eating smoked reindeer and bear-steaks in Helsinki; drinking from the foul tap water of Rio de Janeiro; quaffing large fistfuls of chilli-dogs and fries at fast-food counters all over Los Angeles; and gorging myself on raw fish and cold rice in Tokyo. All because it was either eat that or eat my own dick. But never in all my travels have I come across anything so frankly vomit-inducing as the Chicken Kiev in Moscow. "Why do you think there are no dogs on the streets of Moscow?" whispered Dimitri, our official KGB-approved 'guide' and 'interpreter', conspiratorially as I pushed away my plate again one night.

So, all right, you can't eat. Rule number two: There Is No Such Thing As Russian Money. Well, actually, there is – it's called the Rouble, but no self-respecting Russian accepts any home-grown currency. Officially, a Rouble is supposed to be the equivalent of £1 Sterling. But on the black market, they'll give you up to 10 Roubles for £1. Even then, they're not worth having. The only thing you can buy with Roubles are wooden dolls and big furry hats. The only real consumer variables available are on sale in the Tourist Only stores, which take all major credit cards including American Express. Records or tapes are purchased on the black market.

In fact, the main currency in Moscow is US Dollars. Or better still, packs of Marlboros. At the hotel bar (no beer, no wine, just Teacher's whisky, Vladivostok vodka and a seemingly limitless supply of Bounty Bars) I paid for all my drinks in dollars. If I didn't have the exact amount I'd throw in a pack of Marlboros. For change, I'd receive an assortment of dollar bills, 10-franc pieces and the occasional silver Deutsche Mark. For small change I'd get handed a packet of orange-flavoured Tic-Tacs.

We were staying at a 'five star' £125 a night bread-and-water joint right in the heart of Moscow, one block from Red Square. Prostitutes lined the entrance to the hotel and dark-suited security guards checked the ID of anyone wishing to enter. Fat black cockroaches obviously high on life clung lazily to the walls and ceiling of the lobby. The night I arrived in my £125 a night room up on the 16th floor, I was advised by one of the advance crew to check my bed for bedbugs before settling down for the night. In my bathroom the water running from the taps was the colour of yesterday's piss, in the soap dish there was only a rotting apple-core. The only towel provided was hanky-thin and crisp as an old rag. Two cigarette stubs floated lifelessly in the toilet pan. I was truly baffled. What the fuck happened back there when they had the Great Revolution? Didn't anybody come out on top at the end of it? And if anybody did, where do those guys go to eat? I didn't bother to check for bedbugs. I just pulled back the sheet and got in. I settled my head back on the pillow and turned out the bedside light.

By now you've read the reviews, and/or seen the telecast or heard it on the radio, and the question everybody's lips is: so what the hell was all that actually about? Officially, the Moscow Music Peace Festival was about raising money for the Make A Difference Foundation – an anti-drugs and alcohol abuse agency set up late '88 by Bon Jovi's manager Doc McGhee, as the lion-share of the community service programme McGhee was sentenced to by an American court after he pleaded guilty to funding a multimillion dollar operation to smuggle 18 tonnes of marijuana into the US some years before.

After the 'production costs' all proceeds from the two concerts held in the Lenin Stadium are earmarked by the Make A Difference doyens for various drug and alcohol 'rehabilitation centres' and 'substance abuse awareness' programmes, specifically in the Soviet Union, where until the onset of Gorby's Perestroika it was not officially admitted that a drug or alcohol problem even existed. So far, so worthy. But, as Jon Bon Jovi was the first to admit, there's also the extra icing on the cake of doing something no other rock band has yet done. History and mystery and millions of dollars' worth of free publicity all rolled into one death-defying leap of the imagination...

"You know, at this stage of the game, it's like you ask yourself, what can we do that Zeppelin or the Stones or the Beatles didn't already do?" Jon told me from the back of his Zil. "And being here is it. Not only do we get to come over in a good cause, we also get to put on the kind of rock show never before seen in the Soviet Union."

And the whole world gets to watch. MTV had an American crew on-board the airliner – the Magic Bus – that transported all the bands from the West that would be taking part. If that baby had gone down it would have taken the casts of Bon Jovi, the Scorpions, Mötley Crüe, Ozzy and his band, Cinderella and Skid Row with it. But it didn't, and waiting to greet its arrival at Cheremetyov airport are TV crews from ITN, the BBC, Sky, CNN, some of sombre-faced chaps from the official Soviet TV network, plus a couple of hundred print hacks flown in from various far-flung editorial outposts around the world, all edging for position. It was just the beginning of a media merry-go-round that would test the patience of a saint, never mind a road-hardened rock and roller...

The press conference, like all press conferences everywhere, is a bore. Soft soap and bullshit. De-dum de-dum. Most of the questions from the Western press corps are directed at Jon Bon Jovi. Most of the questions from the Russians are for Ozzy. This comes as no surprise to anybody, except perhaps Ozzy. Doc McGhee paid for a survey to be conducted long before any of the bands arrived in Moscow to determine just how aware his potential Russian audience was of the acts he wanted to bring with him. Ozzy's name came top of the list.

"I was very surprised when they told me that," said Ozzy. "Surprised and flattered. Though looking round, I can see how my music or Sabbath's music makes sense here. It's bleak all round, isn't it?"

Right. Yet 24 hours earlier Ozzy had threatened to pull out of the event after McGhee suddenly changed his (Ozzy's) placing on the bill from third to fourth, upgrading Mötley Crüe – like Bon Jovi, the Scorpions, Skid Row and Gorky Park, all an integral part of McGhee Entertainments – to the slot above Ozzy. McGhee took the threat seriously enough to return Ozzy to his original placing on the bill, just below the Scorpion and Bon Jovi, and Ozzy kept his promise and boarded the Magic Bus. The farce repeated itself on the night before the first show when McGhee made another attempt to have Ozzy accept the fourth spot on the bill below Mötley Crüe. Again, Ozzy threatened to pull out, and again McGhee relented. What Mötley Crüe thought of all this is not generally known, though there were a lot of heated discussions taking place behind closed doors over at the Ukraine Hotel, where all the bands were staying, during the hours leading up to that first show at the Lenin Stadium.

For all their sweet talk to the media about this being a show where it's not important who headlines or who appears where on the bill, privately all of the acts gathered here in Moscow were fiercely competitive on this point. For example, there is no way in the world Bon Jovi are ever going to appear anywhere as anything but headliners ever again. The Scorpions, the only band from the West on the bill to have played before anywhere in the Soviet Union (10 sold-out nights in Leningrad in March '88), rightly lay the strongest claim to the second spot on the bill. As for Ozzy, he's always been happiest second or third on the bill.

"Like at Donington in '84," he explained. "The pressure's all on the headliners You can just go out and enjoy yourself. I've done some of my best shows ever when I've been second or third on the bill at one of these big outdoor festivals..."

Mötley Crüe, who got their first taste of what it was like to play before a big arena crowd opening for Ozzy on his 1983/84 American tour, would these days never dream of appearing so low on a bill of this size – Make A Difference or not – anywhere else in the world. This is Moscow. You do what you're told.

Cinderella, Skid Row, Gorky Park and the other locally-based and government-sponsored (read: no royalties) Soviet acts are all essentially along for the ride. But as long as they get their cut of the prime-time action that comes with it they're happy.

Which is, at heart, what this trip is really all about: free publicity on a global level. And lots of it. And why not? Ask Sting, he'll tell you. The charity thing is pure gold. Bob Geldof's been dining out on it for years...

"I don't know," Jon Bon Jovi shook his head when I talked to him about it. "People are always ready to question the motives behind why a bunch of rock stars would want to get together and do something like this. And, sure, inevitably you get a clash of egos occasionally. It's not exactly the easiest thing to organise in the world, we sure found that out! But at the end of the day, I look at it like this. I wouldn't have known about Nelson Mandela's situation like I do now had I not been drawn to it because of the artists on Amnesty. Or I don't think that I would've ever known about Ethiopia the way I do now if it wasn't for Bob Geldof. So there is a wonderful icing on the cake. You get to see all these big performers that I enjoy too, but there's ultimately a cause behind it. And that's what raises your awareness."

Indeed… and yet a spectre still looms. That of Aerosmith, who not only pulled out of the event at the eleventh hour but also insisted their contribution to the official Make A Difference album (a version of The Doors' 'Love Me Two Times') be lifted from the final pressing. Officially, the word is that Aerosmith are still busy putting last-minute touches to the release of their new album and the start of their own world tour, in Europe in October. Off the record, everybody remains earnest and tight-lipped on the subject. Something's gone down, but nobody's saying what. Besides, there's too much to do. The 48 hours leading up to the first show are spent in a blur of interviews and 'photo-opportunities'.

Everybody gets to go to Red Square. Ozzy is interviewed there for the Derek Jameson show on Sky, and Jon Bon Jovi, Richie Sambora and David Bryan arrive to view the scene armed with a posse of about 50 photographers and at least six TV crews. Ozzy is telling Sky that, "It's not that I make millions out of playing Russia, I just want to play music to them, that's all. Maybe I'll give someone a smile on their face for a day in Russia..."

Meanwhile, back at the Lenin Stadium, I run into Vince Neil and Nikki Sixx and ask them the obvious question: so what the hell are Mötley Crüe, the ultimate all-American sex, drugs and rock'n'roll band, doing in Russia, of all places, appearing at an anti-drugs concert? Sixx bares his teeth and smiles. "It might be an anti-drugs concert for some people, but it's not for us. It's anti-abuse we're talking about. That's our belief. We're not here to preach. If you tell a young kid not to do drugs, he's gonna do it anyway. I know I did," he goes on. "We just say, if you cross the line between use and abuse, then that's really tragic. I've crossed that line, many times. And I know from experience that it's bad, and I try to tell kids not to cross the line. The rest is up to them."

Klaus Meine from the Scorpions had a simpler message. "There's everywhere a drug problem, all over the world. So I think it's good that the bands stand together on one stage and give a message to the kids in the world: forget about the drugs. The best drug is music…"

The last time I saw Jon Bon Jovi was in Red Square on the evening before my departure (we had to be back in London to edit the film in time for Sunday's live broadcast of the concert and so I never got to hang around and see either of the shows). He was still looking for a cold beer. "Have you discovered any of the night life here yet?" he asked me hopefully. I shook my head. I had spent the last three nights prowling the streets of Moscow, TV crew in tow, in search of something even faintly resembling the sort of night life we take for granted in the West. Only, like everything else in Russia, the only bars we discovered that catered for music, live or otherwise, were always closed, or being 'cleaned'. We never found a single club open the whole time we were there. It made the high street in Sheffield on a cold Tuesday night in December seem like the most glamorous place on Earth.

I left Jon Bon Jovi still trying o Make A Difference on the steps of St. Asille's Cathedral in Red Square. It was drizzling rain and the sky was the colour of chilled vodka. The changing of the guard at the gates of the Kremlin was about to take place and a great crowd of tourists and out-of-towners gathered along one side of the Square to watch.

Me, I stick another dime in the jukebox (baby) and watch the discs go round…

First published in Kerrang! Nos.254-255, September 2, 1989

Inevitably, most interviews I did for Kerrang! were of the tell-me-about-the-new-album variety. So when I got a call from Sharon Osbourne asking me to come and speak to her husband about his latest misadventure – being banged-up on an attempted murder charge – I felt a strange mixture of excitement and apprehension. It wasn't every day I got asked to do something like that. But then, that was probably at least half the reason I got into rock writing as opposed to straight news reporting: I didn't see myself as the guy that could write with any insight on a topic as serious as, uh, murder. Naw, getting pissed and stoned and getting my rocks off to some noisy arse-wiggling rock band was about my level. That and pulling chicks – and even that was not always within my reach, as a writer or a fighter.

On the other hand, it wasn't every day a major rock star tried killing someone, and I was just sober enough at the time of the call to understand that this might actually make one hell of a story. Well, I was right about that…

Weirdly, when I reminded Ozzy of this story not long ago he swore blind he couldn't even remember me coming to see him – which says something for the state of mind he was in at the time, poor bastard. Not that it took him long to snap out of it. Just over a year after this story first ran I spent the evening with Ozzy at the apartment he was then renting in LA, drinking brandy, smoking a bong and snorting our brains out together. Not even an attempted murder, it seems, would be enough to stop Ozzy in his tracks for long. Only increasing old age and the even more unexpected success of the realest 'reality show' ever to hit TV would do that…

Ozzy Osbourne, Buckinghamshire, October 1989

Just like everybody else, the first I heard of the arrest of Ozzy Osbourne, at his Beel House mansion in Buckinghamshire, was when I read about it in the newspaper. 'DEATH THREAT' OZZY SENT TO BOOZE CLINIC! screamed the headline in *The Sun*. BAN ON SEEING WIFE! HELL OF DRYING OUT! According to the reports, the police had arrived at the house in the early hours of Sunday morning, September 3, and subsequently arrested Ozzy for allegedly threatening to kill his wife and manager, Sharon, or 'intending her to fear that the threat would be carried out' as the official police report put it.

The phone got to me before I got to it… America's *National Enquirer*, the *Sunday Snort*, the *Daily Angst*... and all with the same questions: what happened? Did he finally go mad? Or better still, has he always been mad? And what about all the, you know, rumours. That Sharon had been having an affair and it was the discovery of this fact that prompted the fight between them. That Sharon's father and a former manager of both Ozzy and Black Sabbath, Don Arden, was about to step in and retake control of his estranged son-in-law's career? And that this move would precipitate the reformation of the original Sabbath line-up, including Ozzy?

I realised straight away that these were the sort of questions only my answer-phone could answer, so I switched the thing on and sat back to think it over. As chance would have it, I had seen both Ozzy and Sharon the day before the incident, at the studios of Capital Radio in London, where Ozzy had been taping an interview. He looked a mess. Eyeballs popping out of his skull, his face a mask of sweat; his mind drifting in and out of the conversation. Sharon smiled indulgently and hid whatever was going on inside her as she always does when Ozzy's having one of his 'bad days'. They were on their way to Hamley's toy shop in Regent Street, to pick up a present for their eldest daughter, Aimee, whose sixth birthday it was the next day.

I asked Ozzy how he was enjoying being home again after his long recent world tour.

He shook his head and frowned: "It's alright… I'm bored already, though; I don't know what to do with myself. Why don't you come up to the house for a drink sometime?"

I said, sure, why not? And that was the last time we talked before the whole shithouse went up in flames. Then a couple of nights after the newspapers broke the story, with Ozzy safely installed in Huntercombe Manor in Buckinghamshire, a private rehabilitation centre for recovering alcoholics and 'substance abusers', Sharon called me at home. Other than checking that she was okay, I found myself asking the same dumb questions as everybody else: what happened? Did he just go mad, or what? "Yes."

Sharon spent her formative years working for her father, Don Arden, whose reputation in the music business for being a hard-boiled example of the Old School, with a bite to back his formidable bark is as well-known as it is well-founded. Later she split acrimoniously to manage and marry Ozzy, one of Don's hottest properties. Following that experience, Sharon is a lady used to dealing with tough situations. "She can be a hard bastard, my old lady," Ozzy once told me. "Anybody who fucks with her – watch out!" On the phone that night, however, Sharon sounded frail, upset, weary and concerned. "Alcohol is destroying his life," she sighed. "To be an alcoholic means you have a disease. If Ozzy had cancer people would feel sorry for him. But because he's an alcoholic people don't understand. He just needs to get help…"

Even though Sharon has since dropped her charges, the legal ramifications have yet to be untangled fully and the police may yet bring a charge to court. It would be unwise therefore to attempt a full blow-by-blow account of what happened that night here. Nevertheless, it's easy to put the pieces together: Ozzy was celebrating his daughter's birthday by getting smashed on his current favourite tipple, Russian vodka. He has a meandering drunken argument with Sharon that begins over dinner and continues throughout the rest of the evening, culminating in Ozzy attacking his wife with such ferocity she felt compelled to call for the police. "It wasn't Ozzy and that's what terrified me," said Sharon. "Ozzy would never, ever, ever have done that to me, or anyone, because he's just not capable of it. But when Ozzy is loaded, Ozzy disappears and someone else takes over..."

Following his arrest, Ozzy spent the next 36 hours in a cell at nearby Amersham police station, while he waited to appear before Beaconsfield Magistrates Court on the Monday morning. Waiting for him inside the courtroom that day were over 50 reporters and photographers from the world's tabloid press. After a brief hearing, Ozzy was placed on bail under three conditions: that he should immediately check himself into an alcoholic rehabilitation programme at a live-in centre of his choice; that he should not make any attempt to contact Sharon; and that he should not return to Beel House. Instead, Ozzy was driven from the courthouse back to Amersham police station, where he was met by his long-time friend and employee, Tony Dennis, who drove him directly to Huntercombe Manor, a £250-per-day rehab joint already familiar to the errant singer. (He had stayed there twice before for brief periods earlier this year and last.)

For the time being he's staying put there. If a trial date is set, it could be as much as three to six months away. Even if he doesn't have to attend trial, it will be at least three months, by his own doctor's reckoning, before Ozzy will be anywhere near ready to go home. "Whatever's wrong with Ozzy, it's not something that's gong to take six weeks in a rest home to cure," says Sharon. "It's going to take a lot longer than that to get Ozzy well again. But no matter how long it takes, the children and I will be there waiting for him. I am not divorcing him. I just want him to get well…"

Though I have been I friends with both Ozzy and Sharon for some years now, that Ozzy might want to meet and talk with me at this precise moment had never occurred to me. I had imagined him far too busy with doctors and lawyers, his senses irretrievably dulled by medication, to even think about doing an interview. So when Tony Dennis called a week after my conversation with Sharon and said Ozzy wanted to talk, I was surprised, to say the least. "He's got a lot he wants to get off his chest," said Tony. "But he doesn't trust talking to anyone else from the press."

Significantly or not, I don't know, it hardly seems to matter under the circumstances and yet in another way it's almost too rueful, but Tony and I decide to meet on the steps of the Hammersmith Odeon, scene of so many triumphant and not-so moments from Ozzy's 20-year career. From there, Tony drives me the rest of the way to Huntercombe Manor, a large building in the style of a traditional English country manor. It lies up a long, winding path shaded by trees somewhere off the M40. We arrived at about 7.30 pm on an already dark Sunday evening, two weeks to the day since Ozzy's arrest. Sundays are one of the two days of the week that the 'guests' at Huntercombe are allowed visitors.

The main reception area is part hotel lobby, part dentist's waiting room. People mill around casually and at first it's hard to distinguish the 'patients' from the 'visitors'. Eventually, a pattern emerges: the patients are the ones smiling and looking relaxed; the visitors are the ones shuffling uneasily in their best shoes, chain-smoking and snatching furtive glances at their watches. I wait in the TV room while Tony goes off to locate Ozzy. He arrives, typically, in a nervous panic, not a little self-conscious perhaps, immediately fumbling for a cigarette, groping for a light. "Allo, Mick. Sorry I kept you waiting... I was in a meeting with my therapist... Have you got a light?"

He keeps the chatter up all the way down the corridor and up the stairs to his bedroom on the first floor. Inside, his room is something like the size and quality of a suite at some well-to-do provincial hotel: one large bedroom with bathroom and shower en suite and a smaller adjoining room, a large bed, the usual bedroom furniture and a couple of chairs. No TV, though. And no smoking allowed in the room.

"It's a bit like a hotel room," I remark casually.

"Yeah, except you can't go downstairs to the bar," says Ozzy, straight-faced, whipping out an ashtray from where he's got it stashed under the bed and lighting up his cigarette.

We settle down in opposite chairs at the table by the window and I pull out the tape-recorder and set it down between us amidst a pile of chocolate bars, packs of Marlboros and cans of Diet Coke that already crowd the table. Despite everything Ozzy looks better than I've seen him in some time. Certainly more focused than the stoned and bamboozled figure I ran into the day before his arrest. And far more alert and together than the lost and distant character that sleepwalked his way through the Moscow Music Peace Festival back in July. Dressed in black T-shirt and black slacks, he looks trim and in very good (physical) shape. Mentally, though, it's harder to tell straight off. It's clear Ozzy's very uptight about the things people have read into, and in some cases read about, his present dilemma, and for that reason says he wants to "set the record straight once and for all, and then everybody can fuck off and leave me and my family alone to get on with the rest of our lives."

The words raced out of his mouth and at one point I feared the torrent of emotion would turn into a flood and that he was on the point of bursting into tears. But just when I thought he might be stepping over the edge and winding himself up unduly, he would suddenly bring the conversation right back down to earth again with a small joke, or, more often, a fitful shrug of the shoulders. Which is exactly where Ozzy says he wants to be these days: back down to Earth. What follows is a 95 per cent verbatim transcript of the conversation we had that night, in Ozzy's room, illicitly smoking cigarettes next to the open window and sipping decaffeinated coffee. Under the circumstances, you'd hardly call it an 'interview'. More a conversation between sober boozing buddies that tends to jump around a lot. Anyway, for better or for worse, Ozzy was on a roll. Mostly I just sat back and watched…

Let's start at the beginning, Ozzy... How, in your own words, have you ended up in this mess? "Well, what happened was I tried touring sober, and I did very well for about four-and-a-half months, and then I started messing around again with it again [drinking] you know? And I came back from Russia, went to Los Angeles, and I had this Russian vodka. So I tried a bit of that. And it was all right for a week or so, on the vodka. Then I became like a closet case, you know? I started drinking in the closet and not telling anybody I was drinking. Till in the end… apparently Sharon and I were having a few words, she was getting on at me for… I think she suspected… I mean, my paranoia stepped in, you know? And I just went into an alcoholic blackout."

How long have you suffered from these 'alcohol blackouts'? "I became a blackout drinker about a year ago… as far as I know. I may have been one for many years before that and never really realised it. Anyway, I went into a blackout and don't remember anything of the incident. I vaguely remember going to a Chinese restaurant with Sharon. Just bits and pieces, you know? I'd drunk a bottle of vodka that day. And then when I woke up in the jail and all my face was scratched where Sharon had tried to defend herself I didn't really know what had happened. I could remember being nicked, but I thought maybe I'd fallen over when they were dragging me out of the house. I just couldn't remember. It was like a mad dream. At the time, in the police car, I thought I was dreaming. I thought, this is not real, you know? Police in my house, taking me out of my house? But I went to jail. They kept me in Amersham jail for two days. They were all right, in the jail. The jail conditions were disgusting, though. I mean, I know they're not supposed to be built like Butlin's, but they were terrible, you know?"

In what way? "Real disgusting places, shit on the walls… not fit for a rat, you know?"

Were you sharing a cell? "No, I was on my own. They were all right to me, though, the people in there. They gave me cigarettes and chatted to me once in a while. What really bothered me was the press. They've built the whole thing way out of proportion. I'm not divorcing Sharon. We've met several times since the incident. I'm not rejoining Black Sabbath. I'm not going back to Don Arden… I just wish everybody would back off and leave me and my family alone, you know? Leave us alone!"

The ugly rumours have certainly been spreading since your arrest. "There's a lot of rumours about Sharon and I breaking up and that she's been having an affair, and all that. As far as I know it's all rumours, it's not true. All I can say at this point is I'd like to thank all the fans who have sent me lots of letters. I am gonna record a new album again with my band. I'm not gonna be touring so much anymore. I mean, I'm not gonna tour for 18 months at a go anymore. I'm gonna cut it down. My band are very loyal to me though, they've all been down to see me. Zakk [Wylde – guitarist] and Randy [Castillo – drummer] flew across from the States especially to see me. So I've still got the thing there, it's just that I went off the rails for a while, you know? The pressure of the tour got to me and I just blew up. That's what happens to me. I've got no other way of getting rid of the frustration, it just happens, you know? Other people go to the pub and have a few drinks and mellow out. I can't do that. I'm a chronic alcoholic and I'm in a chronic phase, and so on the Wednesday before the weekend the incident happened I'd already checked into this place. But my alcoholic mind was telling me, 'Don't go Ozzy, just pull out at the last minute and go up north to some drinking friends of yours and get smashed for a week'. And this was all planned in my sick head, you know?"

Did you go up north? "No, no… I got nicked on the Saturday night, didn't I? I'm just so glad I'm here now, though. I miss my kids and my home, but I have a lot of hope now, you know? I have a real lot of hope, because I don't wanna go any further down the scale than that. That was pretty bad, what I did."

Do you remember attacking Sharon? "I can only take what's been told to me, but I assume she's right because… I mean, it really shook my wife up. Really, what I suppose it's true to say happened, was we had a domestic argument that went a bit over the edge because I was pissed. Which happens every night of the week to some people, but when it happens to me everybody gets to hear about it. Everybody rows. I suppose I was pissed and I took it a little too far and threatened to kill her… But it's snowballed yet again, same as all the other incidents. It's just gone way out of proportion. I just wish everybody would back off. I'm very much still in love with my wife, you know? I don't wish anyone any harm. But just leave us alone."

I heard that both Don I Arden and his son, David, tried to get in contact with you when you checked into this place. "They tried to call me in the jail. I got telegrams and all that. I mean, I appreciate the thought, but I think they need take care of their own business and leave me alone. Me and my family are doing okay as we are. I don't need their help. I'm a big boy now. I'm not the vegetable that they used to call me anymore."

Do you think something like this had to happen before you came to your senses and decided to really do something about your drink-related problems? "Maybe so… It's not fear makes one want to quit drinking, though. Alcoholic people, the same as drug dependent people, don't understand why they're doing it. I don't understand why I get drunk. I don't understand any of it. But you've got to be on your guard 24 hours a day, or suddenly you're lying on the floor the next morning with an empty booze bottle by you and you think, what happened? How did I get here? My intention on Saturday morning wasn't… I mean, I didn't get up and think, 'Oh, it's a good day to go up the pub, get smashed as a rat, come back, drink another bottle of vodka and strangle the wife!' That was not my intention. I just wanted to have a few drinks and mellow out. But I just go crazy with booze now. Today, when my children left me, that was enough for me to want to stop. They were all crying, looking out the back of the Range Rover, and my heart broke. And being in a place like this, it's kind of lonely, you know? You don't know if they're gonna put electrodes to your balls or what…"

What's it actually like here? "It's all right. It's like a therapy thing, you talk in a group to other alcoholics. I really can't give too much more about the place away because it's suppose to be anonymous, you know? But there's a lot of different people here from all walks of life and we sit in a group and we discuss our problems and we recognise similarities. Anybody that's an alcoholic, you always think you're the only one that does these crazy things. But you find out later that everybody who's an alcoholic does exactly the same things. There's a pattern to it, and so you talk it out instead of bottling it up. I'd say something like, whenever I have the third drink I go a bit funny in the head. And the guy in charge will ask if anyone else relates to that and someone will say they can. So it makes you feel a little bit more at ease with yourself. I'm not gonna try any of these aversion therapy things though, where you take this pill and have eight bottles of vodka and throw up. I used to do that without having a pill! I mean, Sharon and I have had a pretty rough year this year, with the work schedule. Sharon's been working her arse off with the Quireboys, Lita Ford and me. She never stops working, which kind of gets on my tits sometimes. Because when I come off tour I wanna be with my wife and family, and she's still a manager for other bands..."

Does that make you resentful? "I get pretty resentful over it, then I get bored. But I've got to work it out somehow or other. I still love her very, very much. But it was hell for me on that last tour: 14 months! Trying to get sober on the road is... Everybody I've met that's got sober said to me, 'Ozzy, you're heading for major destruction, you're heading for a major calamity'. Because you haven't got a chance on the road. I was whacking cortisone in me twice a month, and all that shit just to keep going. And it's all mind-altering. It's all a drug. It's a steroid. I was fucking crazy when I came off that last tour! Absolutely insane! I'm still not sane now. I'm still on medication in this place."

What sort of medication are you on? "Anti-depressants mostly, because the side-effects of cortisone make you very depressed and you think the world's coming down on your shoulders all the time. And I'm on various anti-fit pills, because I became a fit-drinker, I became a spasm-drinker."

What's a 'fit-drinker'? "It's like, when I was withdrawing one time I went into like a spasm, because I didn't have a medical detox. This was about six months ago. It's not such a major thing. It doesn't mean I'm gonna have a heart attack. I'm pretty well healthy, I train every morning on my bike and I run around the field a bit. It's not as bad as it sounds, but if you've got a record of having these seizures they keep you on this medication. I'm on all kinds of different stuff. But I'm glad I'm here, as I said before. It's the best place for me, and it's the only place I've got a chance. Even if I wanted to drink, I can't, you know? And I want to stay here for as long as it takes. I'm not gonna leave here until I feel that I can cope with the real world. I've got to get well this time because it could have been a darn sight worse; I could have ended up killing my wife, which I would never have forgiven myself for till the day I died."

You have spent time in places like this before and it doesn't appear to have had much lasting effect. What makes you think that this time will be any different? "Because I'm not gonna start work until I'm well enough. I'm not even thinking about work, Mick."

So how long are you actually in here for? "Indefinitely... The usual thing is four to six weeks. But I'm not even thinking about that. I'm thinking about three to six months, or maybe even longer. There's no time limit. I'm not gonna go out into the real world until I'm well again. My wife's still in shock. My kids... We're all still in shock over this episode, because it wasn't me in my full... I didn't mean to... You've known me, Mick, for a long time. In my wildest dreams I wouldn't have wanted to do that. I just wanna try and stop these fucking sickos accusing my wife of having affairs, of me having affairs... Everybody's fucking trying to get on our case to destroy the marriage. It's always the same, people want to clean their own doorstep before they start trying to clean mine. There's plenty of shit on everybody else's doorstep to clean. Leave us alone and we'll be all right."

So are you going to have to stand trial eventually? "If it goes to court, it goes to court, you know? I mean, the difference between me and everybody else is all my duty laundry comes out in the open. When we have a row it's in full view of the whole fucking world! That's enough pressure on its own. My wife is in red ribbons, I'm not very well. And the pressure we're under is phenomenal."

What would be the best way things could turn out for you right now, Ozzy? "That Sharon and I are still together. That we're all back to normal, and I can learn a bit more tolerance. And that we have happy days for the rest of our lives, you know? I can't speak for Sharon because I've learnt in this place not to speak for anybody else any more. I presume, at the end of the day, she wants to settle down, though."

But you'd like to keep working, wouldn't you? "Yeah, but keep working in a more civilised manner. I mean, what do I wanna do a fucking gig in all these far off places for? Russia was okay, it was a very interesting place. I wouldn't mind going there again one day. But I don't want to be on the road forever. I've bought a house in Buckinghamshire and in the two-and-a-half years since I bought it, I must have been there about three months! At the most! I mean, what's the point in me buying all this property and buying all this stuff if I'm never there to appreciate it?"

This, it seems to me, is the saddest part of all. You're one of the world's biggest rock stars; your albums have consistently sold in their millions over the years, with or without Black Sabbath. Now you come home from one of your – admittedly longest – but certainly most successful world tours ever, to be with your wife and three beautiful children. And on paper, you should be the happiest man in the world. "Instead, you end up in a rehab joint on an attempted murder charge… Happiness doesn't come from high finance, though. It helps a great deal. I mean, people say, I'd rather be wealthy and unhappy than poor and unhappy. And I'm not going to give it to some far off fucking charities, you can forget that! But it's like, what's the point in working if you don't appreciate what you're working for? I'm never there to take part in anything, so I build up a lot of resentment. Not personally against Sharon, but I build up a lot of resentment within me. Like, why didn't I do that? And why didn't I think of that? Because I'm always working. And then coming home is an anti-climax, you know? I think, when I get home I'm gonna take Jack [Ozzy and Sharon's three-year-old son: they also have two daughters: Kelly, aged four; and Aimee whose sixth birthday it was the day Ozzy was arrested] out on my bike, I'm gonna buy the girls a little paddling pool. I wanna do all those little things that fathers are supposed to do. And when I think about how it's gonna be, I think it's gonna be sunny, it's gonna be this, it's gonna be that. And when you finally get home, it's never how you pictured it. It's either raining, or they've run out of paddling pools, or the bike's broken that you were gonna take Jack out on...

"Also, after living such an active life for a year or so, you come home and people just live ordinary lives, and it's hard for you to wind down. I mean, I understand how people go into meditation and all that, you know? I suppose it's a good way of winding down. You get bored so easily, too. I've got a concentration span of about 30 seconds. I've just been seeing my therapist in that room before you came and he said, you've got to learn some relaxation. I said, I've never relaxed since the day I was born, I can't sit still for a moment…"

Have you actually tried meditation or any other relaxation techniques? "Well, part of the therapy is a kind of a meditation exercise. When I say 'meditation' people out there will probably think I'm talking about the guru and all that. But it's nothing like sitting there going, OOMMMM! We just shout PINTS!" He laughs. "PINTS! And BROWN AALLLEEEE!!! No, it's all right. I feel safe here, you know? It's when I'm out there… I walk out the house, in the yard, in my studio, out of my studio, in my yard, back in the house. I'm like a bloody preying mantis! Yet when I'm on the road for long periods of time, it's worse. I've been on the road for over 20 years, you know? And I really don't enjoy being out on the road for huge long periods of time. It would be worth it if I could go home every two weeks or something. But it don't work like that.

"And I get resentful when I'm away for too long a time. My kid starts to walk, my kid goes to school, my kid takes part in the school sports, and I'm never there for any of it. And I just get pissed off with it. I think, why am I out here on the road all the time? I mean, I get on the phone and they go: 'Aimee came second in a race at school today'. And I go, 'Oh wow, great. What the fuck you telling me for?' You could tell me Aimee just became the first child cosmonaut in the world! I wouldn't know anything about it. And every time I leave my kids, a little part of me dies, you know? I mean, they came today, and they were all crying in the back of the Range Rover when they had to leave me. And I looked at the back of that Range Rover and I thought, that's a good enough reason for anybody to quit fucking boozing.

"At this point, Mick, my number one priority is to get sober and stay sober. I never again want to be in a bar. I've said this a million times before, I know, and always ended up in a bar. But I have hope that I can kick this booze thing and get straight once and for all. It's like a love affair I have with booze. It's like, you know it's killing you but you can't stop. It's like any addiction. You know it's killing you but you just can't put the stuff down. No alcoholic person out there goes, 'Oh shit yeah, I got pissed for a week, I don't wanna talk about it'. I mean, Sharon used to drink a lot of booze many years ago. But she got up one morning, we were in Monmouth, and she said, 'Fucking hell, Ozzy, I feel like shit, I'm never gonna drink again'. And she's never drunk since, as far as I know."

Do you seriously believe you will be able to quit drinking for good? "I hope so. I've got to go to constant therapy classes for the rest of my life, I suppose. I've got to go to meetings. I've got to start reading lots of books. I've got to meet up with other recovering alcoholics."

Do you have any close men friends? "No, not that close!" he guffaws. Then becomes serious again. "I'm involved in a fellowship, where we all sit around chatting about how it was, what it's like now and, you know, how you got here. Two alcoholics can do more for each other than any psychiatrist or therapy. Two alcoholics talking it over can do a lot for each other. And

I've met people a lot worse off than me that got well on this programme. Ultimately, I've got two choices: either get it right this time, or screw up again. And if I don't get it right I'll either die or go insane. I mean, I don't even like I drinking. The feeling of being drunk is oblivion for me. I don't drink for the taste, I hate the taste! I drink it for oblivion from this planet, you know, get me off!"

They say that a lot of alcoholics are actually allergic to alcohol, and that's what makes it so addictive. The body becomes addicted to the poison and the rest is all a major allergic reaction. "I heard that before, yeah. Maybe I am, I don't know. All I know is, I am an alcoholic and my name is Ozzy. And I've got to take certain steps to try and arrest the disease. Because I'm either gonna kill myself, kill someone else, which I very nearly did, or I'm gonna go insane, I'm gonna be locked away in an insane asylum. It's got to that point now where I don't get happy-pissed, I go bulldozing around. I don't even know what I'm doing or where I'm at. Sharon says she's terrified when she sees me drink now. It upsets the whole family, close friends and everybody that works for me. You should do an article on some of the people who have been around me the last 12 months. I've been like Dr Jekyll and Mr Hyde, you know? And I'm really like that when I get drunk – from Dr Jekyll to Mr Hyde, every time. But I can't keep saying, I'm cured, mate! You know, cured in inverted commas. Because I never will be cured from it. I accept that now. I've just got to take certain steps. I've got to be on medication for a while because I became a manic depressive from the cortisone shots. I mean, major depressions. But if I can just reaffirm, I'm in treatment. But there's no guard outside the door. I'm not in shackles. I'm not getting electrodes round my bollocks..."

It's nice to see you've been able to keep some of your sense of humour about this. "All in all, that's about the only thing I have got, which cheers not only me up but all the rest of the people here. We have a scream here. Somehow it's easy to laugh at your troubles. Yet I can have double-platinum records and all the rest of the shit and I'm still unhappy about it. I'll always find a fucking fault in anything. That's the artistic temperament, I suppose."

What was the main reason you asked me here this evening? What is it you want to tell the world the most? "I just wanted to set the record straight. I picked up the newspaper and I read 'Ozzy gets divorced', and it's not that at all! I mean, not as far as I'm aware of. Sharon was round this afternoon. I asked her then, 'Are you going to divorce me?'. She said, 'Absolutely not'. And I want to say that I'm not gonna let people from the outside fuck my marriage up. Nobody thought we would last as long as we have, but we have. And I hope to God that we last as long as the rest of our lives."

It's hard to imagine you and Sharon apart. If the worst came to the worst, though, and you did split up, would you go back on the bottle, do you think? "The very worst thing that could happen to me would be if me and Sharon were to split up. But if it did happen, I wouldn't drink, no. Because I can't drink. Because that would fuck everything up even more. And that's what I've gotta say to myself – no matter what, I don't pick up that first drink. There's no such thing for me any more as just-have-a-half-Ozzy. One's too many and 10 is not enough for me. Once I'm off I'll drink the fucking planet dry! And when you hear of people like Phil Lynott dying, or Bonham and all that, you think: that will never happen to me. But it fucking will! It's catching up with me rapidly. I don't wanna be the next fucking victim, you know?"

Aside from the alcoholism, do you think you suffer from any other problems. Paranoia, insecurity... "Oh yeah, I've always been a paranoid person. Always. Ultra-paranoid. I'm very nervous and shy, too. When I'm performing, that's a different person again. The performing Ozzy is nothing like the person you see now. At least, I fucking hope not. I mean, I don't suppose Laurel and Hardy walked around in the silly hats when they were offstage, and neither do I. But some people look at me and they expect me to walk around with a fucking bag full of bats! Hi there, wanna bat? It's not real, you know? It's called entertainment."

What about the rest of the people in this place – were they at all wary of you when you first arrived? "No, I keep everybody smiling down here. We have a bit of a laugh sometimes. It's all right here, it really is all right here. I mean, it's tough in the respect that sometimes I think, what the fuck am I doing in another dry-out zone? But you know, if you're in a facility like this one and you don't put your heart and soul into it, then you ain't gonna get anything out of it, you know? I mean, I can sit here looking out of my window in my £250 a day fucking room and think, I'm here, what now? But you've gotta get down to some work. You've got to give it your time. When I saw my kids go away today in that car crying, I thought, 'What a fucking arsehole you are Ozzy. What a total dickhead! You're saying goodbye to your kids again and you should be at home with them'.

"I beat myself up about it, you know? I get really down, because it wasn't my intention to fuck everything up again. But whatever happens, I am definitely not splitting up with Sharon. And even if it came to that, I would never go with Don Arden again. And I am definitely, definitely not rejoining Black Sabbath. And that's from the bottom of my heart. You can kiss that one straight off. I will never rejoin Black Sabbath. No fucking way! Not in this life or the next..."

Has Sabbath guitarist Tony Iommi tried to get in touch with you? "Yeah, he's phoned me. I wouldn't pick up his call, though. I haven't spoken to the fucking dickhead since Live Aid and even then he didn't say goodbye. So what's he suddenly become my old pal for? I mean, I'm not that much of a dickhead that I can't see that. I'm stoned, I'm not fucking brain-dead! Not yet, anyway, old bean. Not yet..."

First published in Kerrang! Nos.261-262, October 21, 1989

Although I was hardly a typical fan of their music – it's a long time since I've been a spotty adolescent – I always looked forward to my encounters with Iron Maiden. With the exception of their would-be 'renaissance man' singer, Bruce Dickinson, who always fancied himself a cut above the rest – until his solo career went belly-up, at which point he was more than happy to be 'welcomed' back into the fold – the men in Maiden were a defiantly down-to-earth, unfussy bunch, as epitomised by their staunchly working class leader Steve 'Arry' Harris.

Square of jaw and tattooed of arm, I also liked it that they refused to bend over for a hit single, even when the temptation to do so must have been tremendous. In a parallel universe, Iron Maiden would have been as globally humongous as their former disciples Metallica. But Steve Harris would rather gnaw his own knob off than work with a commercially-sugared producer like Bob Rock. You could argue that it's that kind of bloody-mindedness that has held Maiden back over the years: certainly, they have never been as big in America as they might have been because of it. That said, there has always been so much pride in what Maiden did that Steve would never allow the band to simply cruise amongst the also-rans of the second tier of rock, the way so many bands that now plough the 'classic rock' furrow are happy to.

As a result, Maiden continue to occupy their own unique position in music. They are what they are and fuck what anyone else has to say about it, including me. And I like that. Unlike the writer of the following story, I don't drink anymore. But if I did I would happily raise a glass in their salute. If there was a little bit more of that piss-off attitude in rock generally the music business would be less of a cock-sucking boys' club and more of a place for real men (and women) to feel at ease.

Iron Maiden, Cologne, April 1988

Flight time from Heathrow: 1.30 pm. Arrive Frankfurt: 4.30 pm. Drive to Castle Schnellenberg, arrive: 7.00 pm. Begin interviews: 7.30 pm. Finish: open-ended. It looked like a long day ahead, and another long night. Working, that is. The one subject I failed in at school. The important thing, therefore, at this stage, I decided, was not to get too drunk. I would sink just the one or two on the plane and call it a day until I'd punched the clock on the interviews. Three, maybe, but that was max. There, I'd talked myself into it. At last, I figured, I must be turning pro...

I fill a bag and take a train to the airport. I make it on time, good old me the pro, and when I get there my old mate, Rangi, is there to meet me. Rangi has worked for Steve Harris and Iron Maiden longer than most; part-security, part-crew, and full-time china-plate to 'Arry and the boys, he has a nice line in gritty Kiwi patter, and fists the size of my face.

"Hello, my old mate! How are ya?" I say in greeting. "I'm all right," says Rangi, his eyes scouring the horizon of the over-crowded departure lounge. "But your other old mate isn't here yet and the flight leaves in half an hour..."

The other old mate Rangi refers to is Maiden drummer Nicko McBrain. Nicko isn't late yet, but another ten minutes and he will be. The minutes run away... five... ten... 15 to go before the big metal bird flies...

I hear him coming long before I see him.

"MICKEY!" he hollers.

"Nicko!" I cry.

"RANGI!!" he bellows.

"Nicko!" Rangi cries.

"MICKEEE!! RANGEEEEE!!! Am I late? We've still got time for a wet, surely..."

Suddenly the Mad McBrain is in our midst. With ten minutes to go we manage to make it through customs and passport control and head like men possessed for the bar. DOWN they go, in ones and twos. Then OFF we run like bastards for the plane...

"Always the last to arrive and always the last to leave, my dear," says Nicko in passing to the stewardess with the stopwatch in her hand as we step aboard the plane. I grab the seat next to Nicko and another stewardess leans over and sticks two drinks in our hands. "Now that's what I call service," I tell him.

"MICKEE!" he roars, a big Rasputin smile spreading across his face.

"Nicko!"

"CHEERS!"

And down they go. Just as the plane is starting to go up, up, UP…

We're still doing a forward dance along the ground-to-air diagonal when the next two drinks arrive. At this point the pro in me begins sending out mental reminders about the three-drink-max limit I had set myself. The pro in me sounds very stern, and for a moment I sit there looking at my drink and listening to him go at it. But not for long.

"MICKEE!!"

"Nicko!"

Down they go again, and with them goes the pro in me, on his knees and begging. Nicko calls for the jug. They've just turned the No Smoking sign off. We're still not horizontal, but the pilot takes care of that problem in his way, and me and Nicko take care of it in ours. By the time we've reached our fifth drink, the pro in me is still babbling on. But he's starting to sound like a damn fool, and besides, he sounds like he's been drinking…

"MICKEE!!" the voice goes again, only this time it's mine. We kill the fifth drink.

We arrive in Frankfurt at the same time as Steve Harris and Dave Murray. All of the band have flown in from their various hideouts around the world: Steve from his villa in the Algarve, Dave from a holiday in Tenerife and Nicko from Houston, Texas, via London, where he's been out conducting a travelling drum clinic all over America for the past three weeks. Adrian Smith arrived from Nassau earlier in the day and is already waiting for us at the Castle. Bruce Dickinson, who miraculously has not just returned from a fencing tournament, is already in Germany and has driven direct to the Castle alone. The air is rife with the sound of voices barking out the greetings.

"DAVEE!"

"Nicko!"

"STEEVE!"

"Nicko!"

"Rangi!"

"MICKEE!"

"Steve!"

"Davey!"

"Nicko!"

We're all still shouting at each other as we climb aboard the mini-bus for the two-hour drive from the airport to the Castle. There's a blizzard raging outside. The sky is black but the ground is white-white-white as far as the eye can see. The beers go round the back of the van and the journey is considerably shortened.

"Have you heard the new album yet?" Steve asks me somewhere along the road. I grin and nod my head. "I've had a tape for the last couple of days and I haven't stopped playing it," I tell him. "Well?" he grins. "Well, that's it, isn't it, you've done it," I say, "The ultimate Iron Maiden album! How on Earth are you going to follow it up?" He looks at me and smiles. "I'm glad you feel like that about it. Everyone that's heard it so far has said something like that. We've never quite managed to pull anything off like this before. For me, it's like the enormous leap we suddenly made from our first two albums to releasing 'Number Of The Beast' – very much a step forward, a step up," Steve says, then pauses. "How we're ever going to be able to follow it up, though..." He puffs out his cheeks and blows. "Fucked if I know!" he laughs. "We'll just have to wait and see, won't we..."

We sit there quietly for a moment thinking it over. In the distance, perched upon a clump of dark, snow-capped hills – where else? – lies the good Castle Schnellenberg, home for all of us for the next few days. With its medieval towers and creaky, winding staircase, its cavernous wings and concealed corridors, it is the ideal spot in which to unveil the new Iron Maiden album, 'Seventh Son Of A Seventh Son', in all its atmospheric splendour.

The official playback for the album – the first of some half-dozen such events to be staged around the world over the next few weeks to herald its release on April 11 – is scheduled for tomorrow night, but already the cream of Europe's media establishment is lining up for a piece of the action. Press lizards, TV barons, radio hams, photographers by the swarm, over the next few days they will all converge on the Castle like hungry bees around a honey pot. Every waking moment the band have will be spent entertaining a production line of interviewers, mikes and cameras thrust forward like swinging lights in their faces, lapping up an endless stream of quotes, jokes, anecdotes, stiff one-liners, all the general upbeat gibberish those things eventually lapse into. And it all starts tonight...

Bang on 7.00 pm we pull into the grounds of Castle Schnellenberg and park between two snow-ploughs. Inside the Castle all is warm and cosy and 19th century. I keep expecting an Igor or a Gregor or something to show up with a face like stone and a candle that never goes out in one hand and bid us: "Welcome. The master has been expecting you…" But Shaun Hutson couldn't make it, so it never happens. Although their first TV interviews are due to start at 7.30 pm, the band have only just arrived and nobody has eaten anything yet, so a hasty dinner is arranged and the schedules are unceremoniously pushed back a couple of hours.

Seated around a large round table in a private room to one side of the Castle's main dining hall, everybody – minus Adrian, who's still in his room sleeping off the effects of the long flight from Nassau – tucks into big plates of rich heavy German sustenance. To my right is yet another old mate of mine, Bruce Dickinson. We last met on New Year's Eve and Bruce was talking incessantly about the new album even then, unable to stop himself raving about it being something like "a heavy metal 'Dark Side Of The Moon'," but with a big hit single thrown in there for good measure somewhere along the line. "Or at least as close as we're ever likely to come to it!" he thundered with laughter, his eyes staring past my shoulder.

We met again a few days prior to the trip to Germany. He was still talking about the album. "If 'Number Of The Beast' brought heavy metal properly into the 1980s, which I actually believe it did, then with 'Seventh Son Of A Seventh Son' I think we've shown the way for heavy metal in the 1990s. It sounds like such a boastful thing to say, I know, but that's how it hits me when I listen to it. I hear new stuff on there I haven't heard before every time I play it. I'm completely hooked on the whole bloody thing! Perhaps I need help, what do you think?"

Bruce repeats the question to me over dinner at the Castle. I've had time to think about it since we last met, and of course I've had a tape of the album to help me make up my mind. And what I think is this: this is it, kiddos! The One! 100 per cent Diamond Maiden! Treasure from the deep nobody expected to find. A 'concept' album in the most direct sense – meaning, it has a beginning, a middle and an end, just like all the best stories – 'Seventh Son…' is also, surprisingly, the most plausible feat of magic the band have ever worked inside a recording studio. Eight highly stylised original numbers, all bright and polished enough to stand out on their own, worlds within worlds unto themselves, separate and unique, yet bound quite stealthily together by the continually overlapping layers of the strange and beguiling story that gradually unravels.

Which is? Well, put simply, the Seventh Son of a Seventh Son of the title to our story is born into the world endowed – as befitting his occult status – with certain extraterrestrial powers – the power to heal the sick and to foretell the future being prominent amongst his gifts (though the one thing he cannot foresee is his own horrific demise).

"It's the grandest and most fascinating tale of all," says Bruce at one point. "The classic story of Good versus Evil, only with no guarantees whatsoever that it's the good guys who eventually come through. Nothing and nobody comes out of his story unscathed! Which is everyone's story, really, isn't it? None of us gets through our lives smelling of roses everywhere we go; everything is a constant battle to try and stay sane, to cut through all the bullshit that gets shoved our way. To find some sort of meaning, some pattern. At the same time, there's more to it than that. It's a quite mythical tale, the saga of the Seventh Son of the Seventh Son, and in trying to tell it we really allowed our imaginations to run free."

"We've always been at our best, I think, when we've told a story of some kind through the lyrics to our songs," Steve points out. "'Rime Of The Ancient Mariner', 'Stranger In A Strange Land', 'Number Of The Beast'... all of our best stuff has always told a clear story, really. It's one of the things we're really good at, and it's working in a way that is very inspiring for us. Deciding to extend this particular story into an album came naturally. It didn't make the actual writing any easier though, knowing what the basic outline was; in fact, I probably took longer over the writing I've done on this album than any I've done before. But the stuff we all started coming up with, once we'd agreed that we were definitely going for a fully-fledged 'concept' album, really startled me. It was so much better than anything we'd done in ages, and we all started to get really excited about what we might be able to do with it all once we got inside the studio with Martin Birch, our producer."

Side One opens with the same melancholy chords that later close Side Two: strummed carelessly on an acoustic guitar by Adrian Smith as Bruce Dickinson wails balefully over the intro: "Seven deadly sins / Seven ways to win / Seven holy paths to hell / And your trip begins...'

And then the electric guitars arrive like a siren followed by an explosion, the whole shebang going off like a powder keg, the noise of synthesisers pounding like a strobe in the background, the drums finally raining down in strong, lightning fast blows. The track is 'Moonchild' and it is Maiden at their bones-into-dust best: heightened, exotic rhythms coiled like a snake over everything, the guitars and the drums spinning the world just a little too fast, the voice savage and brutal... I'm not going to sprint through a track-by-track read-out here; that job has already been admirably taken care of elsewhere in this issue by my very old mate, Chris Welch. However, special mention must be made for tracks like the Steve Harris compositions, 'Infinite Dreams' and the title track itself: two of the most awesome moments on a collection bristling with grandeur.

A comment on the first single from the album, 'Can I Play With Madness?', is perhaps appropriate, too. Yes, it is by far the most commercial thing Maiden have recorded since… oh, since 'Run To The Hills', at least. And I'm glad to see it happen. The band have always been finicky about singles. Brushing playfully with commercialism has never been what you would call a hot pursuit of theirs. And now this. Straight out of left field comes an Iron Maiden song with the legs to carry it into the Top Three! Who would've believed it?!

Interestingly, five out of the eight numbers written for 'Seventh Son…' are collaborative efforts. This has reversed the trend for group members to work alone that began around the time of 1983's 'Piece Of Mind' album, and reached its apotheosis with the band's last album in 1986, 'Somewhere In Time', which featured three tracks written by Adrian alone, four by Steve alone, and just one, 'Deja-Vu', co-written by Steve and Dave. On 'Seventh Son…' two of the tracks are credited to Smith/Dickinson/ Harris ('Can I Play With Madness?' and 'The Evil That Men Do'); one to Smith/ Dickinson ('Moonchild'); one to Murray/Harris ('The Prophesy'); one to Harris/ Dickinson ('Only The Good Die Young'); leaving just three credited to Steve Harris alone ('Infinite Dreams', 'Seventh Son…' and 'The Clairvoyant').

Somehow, the spreading of responsibility for the writing has given the album an injection of vigour, of spirit and excitement usually reserved for the band's more inspired live performances. "We didn't consciously decide we must all start writing together more," says Steve Harris, as the dinner things are being trawled away and the first of several TV crews leave the dining room to return upstairs and set up their lights and cameras in time for the first interviews to begin in 15 minutes. "It just worked out like that this time. We probably spent more time checking up on each other to see what everybody else was up to, just to make sure the story fitted properly and went somewhere. As a result, it was only natural that we should end up writing together more this time than we have done perhaps on the last couple of studio albums. But these things happen of their own accord, it's no good trying to force something to work. At the end of the day it doesn't really matter who writes the songs, as long as they're good. That's what it's all about. Keeping the ideas flowing; not writing together because we think we should, but doing it when we get real pleasure out of wanting to create a new number together."

The other mild innovation this time around has been the introduction of synthesisers and keyboards to the quintessential sheet-metal Maiden sound; as evinced best on the new album on tracks like 'Moonchild' and the title track itself. My memory clouds over, but didn't someone from Maiden once say… "That there would never be any keyboards on an Iron Maiden album?" Bruce raises an eyebrow. "Yes, it was probably me, drunk out of my mind in some foreign bar somewhere," he chortles. "Which just goes to prove you should never ever say never to anything! But I was probably a foolish young man back whenever it was that was said. I never knew we'd be able to do this with them."

The lyrics are uncompromisingly forceful on the new album. Maiden are famous, of course, for not mincing their words, and in the past they have suffered the same slings and arrows from right wing fundamentalist groups in the US, like the Moral Majority and the PMRC, that have continued to dog the careers of acts like Ozzy Osbourne, Metallica, the Beastie Boys… you know the names. Particularly hard to shake was the furore that surrounded the band's 1982 Beast On The Road tour of America. With scattered lines littered throughout the new material like, "Don't you dare to save your son / Kill him now and save the young ones / Be the mother of a birth strangled babe / Be the Devil's own / Lucifer's my name..." for example, from 'Moonchild', are the band concerned at all at the predictable reaction such material, pulled out of context as I just did, might receive from the right wing bimbos waiting for them in America with their rolling pins in their hands and their disgusting petitions and vulgar, two-bit pamphlets on full Church day parade? "You mean from people like Mr Jimmy 'Forgive Me For

I Have Sinned' Swaggart?" sneers Bruce. "The man who wrote a book called *Music As Pornography* with a picture of Steve on the cover and has just been discovered crawling around a motel room with a prostitute and then goes on national television to cry about it? You want to know if we're worried about what people like that will have to say about the lyrics on our new album? Listen, the day those people stop having a go at us is the day I'll start getting worried. It rots the brain to even think about the twisted minds of people like that for too long. So we don't. We never give it a thought."

"You can't allow yourself to descend to their level," says Steve. "It's no good getting upset about these fanatics like Swaggart and the PMRC, that's the reaction they want to get out of you. I say let 'em pull any line they like out of any of the songs from any of our albums and twist it around until it suits them, I don't care. I'm not going to let it interfere with writing exactly what I want to. Besides, whatever we write, they'll always find something to pick up on and go mad about. So I just try to completely ignore anything they might have to say about us. It's always the same old clichéd Devil-worshipping thing, too! You'd think they'd have thought of something new by now..."

Indeed, the mention of 'Devil worshipping', however, inevitably leads to the subject of those bands that still trade on their image under such facile banners. "Mentioning no names, but this whole Thrash and Death Metal thing really leaves me cold," says Steve. "Apart from Metallica, who have done some good stuff, most of the other bands completely pass me by. They've got nothing going for them that I look for in a band. For a start, most of them couldn't write a decent melody line – as in write a real song – if their lives depended on it! I often wonder if it's got something to do with the fact that most of these bands don't seem to have very good singers, not in the traditional heavy metal sense of really good singers, anyway. You know, like they can only sing in one really gruff style. I had a similar problem in the early days of Maiden with Paul Di'Anno singing in the band. His singing voice simply wasn't versatile enough, and because of that I could only write songs in the one style he was able to sing them in. With a singer like Bruce in the band, of course, the whole thing changes because there's probably nothing that Bruce couldn't sing if he put his mind to it, which enables me to write songs in any key, any style, any time, any rhythm that I want to because I know Bruce will always be able to handle it."

Nevertheless, bands like Metallica, Anthrax and Slayer, for example, have all been making impressive inroads into the international scene these past two years. How aware were Maiden when they went into the studio to record 'Seventh Son…' that there were now newer, younger bands out there snapping at their heels? "Not in the least bit," says Steve. "We never consider what any other band, no matter who, are doing when we go to work on a new Maiden album. I'm not interested in what everyone else is doing. I'm too into what we're doing ourselves to think any further than that. You say there are all these bands out there waiting to steal our thunder, but I don't feel like that at all. Good luck to whoever comes along next, that's what I say. There are plenty of good new bands around who I do like, and I follow them all, but that's as far as it goes. I don't feel like there's anybody about to overtake us."

The following afternoon at Castle Schnellenberg finds the band trooping from room to room, from interviewer to interviewer, while outside half-a-dozen different TV crews zigzag through the snow in search of the ideal location shot, haggling with the roving press photographers for exclusive rights to the choicest spots they can weigh-up through their viewfinders. Along one wall in the basement bierkeller of the Castle sit a line of journos listening to Walkmans, all with the new Maiden album blasting out of them. Nobody gets to talk to the band until they've heard the album at least once. Every 20 minutes or so another journo will get a tap on the shoulder and be lead nervously away to one of the distant wings of the Castle where one or more of the band will carry out their duties as gentlemen hosts.

By evening another 100 or so media faces have arrived in coaches. The playback, at 8.00 pm, is a huge success, the room erupting into applause at the death of Side Two, the rest of the evening lost in a ferocious feast of back-slapping and yaw-hawing as the wine goes down and the room starts to get loose, everyone relieved as much as anything that the whole new Maiden deal is finally, officially, off the ground and running.

3.00 am and the last guests have long since called it a night and fled the Castle. The last to leave are Steve, myself, Maiden's indestructible manager, Rod Smallwood, and the band's London PR, Roland Hyams. Steve invites us to desecrate the mini-bar in his room, and so, not to be impolite, we agree. Once up there and glasses filled, the talk turns to Steve and the band's forthcoming headline appearance at this year's Castle Donington festival. "One thing we're going to make absolutely sure of," says Steve, "is that on the day every band that plays sounds good – and loud! The big criticism of

Donington for the last couple of years, it seems, has been that no-one except the band headlining ever sounds any good. Well, all that's going to change when we play there. It's going to be our only British date this year and we want to make it the best Donington ever!"

The band's next world tour, already christened the Seventh Tour Of A Seventh Tour, is due to kick-off in Calgary, Canada, in May, and run continuously for the next seven months through 24 different countries, playing to more than two million people along the way. What is it about playing live that makes Steve Harris and Iron Maiden want to do it for up to seven months solid without a break? "Playing live is ultimately what it's all about for a band like us," he says. "The albums are the most important things we do with our music. But once it's written and recorded the real test comes with taking it out live to the Maiden fans and finding out what they've got to say about it all. The strength of the band, the way we've evolved musically, has all come through spending so much time on the road together. We've always been a live band first and foremost. So touring is like the bedrock of everything this band stands for. Without it, our music wouldn't be the way it is. We'll never do another tour as long as the one we did when we released 'Powerslave', though. That went on for eleven-and-a-half months! We were probably lucky to come out of that in one piece. It would have finished off some bands I know.

"And at the end of every tour I'm always glad to be able to go home to my wife and family and forget all about Iron Maiden for a while. But the only reason I can be so relaxed about it then is because I know I'll be back out on the road at such a time as me and the band are ready to go out again. It would be terrible if I didn't know when next I was playing. That's what would really make me go off my head."

Steve's mini-bar went dry about the same time the sun was just starting to creep through his window. Shakily, a bit full of beer and wine and so on, a lot full of it in fact, I get to my feet and point myself in the direction of the door.

"I have to leave now," I tell everybody.

"You're drunk!" cries Rod. "Look at you, you're a bloody disgrace! Go on, bugger off to bed!"

I think it was the seventh sup of the seventh drink that finally did me in. That, or the seven I had after, I don't recall.

Footnote: Nicko McBrain would like to take this opportunity to apologise to the staff and management of the Castle Schnellenberg for breaking the toilet seat in his room. And no, I don't know how he managed to break the toilet seat in his room. But then, according to Nicko, neither does he.

First published in Kerrang! No.183, April 16, 1988

Despite having known and interviewed him for many years, including long before he became nauseatingly world-famous, I still don't really know what I make of Jon Bon Jovi. Happy to play the big giggly kid just thrilled to be here in the days before he made it, once his career took off like a rocket he became so long-faced and serious you wondered what it was he was actually in this for – apart from the money, which was spectacular, of course.

For a pretty-boy, he always seemed so old for his age; so consumed by his own crippling self-absorption that he couldn't even bear to poke fun at himself. Ironically, of course, this has only made him an even bigger figure of fun to the mainstream media than he might have been had he simply owned up to his status as a pop pin-up and forgotten all about his not-so secret dreams of being the new Bruce Springsteen. But he just doesn't seem to have been able to help himself, looking down his nose with contempt at those that treat him like a pop star, while bristling at the very suggestion that he might have anything to do with hairy-assed heavy metal. No, to borrow a phrase, whatever you think Jon is, that's what he thinks he's not.

Maybe that's the tragedy of being such a good-looking and successful rock star: other guys simply don't take you as seriously as they do the singers who look more like Lemmy. Whatever it is, it's hard for the rest of us to really care. When someone as blessed as Jon comes along – dripping chicks, money, fame, even a certain amount of talent – it's almost impossible to feel sympathy for any so-called 'problems' they might genuinely be having. And yet to meet Jon, especially around the time the following interview took place, four years after the chart-molesting 'Slippery When Wet' album first set him on the road to megadom, was to meet a man who clearly felt he was walking around with the weight of the world bearing down on his tanned and gym-toned shoulders. You actually felt sorry for him. Then you went home to your one-bedroom apartment and he went home to his million-dollar mansion…

Jon Bon Jovi, New York, July 1990

It's July and hotter than hell's kitchen in New York City. The heat clings to everything like a second skin; the buildings, the sidewalks, the people. Eyes rolling like hard-boiled eggs in saucepan faces blurred by sweat and car fumes. Jon Bon Jovi and I are perched on the veranda of his manager's second floor suite of offices on Central Park South in Manhattan, elbows resting on the railings, gazing out at the piss-coloured taxi cabs, the hawk-faced pretzel pedlars, the blank-eyed bums and the power-dressed office shirkers pretending to ignore them.

As we look out, Jon tells me this is the very spot he and the rest of Bon Jovi first met with Doc McGhee, their powerful and influential manager, to plot the seeds of a success story that now spans more than 25 million albums and has generated maybe 10 times as many millions of dollars.

"Back then we didn't have the price of a cup of coffee between us," he says, running a restless hand through his long, rust-coloured hair. "That was seven years ago. You ask me has the success changed me since then, I say, sure, man. It changes everybody. Deep down I still have all the energy and enthusiasm I ever had as a kid. But on the outside I'm a lot more cynical these days. A lot more."

Indeed, Jon does looks remarkably cool and unbothered for someone whose new single is rapidly climbing the US charts in a Top 10-bound trajectory, and looks almost certain to do the same here in Britain. The track is 'Blaze Of Glory' – the Bon Jovi-penned theme tune to the upcoming *Young Guns II* movie, in which Jon makes his debut appearance on celluloid as one of the good-looking young guns who gets it (and good) early on in the story. An album – full title: 'Blaze Of Glory: Music From And Inspired By The Movie Young Guns II Written And Performed By Jon Bon Jovi' – follows in the UK on August 6 and features such famous sidekicks as Jeff Beck (the lead on 'Blaze Of Glory'), Elton John (singing harmonies and banging the ivories on 'Dyin' Ain't Much Of A Livin'') and Little Richard (doing much the same on 'You Really Got Me').

In fact, the star of our story looks positively down-in-the-mouth today. Not depressed exactly. Just somewhere else, deep within his own thoughts. He says he's happy enough to do the interview and goes as far as to congratulate *Kerrang!* on reaching the ripe old age of 300. "Three hundred, huh?" he chews his lip. "Well, you don't look it!" he jokes. But it's clear his mind is on other things, other dates, other times, other places.

The first time Bon Jovi received any attention in *Kerrang!* was in 1984 when a positively glowing review of the first 'Bon Jovi' album was ungainly matched by an absolute trashing of one of their early shows in the live reviews section. "I remember it very well," says Jon with a crooked jester's smile. "Bon Jerk-off I think the guy called us. It's funny cos I can't really remember what the album review said. I just remember it was great. It's funny how you always remember the bad things people say about you and very seldom any of the good."

The Happy Birthdays over we get down to business. There's a lot I want to ask him. There's a lot he has to say right now: about his future with or without the rest of Bon Jovi. Specifically, about guitarist and long-time "best bud" Richie Sambora with whom he has reportedly fallen out. And about... oh, a lotta stuff you'll just have to wait for. Meantime, back to that ledge in New York City…

Let's start with the new single, 'Blaze Of Glory'. This is your first solo record, right? "No! I've gotta keep saying that. I don't want anyone thinking this is a solo thing. I have to restate it time and time again. This is a soundtrack. It's for a movie, and that's all it's supposed to be. I mean, I had to write it to fit a certain parameter. So I don't want anyone thinking this is a solo anything. It's not. The parameters I had to write under were so limiting, you know, I could only write songs for particular scenes that some other guy came up with."

How did it all come about? "Well, how it started was they wanted to use 'Wanted Dead Or Alive' [from the 1986 'Slippery When Wet' album] in the movie. I was told that they wrote the first *Young Guns* movie with 'Wanted…' in mind, that it was a big influence on the movie and I was really flattered. I like the first *Young Guns* movie a lot. And I always said that if I'd ever acted in a movie, it would have been in *Young Guns*."

Were you approached to be in the first movie? "No, no, not at all. But anyway, it turns out they decide they wanna feature 'Wanted…' on the soundtrack to the follow-up. Lyrically, though, it wouldn't have really worked. You know, 'On a steel horse I ride…' it just doesn't fit the movie. So I said, if you want, I'll write you something in that vein to fit this part of the movie. I knew where it was going, they told me what it was about, and I went there with a song in my hand, which was 'Blaze Of Glory'. I wrote it just by what they told me over the phone. So I look it to 'em. They liked it. And then I came home and wrote three more. So now we've got four songs, all based on what they'd told me about the movie. So they said, 'Great, let's do an album!'."

But isn't it true that you were looking for some form of solo expression outside of the band, anyway? "I honest to God had no intention whatsoever of doing a solo venture, because to me Bon Jovi records are my solo albums. There's not any songs really that I adamantly didn't want on any of the Bon Jovi records. If I didn't want something, it wasn't there. I mean, my interpretation of what was going to happen to us as we had these discussions in January, was that we were gonna go home and Richie was going to go do his solo record. It was gonna be Richie Sambora & Friends. It was gonna be all his friends playing cover songs, playing some of his songs, playing some things that me and him do together. Meantime, Dave [Bryan] was gonna do a New Age record and I was gonna mix the Bon Jovi live album. And that was what the year was gonna be. That was the plan anyway.

"But come February when the tour was ending, the one thing in my mind was, if something comes up that you don't do every day of your life, do it this time. For the first time when you say you're going to do something, go out and fucking do it! If you finally want to go somewhere where there isn't an arena, then go there, you know? Like, I always say I wanna go to Utah and ride motorcycles and I never fuckin' do. So when Emilio [Estevez, one of the stars of *Young Guns II* and a long-time pal of the singer's] was so adamant about me coming out there, I said, 'Fuck it, I'm gonna get on an aeroplane, without the band, without my road manager, without my wife, all by myself and go and do this!'. That was a big step for me, to go and do something by myself. It's a big deal for me to come to New York City an hour-and-a-half from my house without picking up my dad on the way and saying, 'Hey, you wanna take a ride?' I'm not used to doing anything by myself. I just don't do it."

So are you pleased with the results? "I'm very excited by the album. By playing with those guys. Even if I didn't play with those guys. I was real excited to just get up, cos I wanted to get up, write 10 songs for an album, go produce it and have people be happy with it. When I did it, I was excited. When the single came out here I was waiting with bated breath to see what would happen. Just like I always am before I release a record. But now that it's out, it's beyond me. So now there's a sigh of relief and what happens, happens."

You've got a lot of big names on this album with you - Elton John, Jeff

Beck, etc. How was it they ended up on the record, and why them exactly? "Why them? It was the idea that... Well, I've always loved Beck's playing and I loved his sound. So the idea was, who would you get to play on 'Blaze Of Glory'? It wasn't a matter of four songs or 10 songs, it was one song. My first choice of guitar player was Jeff Beck. I mean, if you're shooting for something you may as well aim for the sky, you know?"

You had already met before, hadn't you? "Yeah, he's been to some shows. He'd been to Wembley, he'd been to Hammersmith, he's been to see us before, yeah. I thought he was a nice enough guy, so what the hell, give him a call and see what he says. He said yes so quickly and hung up the phone, that I would have sworn he wasn't coming. He was like, 'I'd love to do it, man. Have your manager call my manager. It sounds like a great idea. And, er, I gotta go!' I was like, yeah, sure, man. We've all heard the rumours about what he's like, you know. Well, the fucker not only flew out to LA to do it, but he was in the studio in the morning before I was and wouldn't leave until I physically said, 'I'm not gonna do this anymore, go home!' I mean, he worked his ass off! He dispelled all the rumours about him, he was a consummate professional."

What's Beck like as a person, though? "Jeff is a little boy. He loves to play. He wants to go to the movies. We went to see *Total Recall* together [the new Arnold Schwarzenegger flick]. He loves to drive around in this car. He wants to go out to dinner and goof off. I mean, he loves to go play around, but when it came time to work, he was right there on the money every time."

Were you nervous working with someone like that? "No, you see because though I like Jeff Beck, I didn't buy his records when I was a kid. He was a great sounding guitar player, but for me it was always Rod Stewart. I was a singer, I played guitar to write songs. I never grew up wanting to be Jeff, I wanted to grow up and be Rod Stewart."

What about Elton John? What was working with him like? "Ah... again, there's a guy that's a songwriter, consummate songwriter and performer, and Elton is a great guy as well. Fortunately I got a feeling meeting Elton – I think the first time was when he came to see us – I got a feeling meeting Elton that he was one of the guys. He was a real sweetheart who just loves playing piano. Then I played with him at Madison Square Garden and I felt that I had a friend in Elton. When he was in Los Angeles at that time I thought that he would be perfect. It wasn't name value so much as the fact that he was perfect for the part. Roy Bittan was booked, but Bruce [Springsteen] wouldn't let him do it."

Why, because it was you? "I don't think so. I think because he's co-producing his album."

It wasn't a bit of New Jersey boy rivalry? "If Bruce Springsteen is afraid of me then I'm flattered. But I doubt that that is the case. I think that it's just purely that Roy's co-producing the Springsteen album and he couldn't do it. But with Elton being there, he said he'd love to do it. So I had him come over and one song in particular that I wrote on piano really lent itself to Elton: 'Dyin' Ain't Much Of A Livin''. To me it sounds like an Elton John song. To me it was like he's the only guy who can play this song. Then in the control room he started to sing the harmony. All along I was dying to get him to sing the harmony and he started doing it, so there was my in. I went, 'Hey, why don't you sing it?'. So we did it live and the vocal was right there."

Are you an Elton John fan? "Like, the biggest! When he was on the cover of *Time* magazine in '74 or '75, I remember in grammar school as a class project I made a red, white and blue guitar and wrote 'Elton' on it. I had the 'Caribou' album and 'Goodbye Yellow Brick Road'. That whole era, he was the biggest to me, I listened to him religiously. So to have him play on it was real exciting. Then in an old art deco '50s-ish diner right next to the studio – this was prior to Jeff flying in – we said, 'Who else can we get?', just joking around. Like, what legends are there left in this business? And we though, Keith Richards! Let's get Keith Richards!

"The one thing about Keith was, everyone in the room played guitar, everyone, me. Aldo [Nova], and everyone, fought to play on the record. Finally I said to Danny Kortchmar [Jon's co-producer], 'Who's record is this, man? It's mine, I'm playing the parts. It's like everyone wanted to play on this record. Another time, I said, 'Let's get Little Richard to play this song' and everyone dropped their cheeseburgers! Like, 'You know Little Richard?' I said, 'Yeah, I do, he played with us on the last tour'. So I called him up and he came down and it was fucking great cos it was the one thing I could do. Jeff Beck knows the Stones, the Beatles, he's played with everybody. But even he asked me to introduce him to Little Richard, so I did. I asked him to introduce me to Rod Stewart and he did that.

"So I call Richard and he came down and Jeff was so excited and nervous. When Richard walked into the control room – and I know this cos I've done it myself, you feel foolish afterward – but Jeff couldn't help himself and when Richard walked into the control room his fingers started playing 'Lucille'. Richard put his hand out to me and Jeff jumps out of his seat and gives him his hand and says, 'It's so nice to meet you, you're the reason I got into this business', and asks him for his autograph. You have to slap yourself once in a while and say my life is so lucky that I get to be in the company of people like this. To watch those things happen is just a thrill."

It's always been one of the biggest buzzes for you, hasn't it, people such as Jimmy Page getting up onstage with you? "I've been so lucky with that, it's been so much fun."

What happened to the Keith Richards idea? "Well, with five guitar players already we decided to just steal his licks instead!" He laughs. Have you ever met him, though? "Real briefly, at an album launch party for him in Los Angeles."

The $64,000 question, though, is whether there is going to be another Bon Jovi album? "I hope so."

But you don't know so? "I don't know so and I can publicly say it, to you, because the truth is *Kerrang!* started this whole fucking fiasco. We were in Mexico, at the end of the last tour, with nothing but wonderful things happening. We were finishing the tour doing stadiums, which is just how we wanted it to end, and we were feeling real good. Then *Kerrang!* says Tico [Torres] is leaving the band [America Calling column, issue 274]. Suddenly we got drummer tapes and pictures and everything coming in. It was like, 'Hey, Tico, are you quitting the band?' He was like, 'First I've heard of it. man!' That was amazing, but that's when it started. But we pushed it away, I threw the magazine out the window. I was upset cos I knew it wasn't true. I think the quotes were like the drummer's quitting and the band is breaking up. I thought, what the fuck's this?

"So then the English papers, I think it was *The Sun*. or one of those gossip rags, got hold of it. The headline ran 'All Ovi For Bon Jovi'. It said that Sambora was out and there were money problems, that he wasn't happy with his cut and he was leaving for Cher and all this shit. I'm reading it out of the fax thinking what is all this shit? Then phone-calls start coming in, people calling me saying they want the gig. I tell you, four months later I'm not entertained by it any more. It's got to this point because the five of us haven't been in the same room together since before the last show and it's added fuel to the fire. So now all of us are believing there are problems. I can't tell you what the problems are about, but we think we've got problems."

Jonathan King asked me when we were in Moscow last year whether you and Richie were having problems. He said in the early days you were never apart. Now it's like one walks in the room and the other walks out. Have you grown apart? "In the state of things at this time, yeah. Right now, in July 1990, yeah. Things are not happy in the Bon Jovi camp, that's for sure, they're not happy at all. I don't want the band to break up. cos the five of us… It's like, you can only play your first time at Donington once. Your first headline show in London [at the Dominion, in 1985]. Those gigs were what made us. We were spitting in the eye of the fire and we didn't give a fuck about anyone. It was us and we were gonna make it. Regardless of money and stadiums, or who I played with, if that was the band tomorrow and Elton was my new keyboard player, it would never be the same. All of that would be lost and I don't want that to happen. I definitely don't want that to happen. I want to keep it together cos these are the guys who seven years ago were here when we sat on this ledge for the first time, when we didn't have enough money for a pretzel across the street and no-one knew whether Bon Jovi was jeans or what the fuck it was. We had to fight for everything we got and we had to fight even on the 'New Jersey' album to prove that we were gonna be around. It's a rewarding feeling to know that the band as a unit did this. I could play with better musicians, or different musicians, and they could play with a better songwriter and singer, but it wouldn't be the same – ever."

Do you think that everyone has to get their solo albums out of their system first? "I don't know, you'd have to ask them. Richie was always, 'Oh, I'm gonna do it', to the point where things weren't happening for him and he joined this thing. Everyone gives Rich a lot of attention-and well-deserved it is, he's a fine musician and a fine singer – but I don't think it's fair to harp on about him all the time because it was us and the band. For the first two albums, he never wrote any of the singles. Dave Bryan co-wrote the singles. It was Dave and I who did it. Richie came in on the third album when he had begun to understand the way I like to write. It wasn't until the third album so it's not fair for everyone to pick on him because it's… the press I mean, it's not fair."

It's like the Jagger/Richards thing, though, isn't it? You and Rich always were the stars of the show. "It's so stereotypical of what's supposed to be, though: John Lennon and Paul McCartney, it's the same tiling."

With respect, though, if the drummer leaves the band, it's not the same story. But when the lead guitarist leaves, that's news. "Yeah, you're right. I don't know how much I like that or dislike that but it's true. I missed him very much when Little Steven left Bruce, it just wasn't the same anymore. I don't want this band to break up. But there aren't any plans to make a record at the moment."

Where does that leave your career at this point? "Promoting the 'Young Guns' record first and foremost. Promoting the 'Young Guns' record as a soundtrack for a movie, and then I'm going to go and produce other things and get them out. I just produced Hall & Oates' next single. I wrote that with a couple of other guys."

Sooner or later, though, you're going to want to get back on the road, right? "I went to see Alec [Jon Such] and he said to me, 'The Al that was out there in South America and Mexico isn't the guy that you know now'. I didn't think he was being any weirder than usual. But he says, 'I was so burned-out I couldn't take it any more, but you wanted to keep going so we had to keep going'. I didn't know what to say. I felt great this tour so I kept pushing and pushing, I didn't give a shit. I'd have stayed out there forever. I love touring but I can turn it off, when I'm done touring I'm done. I don't have any desire to go down the Stone Pony [a club in the Asbury Park area of New Jersey] on a Sunday night and play a song. I don't have any desire to do that at all.

"I'm really excited by the avenue that's opened up, though, doing this soundtrack. And I'm blown away that Daryl Hall and John Oates have asked me to work with them. I was even happier afterwards when they would tell people, 'He's a real producer'. I guess coming from them, that's a compliment. But Aldo [another long-time buddy] on the other hand, I've got 15 tunes with Aldo and we're gonna go into the studio in October. So that's my next project, to get Aldo out on the road. We'll see what happens. Skid Row are gonna want to do their own album next time too. I don't think I'll be writing anything with them this year. So there's a lot, you know. But in the meantime I'll be watching, I'll be checking out what's happening..."

Briefly, the acting thing in the movie when you get shot, is it like a Sam Peckinpah slow-mo bloodbath or a John Wayne trickle down the cheek?

"It's in the middle of the two. I'm in it for 30 seconds. Don't mistake this for an acting career! I was freezing my ass off in Santa Fe, New Mexico, in February, dressed the way you would dress your three-year-old kid, you know, snowsuit, gloves, feet-warmers, just freezing my ass. I was thinking, why am I out here with these idiots, you know? I was miserable, while the stars of the movie are running around in T-shirts and jeans, riding horses, moving around, running, shooting and I'm going, 'Fuck this, I'm a spoiled brat, I wanna go home!'

"They said, 'Be in the movie then' and I said, 'Great, give me something to do, I hate this!' And they did. So, for 30 seconds I escape from this jail with the writer of the movie, who was the fan who started all this off. I escape from this jail with him. We grab the deputy in the jail. The sheriff sees me and loads up his gun and I take one hit to the chest and there's blood everywhere. It's in slow motion and in close-up. And that's it. It took me longer to explain it than it did for it to happen."

Do you think there will be any teenage girls having heart attacks seeing Jon Bon Jovi being splattered like that? "Do you know what their really gonna have heart attacks over? The seven bucks it costs them to get into the movie – cos I'm in it for 30 seconds max! Nobody blink!"

Considering you're hardly in the movie, the publicists in Hollywood are certainly making a meal out of the fact that it Jon Bon Jovi in it. "Tell me about it. I mean, I don't want 'em taking advantage of our fans, making believe like this is my first big film part or anything. Like the album. I'm pissed off because first they were gonna use at least four of the songs in the movie. Then it was three. Now I'm afraid that the last cut was only two. So here's gonna be my friends and fans and family going to see a movie that I'm in for 30 seconds and I have two songs in. But they're marketing it like it was my first major film role or something."

How, in your own mind, is the soundtrack record different from a Bon Jovi record? "Musically, it's real different. If I were to do a Bon Jovi record for this film, I would look foolish and they would look foolish for hiring me. It had to be different. It had to be a little off the wall. With that in mind, that's why I did it."

What is it about the cowboy image that appeals to you, though? Is it the same as the rock and roller type of thing? "I think it's that kind of lifestyle. The truth of the matter is, like the way we wrote 'Wanted Dead Or Alive', I feel that you ride into town, you don't know where the fuck you are. You're with your 'gang', stealing money, getting what you can off any girl that'll give it to you, drinking as much of the free alcohol as you can and being gone before the law catches you – before someone wakes you from this wonderful dream and says, 'You're an asshole, you're going to jail'. Because it's not the real world I'm living in, it's a dream sequence, a big fucking wet dream."

Ratt's new album features you doing backing vocals on a track called 'Heads I Win, Tails You Lose'. It's a great track. How did you end up doing that? "Well, they asked me and I said, 'Yeah!' I was doing my record in LA at the same time as they were [and] I think that the years that have passed have helped both of us as bands to be allies. When we opened for them in '85 it was hell. Me and [singer] Stephen Pearcy definitely didn't get along. Now, I truly like Stephen a lot and I think both of our bands are very good friends. The thing is we both grew up, I think, and have seen the highs and the lows and realise that there is room enough for everyone. Both of us came down off of our high horses and realised that it's a friendly sport, you know? I like the new Ratt record, they've got some good shit in there."

Do you think that you're a nicer person than you were five years ago, before the fame and the money? "Maybe, I hope so. I think I'm a little more cynical and sceptical. I hope I am nicer, but you'd have to tell me that. Other people would have to tell me whether I am or not."

All I remember is a very energetic and excited kid. "I still think I have a lot of energy and I am excited. That's probably another reason why the band is going their own ways. We are supposed to, like human beings do, take some time off. I gotta settle down. The way I figure it is, if I was to sit with Freud or one of those guys, he'd tell me it was because I hate my wife or my mother or something. Because all I like to do is go and work. I dig making records."

Do you think that your individual fame has forced you to make a conscious decision not to turn into an asshole and to try and stay a 'human being'? "No. People will say about you what they want. I mean there's a DJ here in New York named Howard Stem who went on a rampage for about a year saying what scumbags me and my organisation are."

Why? "Because I couldn't go to his radio station the week 'Bad Medicine' came out. He literally went on a tirade for a year and it really upset me. I was a true friend of his. Then there's the good stories about how I helped a little girl across the street one day. Everyone's got their stories, you gotta deal with them. I just hope there's more good than bad."

Mike Tramp of White Lion told me that when he was having problems with his voice, he got you on the line straightaway trying to help him. That's unusual in this business, isn't it? Something for nothing? "Sure. I guess it is. But I just don't get it. To me, when I was in a young band all I wanted was for the Scorpions – or whoever we were playing with – to say, 'I dug this band'. No one ever said that. As a headliner now I look down on my opening bands as a part of my organisation. With Cinderella, every night we would bring them out on stage with us at the end, every night. What's great is that now Cinderella are doing that with their support bands, Winger and the Bullet Boys. Every night they do a jam. I had something to do with that. Tommy [Keifer] is a great guy, he has no ego."

Are you disappointed with the Skid Row situation, where Sebastian Bach – who bad-mouthed you from the stage while supporting Bon Jovi – doesn't appear to appreciate what you've done? "I guess he doesn't. But I can punch the bastard in the face and be very happy I did it."

Does that kind of thing make you less inclined, though, to be so charitable to be your support bands? "No, definitely not, that would never happen. One thing that I heard someone say, I think it was Billy Squier, was, 'If you're ever afraid of your support band then you don't deserve to headline'. So I would give my support band anything to help them. It only makes the show better for the people who come to see us. I don't give a shit about the ego involved. All I expect is, like, if this is my house then treat it nicely, don't spit in the house, you know? That's all I would ask of anyone. If you don't like us then fine, go about your business but don't ever slag it because that's why you're here.

"Fortunately for us, we don't need a support band – it's like whoever we want to put on our bill. When you're the one selling all the tickets then who gives a shit? Then you're doing it because they are your friends. The Skids are wonderful guys though. I just spent a week's vacation with [guitarists] Snake and Rachel. I still love them very much – and Sebastian's probably a good kid too. I don't spend enough time with him to find out. It's tough for him to grow out of my shadow. I mean every fuckin' interview they were saying 'Jon did this for you, Jon did that'. I'm sure he got sick of it, like 'Fuck Jon!'. I understand that."

So after two of the most successful rock albums of the '80s – 'Slippery When Wet' and 'New Jersey' – what comes next? What are you actually going to do? "I don't think I can write 'Livin' On A Prayer' again. I just think that it is old. We did it. I think that our public is more intelligent than to expect that. I think that our organisation is more intelligent than that. It wouldn't be fair to us or our audience to do the same thing. I think that the songs on 'New Jersey', like 'Wild Is The Wind', which were never released as singles, are bridging the gap to where we're going."

Which is where? "Just to do something different. I see big bands on MTV now with their new albums and it just looks and sounds the same. That's great and all but fuck, I can't do it again. It's just not right."

I was reading someone who said that arena rock has become 'the professional wrestling of the '80s': just going through the moves, the formula, knowing what gets the crowd crazy, and that's it. "I agree with that. I figured that out. I don't think that that's the way we're going, that's for sure. From what I hear of what Richie's doing and judging by this soundtrack that I just spat out, that's not where we're going."

Would you risk your commercial impact to diversify artistically? "Yeah, yeah. But defending Bon Jovi albums, I never in a million years thought: 'This is a commercial album therefore it's gonna sell a lot of records'. I didn't set out to do that on 'New Jersey'. With 'Slippery...' who knew? We had no fuckin' idea. And definitely not with 'New Jersey', no way. With this soundtrack it's the same deal. I set out to write 10 songs. I hope you like them, end of story."

Is there one person of whom you could say 'That's the nicest superstar I ever met'? "When I was a gofer at the Powerstation studio Mick Jagger was very nice to me. The second time he came in he remembered me enough to say, 'You keeping up those demos? You keep on it'. I never forgot that. Maybe that's a part of the reason I'm here today. I mean, that was a buzz cos I was just a shit-head little gofer with a tape. It was very nice of him, you know. You don't forget. The Scorpions were also very good to us on our first tour. .38 Special were real good to us on the 'Slippery...' tour. They were legitimately nice guys. Southside Johnny has always been a great guy. 10 years ago Johnny let me open for him and he's still a great guy."

I hear that you met Prince. I'm intrigued by the idea of you and Prince working together. "I'm intrigued, too! Prince and I met at Tramp [club in London] one night. We chatted over a bottle of wine – seeing Prince drunk is great."

I didn't know he drank. "He did that night! He was a real sweetheart, he was great, he was funny. He was real candid. He came to see us in Minnesota and invited us back to his place after and we all went, it was a lotta fun."

What's his Paisley Park place like? "Oh, it's ridiculous, amazing – a $10 million recording studio. I'd like that. I think that he is a genius lyrically, and somewhat musically. 'Sign Of The Times' is a real good indication of that. I would like to do that. I would like to write a 'Sign Of The Times'. I'm intrigued by guys like him. It's something different. I'd like to be responsible for going 'left'."

Have you discussed this with him? "Yeah."

Why does he want to work with you? "Good point, I don't know. I couldn't honestly give you an answer, so it's not fair to guess. He told us he liked our music. He came to our show, right?"

Did he get up onstage and jam? "Nah, he chickened out! Well, it's a whole different vibe than his kinda thing. We had rehearsed a version of 'All Along The Watchtower' at the soundcheck, but he backed out. We were ready to do it, but between the encores he said he didn't want to do it. But later that night he had an all night jam session at his studio with us and Living Colour.

"But the idea behind working with Prince is to do something different. We have a couple of tracks – we never save songs usually, I throw them away – from the last album where you'd never guess it was us. One song is called 'Let's Make It Baby' and it's just about fucking. Just a nasty Prince-style fucking-song! The other one is called 'Diamond Ring', that's about what a wedding ring can do to you. It's like that song 'Fever' by Peggy Lee or something like that. It's just slinky and quiet and spooky. It doesn't have a fully fledged chorus and it's real different for us. With that in mind, that's where we need to go. That's where we want to go. Somewhere just a little left of where we've been before. It might fail miserably, but at this point there's no timetable and there's no parameters which we have to keep in. So we can make an album and if it sucks then we can throw that album in the garbage and write another one. For the first time we have my studio, which is finished now. It's a full 24-track studio. So nobody has to hear it if… it won't get stolen and sold as bootleg demos."

I was talking to somebody about how bands around today will stand in history. Who do you think will still figure in 20 years? "Prince will still be important. And Madonna, I think Madonna has been incredibly important to the 1980s, musically. She was a little disco queen who lost the baby-fat and became an icon, an '80s version of Marilyn Monroe."

What about Bruce Springsteen? "I wanna hear Bruce's new stuff as much as anyone else cos I wanna hear which way he goes. Nobody, except the people who've played on the record, who say it's real good, have heard it yet. I don't know what Bruce means to everyone else. For someone from New Jersey that's not a fair question. He was the hometown boy, so to us he was Jesus when I was in high-school... [But] I really don't know about Bruce."

Any rock artists? How about Aerosmith? "I don't know if they count or not: they've been around for 17 years as it is. But they have influenced so many bands who came up when I did. Not us particularly but Rätt and Mötley and all those kind of bands."

Guns N' Roses? "Good question. They've still yet to be proven. I don't know whether Axl is a genius or a psycho. I've heard that this song 'Civil War' is amazing and I think that lyrically if he is going after that then he has real potential of being there [in 20 years]."

How about Metallica? "I don't know any of their music except for that song 'One', which I saw on MTV. They were better than I previously thought they'd be. But I've still never heard a Metallica album and I never saw them when I played with them. It's not that I'm not interested, I respect those guys a lot. But they have given Bon Jovi a lot of stick. I actually sent them a telegram when their bass player, Cliff Burton, got killed because I knew that the bond that they have is similar to what we have and I really felt bad for them. Apparently they never received it. When we played Donington they thought we cleared the backstage area but of course the band never knew anything about it and Metallica carried a chip... Metallica have been important to heavy metal, but I don't know enough about them."

Mötley Crüe? "I don't think that the Mötleys are at all influential. I don't think that they ever had enough to say lyrically, musically or personally. Again, because of the mud they've thrown over here, it made better press for them to slag us than to slag Doc McGhee [one-time co-manager of both bon Jovi and the Crüe] cos no-one knows who Doc McGhee is. But I swear that I did not set off those lasers and pyro in Russia. If that was so important to them then maybe they didn't deserve to headline. All power to them, they just made their most popular album yet ['Dr Feelgood'], but I don't think they'll stand the test of time..."

Where do you think Bon Jovi will be in 20 years time? "I want us to be together because it's afforded me all these things. It's really been my love and I feel a loyalty to those four guys that I only feel toward my immediate family. I hope that I can keep it together, but I'll only keep it together if it's fun. I can't do it for money and I can't do it to keep the record company happy. I can't do it unless it's going to be a good time. Unless I still want to have a beer with those guys every night like we always have, then..."

He pauses, looks over the railing, thoughts elsewhere, then continues… "We always grew up hearing 'Boy, Van Halen were so dumb to split'. But none of us in the general public know what the real problem was. Same with Journey, same with Aerosmith... I'm giving you these examples so you can tell your readers that I'm as confused as anyone. I want it to stay together because it's been so good but I don't want it if it is no longer good. [Former Journey singer] Steve Perry said to me, 'You're right where I was when I walked away from it and I miss Journey'. You go like, 'Wow, I don't know if I should walk away from it'.

"I know that I'll still make records and I'll still be able to tour but who cares about the money? That's not why I'm doing it. It's only if it's going to be fun that I'll continue with those four guys. Time will tell…"

First published in Kerrang! Nos.300-301, July 28, 1990

Because they came out at about the same time, people have understandably tended to assume that the reason my name ended up in 'Get In The Ring' from the 'Use Your Illusion II' album is because Axl Rose objected to my 1991 Guns N' Roses book, The Most Dangerous Band In The World. *Not so. There were many reasons why Axl got his knickers in such a twist over me, but, essentially, the main one revolved around the following article. As we now know from the Mötley Crüe autobiography,* The Dirt, *published 11 years later, Vince Neil was so pissed off when he read Axl's rant about him in the interview with me, he decided to take Axl up on his offer and agree to duke it out with him. Of course, as we now know, Axl, whose mouth has always exceeded his trousers by some considerable distance, then decided he'd never said any such thing and went as far as telling friends and associates that I had made the whole thing up. Gee, thanks, pal.*

This, in turn, led to a series of verbal skirmishes that eventually led to me leaving Kerrang! *after the then editorship was told they would be denied all further access to the band until they had eradicated the 'problem' – i.e. me. In fairness to the lily-livered hierarchy at the magazine back then, I had not helped my cause by becoming almost as megalomaniacal as Axl himself by that point, and when I deliberately failed to turn up for the party to celebrate the magazine's 10th anniversary at the end of 1991, it was a snub that effectively signed my own death-warrant. My name was unceremoniously dropped from the editorial masthead a week later.*

For all those reasons – and several more it would take a separate book to try and explain adequately – this turned into quite a momentous article, for me and Axl both. The moral might be: don't ever bite the hand that feeds you. If only morality had been something people like me and Axl Rose cared about back then…

W. Axl Rose, Los Angeles, April 1990

W. Axl Rose is pissed off. Not, thankfully, in the grand manner to which he is sometimes accustomed: no glass smashing, no room wrecking. But he has a bee in his bonnet that he wants squashing, and so what if it's nearly midnight, why don't I come over right now and take down some kinda statement?

Well... why not? Sleep's for creeps anyway, or so they say in LA. So I hot-rod my tape-machine, scuttle down a coupla quick beers and head over to Axl's West Hollywood apartment.

Axl meets me at the door with eyebrows like thunder clouds. "I can't believe this shit I just read in *Kerrang!*" he scowls.

"Which shit are you referring to?" I ask.

"This shit," he growls, holding up a copy of *Kerrang!* dated November 4, 1989, in his hand, yanked open at a page from Jon Hotten's interview with Mötley Crüe. "The interviewer asks Vince Neil about him throwing' a punch at Izzy [Stradlin GN'R rhythm guitarist] backstage at the MTV awards last year, and Vince replies," he begins, reading aloud in a voice heavy with sarcasm: "'I just punched that dick and broke his fuckin' nose! Anybody who beats up on a woman deserves to get the shit kicked out of them. Izzy hit my wife, a year before I hit him'. Well, that's just a crock of shit! Izzy never touched that chick! If anybody tried to hit on anything, it was her trying to hit on Izzy when Vince wasn't around. Only Izzy didn't buy it. So that's what that's all about..."

He goes on, still furious. "But this bit, man, where Vince says our manager, Alan Niven, wasn't around, and that afterwards [Vince] walked straight past Izzy and me and we didn't do a thing, that's such a lot of bullshit, I can't believe that asshole said those things in private, let alone to the fuckin' press! The whole story is, Vince Neil took a pot-shot at Izzy as he was walking' offstage at the MTV awards, after jamming' with Torn Petty, because Vince's wife has got a bug up her ass about Izzy. Izzy doesn't know what's going on, Izzy doesn't fuckin' care. But anyway, Izzy's just walked off stage. He's momentarily blinded, as always happens when you come offstage, by comin' from the stage-lights straight into total darkness. Suddenly Vince pops up out of nowhere and lays one on Izzy. Tom Petty's security people jump on him and ask Alan Niven, our manager who had his arm 'round Izzy's shoulders when Vince bopped him, if he wants to press charges. He asks Izzy and Izzy says, 'Naw, it was only like being' hit by a girl' and they let him go."

He smiles mirthlessly. "Meantime, I don't know nuthin'... I'm walking' way up ahead of everybody else, and the next thing I know Vince Neil comes flying past me like his ass is on fire or something'. All I saw was a blur of cheekbones! I tell ya, man, it makes my blood boil when I read him saying' all that shit about how he kicked Izzy's ass. Turn the fuckin' tape recorder on. I wanna set the record straight..."

He carries on ranting about wanting to give Vince "a good ass-whippin' as I hurriedly set up the tape-recorder; about how he wants to "see that plastic face of his cave in when I hit him." Referring to the fact that Vince had recently reportedly had plastic surgery.

Are you serious about this, I ask him? He nods vigorously. "There's only one way out for that fucker now and that's if he apologises in public, to the press, to *Kerrang!* and its readers, and admits he was lying' when he said those things in that interview. Personally, I don't think he has the balls. But that's the gauntlet, and I'm throwing it down... Turn on the machine!"

We settle back in the only two available chairs not smothered in magazines, ashtrays, barf-balls (one squeeze and fzzzttttt, it's Johnny Fartpants a-go-go) and other assorted crap. I fix up my machine and we start to roll...

Axl scrunches up on the balcony window which affords an impressive cinema-scope view of the twinkling footlights of the billowing Hollywood hills below. It reminds me of the sort of backcloth you might see on something like 'Late Night With David Letterman' (the American TV talkshow Jonathan Woss wipped off). I wait for the band to cool out and the applause from the studio audience to die down before I hit tonight's star turn with my first question...

You don't seriously believe Vince Neil will take up the gauntlet and arrange to meet you and fight it out, do you? "I've no idea what he will do. I mean, he could wait until I'm drunk in the Troubadour one night and come in because he got a phone call saying I'm there and hit me with a beer bottle. But it's, like, I don't care. Hit me with a beer bottle, dude. Do whatever you wanna do but I'm gonna take you out... I don't care what he does. Unless he sniper-shoots me – unless he gets me like that without me knowing it – I'm taking him with me and that's about all there is to it."

What if Vince was to apologise? "That'd be radical! Personally, I don't think he has the balls. I don't think he has the balls to admit he's been lying out of his ass. That'd be great if he did though, and then I wouldn't have to be a dick from then on."

I heard that David Bowie apologised to you after the incident at your video-shoot.

(The story goes that Axl got pissed-off with the ageing soopastar after he appeared to be getting a little too well acquainted with Axl's girlfriend, Erin, during a visit last year to the set where the Gunners were making a – yet to see the light of day – video for 'It's So Easy'. The upshot, apparently, was that Axl ended up aiming a few punches Bowie's way before having him thrown off the set.)

"Bowie and I had our differences. And then we talked and went out to dinner and then went down the China Club and stuff. And when we left, I was like, 'I wanna thank you for being the first person that's ever come up to me in person and said how sorry they were about the situation and stuff. It was cool, you know? And then I open up *Rolling Stone* the next day and there's a story in there saying I've got no respect for the Godfather of Glam even though I wear make-up and all this bullshit. It's laughable.

"I was out doing a soundcheck one day when we were opening for the Rolling Stones [at the LA Coliseum in October '89] and Mick Jagger and Eric Clapton cornered me. I'm sitting on this amp and all of sudden they're both right there in front of me. And Jagger doesn't really talk a lot, right? He's just real serious about everything, and all of a sudden he's like..." He adopts an exaggerated Dick Van Dyke-style Cockney, "... 'So you got in a fight with Bowie, didja?' So I told him the story real quick and him and Clapton are going off about Bowie in their own little world, talking about things from years ago. They were saying things like when Bowie gets drunk he turns into the Devil From Bromley... I mean, I'm not even in this conversation, I'm just sitting there listening to them bitch like crazy about Bowie. It was funny."

But you and the Thin White Duke are now best of buddies, is that right?

"Well, I don't know about 'best buddies'. But I like him a lot, yeah. We had a long talk about the business and stuff and I never met anybody so cool and so into it and so whacked out and so sick in my life. I remember lookin' over at [GN'R guitarist] Slash and going, 'Man, we're in fuckin' deep trouble' and he goes, 'Why?' and I go, 'Because I got a lot in common with this guy. I mean, I'm pretty sick but this guy's just fuckin' ill!' And Bowie's sitting there laughing and talking about, 'One side of me is experimental and the other side of me wants to make something that people can get into, and I DON'T KNOW FUCKIN' WHY! WHY AM I LIKE THIS?!' And I'm sitting there thinking, I've got 20 more years of... that to look forward to? I'm already like that... 20 more years? What am I gonna do?" He laughs.

Speaking of the gigs you did supporting the Stones last year, you announced at the first show that you were going to 'retire' and that the band was going to split up. Was this a serious-minded statement at the time? Or was it nothing more than a publicity stunt? "No, no... The thing at the Stones show was definite and it was serious. I mean, I offered to go completely broke and back on the streets, you know, because it would have cost us an estimated $1.5 million to cancel the show. That means Axl's broke, OK? But I didn't do that because I didn't want the band to have to pay for me cancelling the show. I don't want Duff to lose his house because Axl cancelled two shows. I couldn't live with that. But at the same time, I'm not gonna be a part of watching them kill themselves. I mean, we tried every other angle to get our shit back together, and it didn't work. It had to be done live. Everybody else was pissed off with me but after the show Slash's mom came and shook my hand, and so did his brother."

They say that every successful band needs a dictator in the line-up to kick butt and keep things moving. Do you think that's one of the roles you fulfil in Guns N' Roses – the dictator of the band? "Depends who you ask and on which day. We got into fights in Chicago, when we went there last year to escape LA and try and get some writing done. Everybody's schedules were weird and we were all showing up at different times. But when I would show up I was like, 'OK, let's do this, let' do that, let's do this one of yours Slash. OK, now let's hear that one Duff's got...' And that's when everybody would decide I was a dictator. Suddenly I'm a total dictator, a completely selfish dick, you know? But fuck, man, as far as I was concerned we were on a roll. Slash is complaining we're getting' nothin' done and I'm like, 'What do you mean? We just put down six new parts for songs!' We've got all this stuff done in, like, a couple of weeks. So suddenly, like, everything's a bummer and it's all my fault.

"And he was like, 'Yeah, but I've been sitting here a month on my ass waiting' for you to show up'. I'd driven cross-country in my truck to Chicago from LA and it had taken me weeks. So suddenly, like, everything's a bummer and it's all my fault. But after working with Jagger it was like, 'Don't anybody ever call me a dictator again. You go work for the Stones and you'll find out the hard way what working for a real dictator is like!'"

Apart from that one brief conversation about Bowie, did you get to 'hang' with Jagger or any of the Rolling Stones when you supported them last year? "Not really. Not Jagger, anyway. That guy walks offstage and goes and does paper work. He checks everything. That guy is involved in every little aspect of the show, from what the backing singers are getting paid to what a particular part of the PA costs to buy or hire. He is on top of all of it. Him and his lawyer and a couple of guys that he hangs with. But basically, it's all him. And this is where I sympathise. I mean, I don't sit around checking the gate receipts at the end of every show, but sometimes the frontman… I don't know. You don't plan on that job when you join the band. You don't want that job. You don't wanna be that guy to the guys in your band that you hang with and you look up to. But somebody's got to do it. And the guitar player can't do it because he is not the guy who has to be communicating directly with the audience with eye-contact and body movements. He can go back, hang his hair down in his face and stand by the amps and just get into his guitar part…"

How do you manage to 'communicate directly' with the crowd when you're playing in one of those 70,000-seater stadiums like the one you played in with the Stones? "You have to learn how, but it can be done. You know, like someone goes, 'You're gonna have this huge arena tour next year, dude!' And I go, 'I know, but that's the problem. I can work a stadium now'. And I can. And if I can work it, then that's what I wanna do. It's just bigger and more fun."

Tell me about how things are coming together for the new LP. "It's comin' together just great. Cos Slash is on like a motherfucker right now. The songs are comin' together – they're comin' together real heavy. I've written all these ballads and Slash has written all these really heavy crunch rockers. It makes for a real interesting' kinda confusion..."

What about Steven [Adler], your drummer? First he's out of the band, then he's back again… What's the story right now? "He is back in the band. He was definitely out of the band. He wasn't necessarily fired, we worked with Adam Maples, we worked with Martin Chambers, and Steven did the Guns N' Roses thing and got his shit together. And it worked, and he did it, and he plays the songs better than any of 'em, just bad-assed, and he's GN'R. And so if he doesn't blow it, we're going to try the album with him, and the tour and, you know, we've worked out a contract with him..."

So you told him he had to stop taking drugs or he was out of the band? "Yeah, exactly. But, you know, it's worked out. It's finally back on and we're hoping it continues. It's only been a few days so far. It's only been since Thursday last week, and he's doing' great. We're all just hoping it continues."

How different has it been writing these new songs compared to the way you wrote the songs for 'Appetite For Destruction'? "One reason things have been so hard in a way is this. The first album was basically written with Axl comin' up with maybe one line and maybe a melody for that line, or how I'm gonna say it or yell it or whatever. And the band would build a song around it. This time around, Izzy's brought in eight songs, at least, OK? Slash has brought in an album. And Duff's brought in a song. Duff's said it all in one song. It's called 'Why Do You Look At Me When You Hate Me' and it's just bad-assed! But none of this ever happened before. I mean, before the first album I think Izzy had written one song in his entire life, you know? But they're comin' now. And Izzy has this, like, very wry sense of humour, man. He's got this song about..." He half-sings the lyrics, "... 'She lost her mind today / Got splattered out on the highway / I say that's OK...' Hahaha! It's called 'Dust And Bones', I think, and it's great. The rhythm reminds me of something like 'Cherokee People' by Paul Revere And The Raiders, only really weird and rocked out. It's a weird song. But then it is by Izzy, what can I tell you?"

You seem very happy now you're back with the band in a recording studio. You like recording? Yeah, I do. I prefer recording to doing a live gig, unless I'm psyched for the gig. Before the gig I always don't wanna do the fuckin' show, and nine times out of 10 I hate it. If I'm psyched it's like, let's go! But most of the time I'm mad about something', or something's going fuckin' wrong... I don't enjoy most of it at all."

Is that partly your own fault, though? Some people have accused you of having a very belligerent attitude. "I don't know exactly... Something' always fuckin' happens before a show. Something' always happens and I react like a motherfucker to it. I don't like to have this pot-smoking' mentality of just letting things go by. I feel like Lenny Kravitz: like, peace and love, man, for sure, or you're gonna fuckin' die! I'm gonna kick yer ass if you mess with my garden, you know? That's always been my attitude."

Do you think that attitude has hardened, though, with the onset of this enormous fame and notoriety you now enjoy? "Meaning what exactly?" Do you act the way you do because your fame and popularity allows you to, or would you act that way anyway? "I've always been that way, but now I'm in a position to just be myself more. And the thing is, people do allow me to do it, whether they like it or not. It's weird."

Do you ever take unfair advantage of that, though? (Long pause) "... No. No, usually I'm just an emotionally unbalanced person," he smiles. "No, really. I'm usually an emotional wreck before a show because of something' else that's going on in my life. I mean, as I say, something' weird just always happens to me two seconds before I'm supposed to go onstage, you know? Like I found William Rose..." Axl's natural father, estranged from the family since his son's infancy. "Turns out, he was murdered in '84 and buried somewhere in Illinois, and I found that out like two days before a show and I was fuckin' whacked! I mean, I've been trying to uncover this mystery since I was a little kid. I didn't even know he existed until I was a teenager, you know? Cos I was told it was the Devil that made me know what the inside of a house looked like that I'd supposedly never lived in. So I've been trying to track down this William Rose guy. Not like, I love this guy, he's my father. I just wanna know something about my heritage – weird shit like am I going to have an elbow that bugs the shit out of me when I get to 40 cos of some hereditary trait? Weird shit ordinary families take for granted."

You say your father was murdered? "Yeah, he was killed. It was probably like at close-range too, man. Wonderful family..."

You've taken a lot of personal criticism for the more brutal aspects of the lyrics to your songs – 'One In A Million' being the most obvious example. Do you think your critics miss a lot of the humour in your songs? "To appreciate the humour in our work you gotta be able to relate to a lot of different things. And not everybody does. Not everybody can. With 'One In A Million' I used a word ['nigger']. It's part of the English language whether it's a good word or not. It's a derogatory word, it's a negative word. It's not meant to sum up the entire black race, but it was directed towards black people in those situations. I was robbed, I was ripped-off, I had my life threatened. And it's, like, I described it in one word. And not only that, but I wanted to see the effect of a racial joke. I wanted to see what effect that would have on the world. Slash was into it... I mean, the song says: 'Don't wanna buy none of your gold chains today'. Now a black person on the Oprah Winfrey show who goes,

'Oh, they're putting down black people' is going to fuckin' take one of these guys at the bus stop home and feed him and take care of him and let him babysit the kids? They ain't gonna be near the guy!

"I don't think every black person is a nigger. I don't care. I consider myself kinda green and from another planet or something', you know? I've never felt I fit into any group, so to speak. A black person has this 300 years of whatever on his shoulders. OK. But I ain't got nothin' to do with that. It bores me, too. There's such a thing as too sensitive. You can watch a movie about someone blowing the crap outta all these people, but you could be the most anti-violent person in the world. But you get off on this movie, like, yeah! He deserved it, the bad guy got shot...

"Something I've noticed that's really weird about 'One In A Million' is the whole song coming together took me by surprise. I wrote the song as a joke. West [Arkeen; co-lyricist of 'It's So Easy', amongst other GN'R songs] just got robbed by two black guys on Christmas night, a few years back. He went out to play guitar on Hollywood Boulevard and he's standing there playing in front of the band and he gets robbed at knife point for 78 cents.

"Coupla days later we're all sitting around watching TV – there's Duff and West and a couple other guys – and we're all bummed out, hung-over and this an' that. And I'm sitting there with no money, no job, feeling guilty for being at West's house all the time sucking' up the oxygen, you know? And I picked up this guitar, and I can only play like the top two strings, and I ended up fuckin' around with this little riff. It was the only thing I could play on the guitar at the time. And then I started ad-libbing some words to it as a joke. And we had just watched Sam Kinison or something' on the video, you know, and I guess the humour was just sorta leaning' that way or something'. I don't know. But we just started writing this thing, and when I sang 'Police and niggers / That's right...' that was to fuck with West's head, cos he couldn't believe I would write that. And it came out like that.

"Then the chorus came about because 1 like getting really far away, like 'Rocket Man', Elton John. I was thinking about friends and family in Indiana, and I realised those people have no concept of who I am any more. Even the ones I was close to. Since then I've flown people out, had 'em hang out here, I've paid for everything. But there was no joy in it for them. I was smashing' shit, going fuckin' nuts. And yet, trying to work. And they were going, 'Man, I don't wanna be a rocker any more, not if you go through this'. But at the same time, I brought 'em out here, you know, and we just hung-out for a couple months – wrote songs together. had serious talks, it was almost like being on acid cos we'd talk about the family and life and stuff, and we'd get really heavy and get to know each all over again. It's hard to try and replace eight years of knowing each other every day, and then all of a sudden I'm in this new world. Back there I was a street kid with a skateboard and no money dreaming' 'bout being in a rock band, and now all of a sudden I'm here. And it's weird for them to see their friends putting up Axl posters, you know? And it's weird for me too. So anyway, all of a sudden I came up with this chorus, 'You're one in a million', you know, and 'We tried to reach you but you were much too high…'"

So many of your lyrics are littered with drug analogies. Is that a fair comment? "Everybody was into dope then and those analogies are great in rock songs – Aerosmith done proved that on their old stuff, and the Stones. And drug analogies… the language is always like the hippest language. A lot of hip-hop and stuff, even the stuff that's anti-drugs, a lot of the terms come directly from drug street-raps. Cos they're always on top of stuff, cos they gotta change the language all the time so people don't know what they're saying, so they can keep dealing. Plus they're trying to be the hippest, coolest, baddest thing out there. It happens. So that's like, 'We tried to reach you but you were much too high' – I was picturing 'em trying to call me if, like, I disappeared or died or something. And 'You're one in a million – someone said that to me real sarcastically, it wasn't like an ego thing. But that's the good thing, you use that 'I'm one in a million' positively to make yourself get things done. But originally it was kinda like someone went, 'Yeah, you're just fuckin' one in a million, aren't ya?' and it stuck with me.

"Then we go in the studio, and Duff plays the guitar much more aggressively than I did. Slash made it too tight and concise, and I wanted it a bit rawer. Then Izzy comes up with this electric guitar thing. I was pushing him to come up with a cool tone, and all of a sudden he's coming up with this aggressive thing. It just happened. So suddenly it didn't work to sing the song in a low funny voice any more. We tried and it didn't work, didn't sound right, it didn't fit. And the guitar parts were so cool, I had to sing it like HURRHHHH! So that I sound like I'm totally into this."

It certainly doesn't sound like you're pretending on the record, though, does it? "No, but this is just one point of view out of hundreds that I have on the situation. When I meet a black person, I deal with each situation differently. Like I deal with every person I meet, it doesn't matter."

Have you taken any abuse personally from any black people since this whole controversy first started raging? "No, not actually. Actually, I meet a lot of black people that come up and just wanna talk about it, discuss it with me because they find it interesting. Like a black chick came up to me in Chicago and goes, 'You know, I hated you cos of 'One In A Million''. And I'm like, 'Oh great, here we go'. Then she goes, 'But I ride the subway...' All of a sudden she gets real serious. She says, 'And I looked around one day and I know what you're talking' about. So you're all right. I've got a lot of that..."

What about from other musicians? "I had a big heavy conversation with Ice Cube [former member of hard-line LA rappers NWA - Niggaz With Attitude]. He sent a letter, wanting to work on 'Welcome To The Jungle' cos he'd heard I was interested in turning it into a rap thing. He wanted to be part of it. Anyway, we ended up having this big heavy conversation about 'One In A Million', and he could see where I was coming from all right. And he knows more about that shit than most."

At last the grisly subject of 'One In A Million' is allowed to drop. Axl lights another cigarette, unzips the top from another can of Coke, rubs a tired eye with the back of a thumb, and the conversation drifts towards the next Guns N' Roses album. "There's, like, seven [finished] songs right now, but I know by the end of the record there'll be 42 to 45 and I want 30 of them down."

A double album then? "Well, a double album or a single 76 minutes or something like that. Then I want four or five B-sides – people never listen to B-sides anymore – and that'll be the back of another EP. We'll say it's B-sides, you know. Plus there should be four other songs for an EP, if we pull this off. So that's the next record and then there's the live record from the tour. If we do this right, we wont have to make another album for five years!" he cried triumphantly.

Why wouldn't he want to make another album for five years? "But it's not so much like five years to sit on our asses. It's like five years to figure out what we're gonna say next, you know? After the crowd and the people figure out how they're gonna react to this album."

What kind of direction do you see the band taking on this next album? Do you plan to expand your usual themes somewhat, or are you sticking pretty much to the sleazy half-world undercurrents of the first album for inspiration? "This record will show we've grown a lot, but there'll be some childish, you know, arrogant, male, false-bravado crap on there, too. But there'll also be some really heavy serious stuff."

It's been such a long time since the release of 'Appetite For Destruction', and what with everything that's gone down in between, do you sense the possibility of a backlash building up in time for the new album?

"It doesn't fuckin' matter. This doesn't matter, man. It's too late. If we record this album the way we wanna record this album, it could bomb, sure. But five years from now, there'll be a lot of kids into it in Hollywood. Ten years from now, it'll be an underground thing like Aerosmith and Hanoi Rocks. The material has strong enough lyric content and strong enough guitar parts, you'll have no choice, it'll permeate into people's brains one way or another. If the album doesn't sell and be successful, someday in 10 years from now someone's gonna write a record and we're gonna be one of their main influences, and so the message is still gonna get through. Whatever we're trying to say and the way in which we try to say it, we pay attention to that. If we get that right, the rest just takes care of itself. There is an audience for what we're saying that's going through the same things we are, and, in a way, we are leading."

How conscious are you of the role as 'leaders', in terms of your position – both critically and commercially – at the forefront of modern rock music? "It's been... shown to me in a lot of ways. I didn't want to accept the responsibility of it really, even though I was trying, but I still was reluctant. Now I'm kind of into it. Because it's like, you have a choice, man, you can grow or die. We have to do it – we have to grow. If we don't grow, we die. We can't do the same sludge, I'm not Paul Stanley, man! I can't fuckin' play sludge, man, for fuckin' 30years. Sludge, man. It's sludge rock.

"That's one of the reasons why 1989 kinda got written off. We had to find a whole new way of working together. Everybody got successful and it changed things, of course it did. Everybody had the dream, when they got successful they could do what they want, right? That turns into Slash bringing in eight songs! It's never been done before, Slash bringing in a song first and me writing words to it. I've done it twice with him before and we didn't use either of those songs, out of Slash's choice. Now he's got eight of 'em that I gotta write words to! They're bad-assed songs, too.

"I was working on, like, writing these ballads that I feel have really rich tapestries and stuff, and making sure each note, each effect, is right. Cos whether I'm using a lot of instrumentation and stuff or not, I'll still write with minimalism. But it has to be right; it has to be the right note and it has to be held the right way and it has to have the right effect, do you know what I mean?"

I didn't know you were such a perfectionist. "What people don't understand is there was a perfectionist attitude to 'Appetite…' There was a definite plan to that. We could have made it all smooth and polished. We went and did test tracks with different people and they came out smooth and polished. We did some stuff with Spencer Proffer and Geffen Records said it was too fuckin' radio. That's why we went with Mike Clink, we went for a raw sound because it just didn't gel having it too tight and concise.

"We knew what we were doing, and we knew this: we know the way we are onstage, and the only way to capture that energy on the record, okay, is by making it somewhat live. Doing' the bass, the drums, the rhythm guitar at the same time. Getting the best track, having it a bit faster than you play it live, so that brings some energy into it. Then adding lots of vocal parts and overdubs with the guitars. Adding more music to capture… because Guns N' Roses onstage, man, can be out to lunch! But it's like, you know, visually we're all over the place and you don't know what to expect. How do you get that on a record? That's the thing.

"That's why recording is my favourite thing, because it's like painting a picture. You start out with a shadow, or an idea, and you come up with something and it's a shadow of that. You might like it better. It's still not exactly what you pictured in your head. But you go into the studio and add all these things and you come up with something you didn't even expect. Slash will do, like, one slow little guitar fill that adds a while different mood that you didn't expect. That's what I love. It's like you're doing a painting and you go away and come back and it's different. You allow different shading to creep in and then you go, 'Wow, I got a whole different effect on this that's even heavier than what I pictured. I don't know quite what I'm onto, but I'm on it', you know?"

You're using Clink again to produce the new album, and you're recording in the same studios you made 'Appetite…' in. Are there any ingredients you plan to add to the recording that you didn't use first time around? "Yeah. We're trying to find Jeff Lynne." Jeff Lynne? Leader of '70s monoliths Electric Light Orchestra – ELO – last seen hobnobbing it with the Travelling Wilburys? "I want him to work on 'November Rain', and there's like three or four possible other songs that if it works out I'd maybe like him to look at."

As an additional producer to Clink, or to contribute some string arrangements, or what? "Maybe some strings, I don't know. Cos this record will be produced by Guns N' Roses and Mike Clink. I might be using synthesiser – but I'm gonna say I'm using synthesiser and what I programmed. It's not gonna be like, 'Oh, you know, we do all our shows live', and then it's on tape. That's not gonna be the thing. I mean, I took electronics in school. It's like, I don't know shit about synthesisers but I can take a fuckin' patch-chord and shape my own wave-forms and shit, you know? So now I wanna... you know, jump into today. I've never had the money to do it before. Maybe someone like Jeff Lynne can help me. It's a thought."

This song, 'November Rain', I read somewhere that you said if it wasn't recorded to your complete satisfaction you would quit the music business. "That was then. At that time it was the most important song to me."

Were you serious, though, when you said you'd quit the music business if it wasn't done right? "Yeah, that's the fuckin' truth, all right. But the worse part of that is, like, if you wanna look at it in a negative way, I've got four of those motherfuckers now, man! I don't know how I wrote these, but I like 'em better than 'November Rain'! And I'm gonna crush that motherfuckin' song, man!

"But now I've got four of 'em I gotta do, and they're all big songs. We play them and we get chills. It started when I came in one day with this heavy piano part, it's like real big, and it fits this bluesy gospel thing that was supposed to be a blues-rocker like 'Buy Me A Chevrolet' by Foghat or something'. Now it's turned into this thing, like, 'Take Another Piece Of Heart' [by Janis Joplin] or something'..."

I'm still mulling over the giddy prospect of Jeff Lynne working on the next Guns N' Roses album... Why him? Were you an ELO fan? "Oh yeah, I'm an ELO fanatic! I like old ELO, 'Out Of The Blue', that period. I went to see 'em play when they came to town when I was kid and shit like that. I respect Jeff Lynne for being Jeff Lynne. I mean, 'Out Of The Blue' is an awesome album. So, one: he's got stamina. And two: he's used to working with a lot of different material. Three: he's used to working with all kinds of instrumentation for all kinds of different styles of music. Four: he wrote all his own material. Five: he produced it! That's a lot of concentration, and a lot of energy needed. Hopefully, I would like, if he's available, to have him. He's the best. But I don't know if we can get him or not."

You'd work with him just on certain tracks? "That's what I'd like to start with. I mean, who knows, maybe him and Clink will hit it off just great, and everybody'll be into it. If it works, then great, welcome to it, you know?"

Silence reigns for a brief moment, Axl's attention turned suddenly to the low distant hum of his hi-fi which has been spinning taped music throughout the conversation, his gaze frozen between the ashtrays and magazines littered on the table before us, a pinched little smile creasing his lips. I ask who it is we're listening to.

"Cheap Trick, 'In Colour', featuring Rick 'The Dick' Neilsen," he says. "What a fuckin' asshole! I love Cheap Trick, too. It's kinda funny now, cos I listen to it and just laugh at him."

Why? What happened? "There was a thing in *Rolling Stone* where he said he fuckin' decked Slash! He didn't deck Slash! Do you think anyone is gonna fuckin' deck Slash when Doug Goldstein [GN'R tour manager] is standing right there between them? It's not gonna happen."

Why does everybody want to tell the world they beat up one of Guns N' Roses? "Because Guns N' Roses has this reputation for being bad, you know, the new bad boys in town, and so, like, hey, man, it perpetuates down to fuckin' Rick Neilsen wanting to get back in good with the youth market by claiming' he's badder than Guns N' Roses, you know? If he had any real balls, he'd apologise to Slash in the press. Not in person, he can come up to me and say he's sorry all he wants, it doesn't mean shit till he says it in the press.

"Now Bowie's a different situation, because Bowie hasn't talked to the press about our bust up. So Bowie can apologise to me, and then when they see photos of me and him together they'll go, 'Fuck, we tried to start a war and look at these guys, they're hanging' out!' Ha! That's cool, you know? Like Jagger was supposed to have told me off and the next thing you know I'm onstage singing with him – that fucked with a lot of 'em. I mean, it's either somebody kicked our ass or it's how some chick is scared I'm gonna come kill her cat. I mean, I could make a joke about it, but..."

Speaking of bad boys, did you get to meet Keith Richards when you supported the Stones? "I got to meet him and talk to him for a little bit. I just kinda watched the guy. Basically, I told him I gotta go shopping, cos he has the coolest coats in the world. He just loved that. And I asked him about Billy Idol ripping' the idea of for the 'Rebel Yell' album off him, kinda joking. And he goes..." [Adopts the tie-dyed Cockney again], 'Stole it off my fucking night-table, he did!' Hahaha! I thought that was great!

"It's like, I met John Entwhistle from the Who, man, and I said I'd always wondered about these rumours about 'Baba O'Riley', you know. Like for the keyboard parts they went and got brainwaves and then programmed 'em through a computer, you know? So I asked Entwhistle, and Entwhistle's annihilated out of his mind, right? He's in his own little world, and he looks at me and goes: 'Brainwaves? What fuckin' brainwaves? Townshend's got no fuckin' brainwaves!" He sniggered.

"Then I asked him about the time he was supposed to have shot up all his gold records, and he said, 'I'll let you in on a secret, mate. Those were all Connie Francis's gold records, I fucking stole 'em!' I said, 'Wow, okay, I've had enough of this guy. I can't deal with him anymore! He was just fuckin' lit and ready to go..."

You seem very settled at the moment, relaxed, not a bit like your image. "I'm happy to kick-back tonight and sit around jawing, because today everything is under control. Tomorrow – wait and see – it's fuckin' over! Something will come up. There's only one thing left, and that's this damn album, man. That's it. I mean, we may do another record but it's like, Guns N' Roses doesn't fully function, nothing ever really happens, to its utmost potential, unless it's a kamikaze run. Unless it's like, this is it, man! Like, fuck it, let's go down in fuckin' flames with this motherfucker! That's how we are about the record, everybody's like, we're just gonna do this son of a bitch..."

The hour, as the prophet sang, is getting late. We wind up with the obligatory, 'What now?' questions, Axl casting a slant-eyed glance into the immediate future for himself and his hand. "The main thing about the next record is this is our dream, to get these songs out there into the public. Then once we get out there we'll fight for them with the business side and stuff. But at this point that's not what's important. What's important is the recording of the songs. If the business comes down really hard on us in a weird way, then we'll make our choices – do we wanna deal with this, or do we not wanna fuckin' deal with this?

"The record will sell a certain amount of copies the minute it comes out anyway, and we could live off that for the rest of our lives and record our records on small independent labels, it doesn't matter. I mean, that's not in the plans, but, ultimately, it just doesn't matter, you know? It's all down to what we want to deal with. Do we wanna be giving everything that we feel we have inside of ourselves, to do the shows, to our top potential? Yes, we do. But I don't choreograph things. I don't know when I'm gonna slam down on my knees or whatever. It's like, you have to ask yourself, do I wanna give all that, and have someone fuckin' spitting' in my face? Does it mean that much to me? No! I dig the songs. If you don't want 'em, fine. But I don't have to give them to you."

I know you've often threatened it, but if you wanted to, could you really leave all this behind? The band, your career in the music business – not just financially, but emotionally, artistically? "If I wanted to badly enough, sure. This is all right, in bits and pieces, but whether it'll take up all the chapters in the book of my life, I don't know. I would like to record for a long time… I have to make this album. Then it doesn't matter. This album is the album I've always been waiting' on. Our second album is the album I've been waiting' on since before we got signed. We were planning out the second album before we started work on the first one! But as much as it means to me, if it bombs, if that happens, yeah, I'm sure I'll be bummed business-wise and let down or whatever, but at the same time it doesn't matter. It's like, I got it out there. That's the artistic thing taken care of. Then I could walk away…"

What about the money, could you walk away from that? "I'd like to make the cash off the touring, and then I'd like to walk away knowing that I can support my kids, for whatever they want, for the rest of my life, you know? And that I can still donate to charities. I'd like to have that security. I've never known any security in my whole life. The financial aspect is just to get that security. If I have that in the bank I can live off the interest and still have money to spend on whatever – including, top of the list, the welfare of my own immediate and future family."

Last question. First question. Same question, in fact, I've been asking for the last couple of years. "When will the album actually fuckin' come out?" I nod. He doesn't. "It's taken a lot of time to put together the ideas for this album. In certain ways, no-one's done what we've done – come out with a record that captured that kind of spirit, since maybe the first Sex Pistols album. No-one's followed it up, and we're not gonna put out a fuckin' record until we're sure we can. So we've been trying to build it up. It's like, it's only really these last couple of months that I've been writing the right words. Now suddenly I'm on a roll, all the words for Slash's songs are there. But it's taken this long to find 'em.

"I just hope the people are into it, you know? I think that the audience will have grown enough, though. It's been three years – they've gone through three years of shit too, so hopefully they'll be ready to relate to some new things. When you're writing about real life, not fantasy, you have to take time to live your own life first and allow yourself to go through different phases. Now I think there's enough different sides of Guns N' Roses that when the album is finally released no-one will know what to think, let alone us! Like, what are they trying to say? Sometimes even I don't fuckin' know..."

First published in Kerrang! Nos.286-287, April 21, 1990